# Feather Brain



## Developing, Testi
## and Improving
## Saltwater Fly Patterns

**Drew Chicone**

HEADWATER
BOOKS

STACKPOLE
BOOKS

Published by
STACKPOLE BOOKS
5067 Ritter Road
Mechanicsburg, PA 17055
www.stackpolebooks.com



First edition

Distributed by NATIONAL BOOK NETWORK

*All photos by the author*

*Cover photo from iStockphoto; photos of flies by the author*
*Cover design by Caroline Stover*

**Library of Congress Cataloging-in-Publication Data**

Chicone, Drew.
Feather brain : developing, testing, and improving saltwater fly patterns / Drew Chicone. – First edition.
pages cm
Includes index.
ISBN-13: 978-0-8117-1196-8 (pbk.)
ISBN-10: 0-8117-1196-X (pbk.)
1. Fly tying. 2. Fly fishing. I. Title. II. Title: Saltwater fly patterns.
SH451.C48 2013
799.12'4–dc23

2012047779

*This book is dedicated to my father, David H. Chicone,*
*for having the patience to impart skills that*
*have proven to be the gift of a lifetime,*
*and my daughter Lucy, to whom someday*
*I hope to pass along the same gift.*

# Contents

# Acknowledgments

I thank my wife, Susan, first and foremost for understanding and supporting my undying passion for fly tying. Her patience with the "dead animals," airborne feathers, and frequent strands of flash stuck to the dog does not go unnoticed.

Many thanks also go to my friend and mentor, Eric Leiser. No one else has more knowledge of everything fly tying. You are one of a kind, and I treasure the time you gave to me. Your lessons, guidance, and encouragement have inspired me, and as promised, I will always share my knowledge with others.

I cannot forget Stackpole's Jay Nichols and Amy Lerner for their hard work and continued support.

To Warren Weatherford: Any man who covertly trims his dog, Halloween wigs, or his wife's sweaters for fly-tying materials is an innovator and a genius in my book. Thank you for encouraging me to write this book, always listening to my featherbrained ideas, and throwing fuel on the fire that is my passion for fly tying.

And to the hundreds of other fly tiers that have helped and encouraged me along the way, I cannot thank you enough. I only hope I can do the same for the next generation of tiers to come.

# Introduction

Having spent a fair amount of time behind the vise or around others tying, I believe that the reasons for tying fur and feathers onto a hook go much beyond catching fish, further than any who don't tie could ever imagine. Whether it's the camaraderie or the creativity, art, or simply a means to catch fish, people are passionate about tying flies for a lot of different reasons. For me, it's all those reasons and more. Tying has become part of my daily routine, and teaching people how to tie is one of my favorite activities. When I started tying somewhere around the age of six or seven, it was simply a way to be with my dad and fight off cabin fever during the seemingly endless winters in upstate New York. Saturday morning cartoons were replaced with tying the Leadwing Coachman, and the trout flies I learned to tie in the winter lead to a passion for deer hair bass bugs in the summer. The flies seemed to change with the seasons of my life. Wherever I was, I was fishing and tying flies for the fish at that particular time and place.

I live in Florida now, and the seasonal changes are not quite as noticeable. Sometimes I tie to get away from the distractions and general busyness of everyday life. I find it calms my

I have learned a lot about tying flies from books, videos, or the Internet, but the lessons that I hold closest to my heart I learned while sharing the bench with friends. There are very few things that I enjoy more than tying flies and telling stories, and no one has better stories than Eric Leiser.

nerves and relaxes my mind . . . I guess it's kind of like therapy for me. Other times I am sick of channel surfing, or my need to be doing "something" takes over, but most of the time I tie to try and pacify my insatiable yearning to convince, trick, or outsmart fish. The thrill I get and the sinister grin on my face is not just from actually catching the fish I have cast my fly to . . . well, not completely. The gratification also comes more from solving a constantly changing puzzle with infinitely different rules: knowing what it will take to make a specific fish, at a specific time and place, turn on and eat even if it doesn't want to. Tomorrow the game will change, and solving the puzzle that convinces another fish will take a new solution.

## My Process for Creating Flies

Teaching fly tying is rewarding for me because I get to watch students evolve from technicians to artists, usually within a short time. It doesn't take more than a couple of classes and a little practice before their interests change from "How do I tie that fly?" to "Check out this new fly I invented!" Almost every week one of my younger students hands me his or her new pattern and asks me what I think of it. I carefully look the creations over and give him or her a few tips or pointers on technique, and then I ask, "What's it supposed to do?" This is usually followed by one of two responses: "Look cool" or "Catch fish." It never fails. "Look cool" is easy; it's the "Catch fish" response that takes a little more explaining and is ultimately the reason for writing this book.

This book was not written for tiers of one skill level, but for those who have caught the bug. "Feather brain" is not a symptom of bird flu but describes what some people would call a sickness. This type of person has discovered a passion for fly tying and that leads sufferers to think about some aspect of the craft on a regular basis or sit at the vise as part of their normal routine. More and more they may find themselves spending time surfing the Internet or scouring magazine articles in search of new patterns, innovative techniques, or the latest material. Wondering why specific materials or techniques are used to create a pattern is standard thinking for a feather brain, and researching the best flies for a specific species of fish is a given before any fishing trip. These obsessed individuals have an insatiable desire for knowledge and just can't seem to take in enough information. I wrote this book for people who live by the creed that you can always improve, and anything worth doing is worth overdoing.

If you have ever wanted to create your own patterns, improve the flies you tie, or just catch more fish, this is your turn-by-turn road map for material selection and your guide for pattern development. My goals are to explain and demystify when to use specific materials and colors. The clear illustrations and pragmatic approach to fly tying that follows takes the guesswork out of which materials should be used for a specific type of fly, and the tips and tricks will help you create your own patterns. This is the book I wish I had when I started.

Whether you are a weekend warrior with a bucket list of fish or a world traveler in search of rare species in remote locations, this book will arm you with the knowledge to select materials and apply techniques to create patterns for any species in any saltwater situation.

PART I

# The Foundation

## Fly-Tying Materials and Hints

# CHAPTER 1 Designing a New Pattern

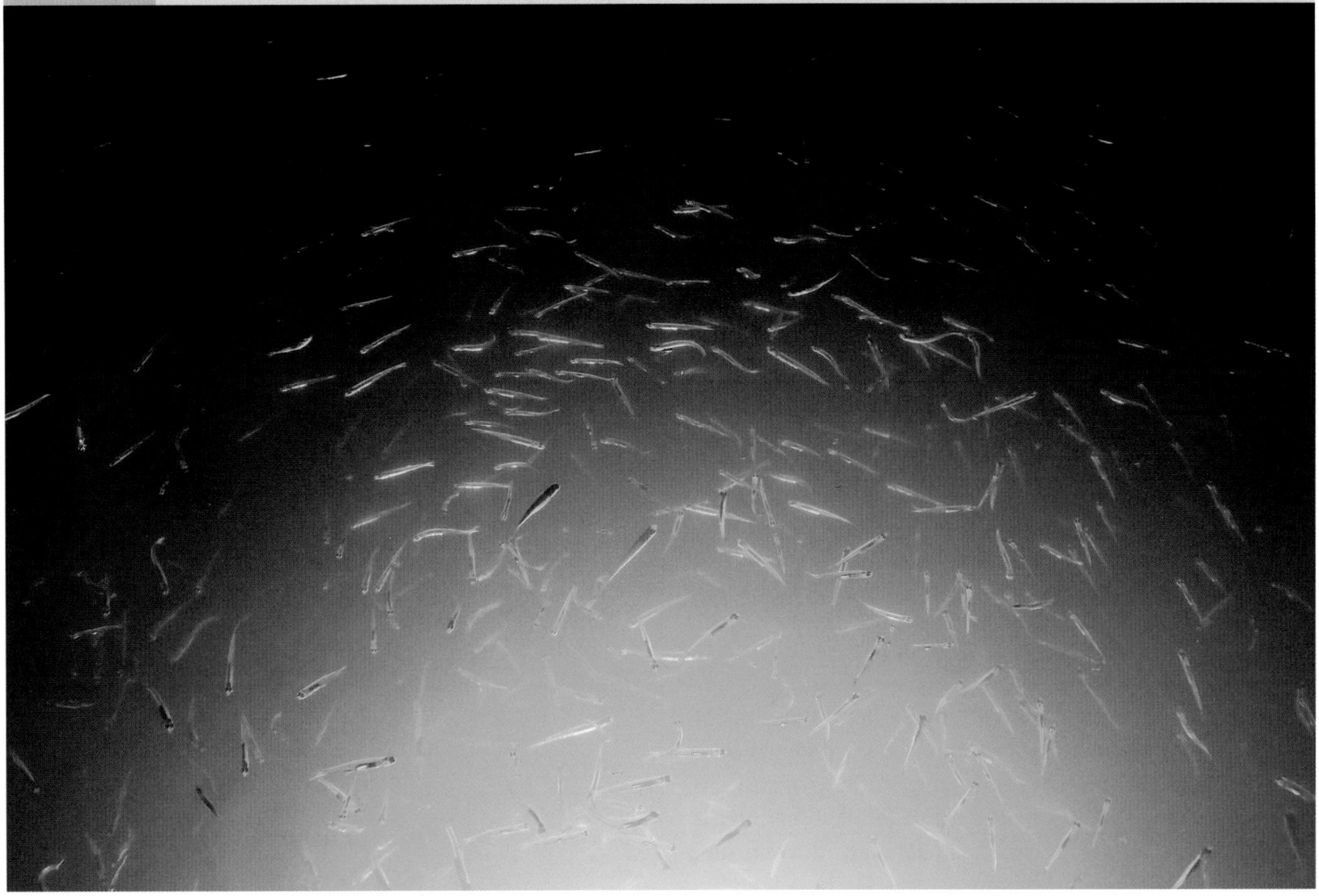

Although there are how-tos for my favorite patterns, my goal is not only to teach you how to tie a particular fly, but rather to explain how to create new productive flies and the reasons why one material may work better in a given situation than another. If you understand why historically productive patterns work so well, it will help you design flies that look cool and catch fish too.

My process starts with the fish. I am and have always been enamored by fish. Even the smallest glass minnows are mesmerizing to me, and I still get a tickled feeling and often laugh out loud watching fish like snook or tarpon smash bait on the surface. The only thing better is catching them.

Analyzing feeding behavior by asking myself a few questions has shaped the way I create flies. Most of the time each question has multiple possible answers, and maybe there is no way of knowing the exact answer. However, after working through these questions, I have a pretty good idea of what types of materials I need to be lashing to the hook and what kind of hook I need to use as a foundation. The exercise is really a way of collecting and organizing my thoughts, and the nerdy consulting diagrams work as a road map for getting from what I want to emulate to what materials I need to use to do that effectively.

The first two questions to answer are "What are they eating?" and "Where are they eating it?" What type of prey item are you going to try to imitate? Some type of baitfish, shrimp, crab, worm . . . Is it on the surface, on the bottom, or somewhere in between? Once I have an answer or even

*Above:* Thousands of tiny glass minnows are attracted to the green glow of an underwater light. This is a great spot to observe snook eating and think about creating new patterns to match glass minnows.

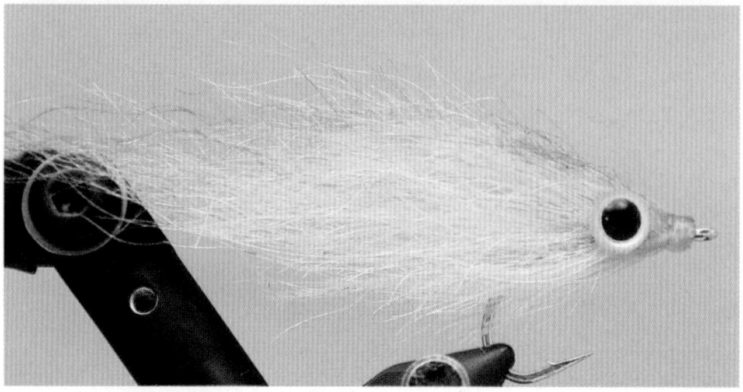

The term "matching the hatch" is commonly used in freshwater trout fishing to refer to the process of selecting flies to emulate the type of insect that the trout are feeding on. The same principle applies to creating saltwater patterns: once you have an idea of what the fish are feeding on, then you can create flies to match it. Here is a scaled sardine (aka white bait or pilchard), and my matching Sanibel Cannibal pattern tied with yak hair.

a general idea of what the answer might be to those major questions, the rest of the process almost takes care of itself.

Let's start with what they are eating, and move on to its specific attributes. What makes a fish think something is food? The answers are endless, and I certainly don't presuppose to know all the reasons why fish eat, but here is an example of how I start to lay it out.

Having a good picture or idea of what you're trying to mimic is a good starting place. Being able to create nearly exact replicas of a shrimp or baitfish on a hook is a great skill to have, but those picture-perfect imitations don't always catch fish. Oftentimes a fly is not designed to look exactly like one particular prey item, but its appearance could be easily mistaken for a number of common foods. These types of flies are commonly referred to as impressionistic flies.

I think Dr. Aaron J. Adams explains it best in his book *Fly Fisherman's Guide to Saltwater Prey* when he writes, "In general, I think fly-tying strategy can be broken down into two types–impressionistic and imitation. Both strategies can be effective, and often a mixture of impressionistic and imitation yields the best result." He goes on to say, "I use my understanding of the gamefish and their habitats in an attempt to figure out which prey characteristic triggers a feeding response from gamefish." Some flies are tied to look exactly like a specific baitfish or crab, with lifelike detail–those flies fall into the category of imitation. Flies that are designed to look like food in general are classified as impressionistic. Mixing imitation and impressionistic tying styles in your fly patterns will more often than not increase the number of fish you catch.

So once you have figured out the prey characteristics, how do you design flies that emulate them? Teaching fly tiers how to mimic those characteristics by selecting the right materials and teaching the proper techniques to apply them to a hook is what I hope to achieve with this book. Ultimately, you will create better flies and catch more fish as a result.

Studying and taking note of the prey's characteristics is a great starting place, but fly tiers need to drill down one step further and recognize specific movements and physical traits, such as size, shape, profile, and color–or lack thereof. This will help you select materials. Whether the pattern ends up being classified as impressionistic or imitation is irrelevant as long as it does what you intended it to do and ultimately catches fish.

Matching the size, shape, and profile doesn't take much analysis, and you can adjust these features on the water if need be; however, mimicking the underwater appearance and specific movements of prey takes a little more thought. Knowing how the fly needs to look and act in the water determines what types of materials you should select and what techniques to use to apply them.

In the mind of the obsessed fly tier, anything and everything is a potential new material and most likely will be

I designed the Disco Shrimp pattern to make a noise and surface disturbance to imitate a common pink shrimp, which snaps and pops the water on the surface when a predator fish is chasing it.

I use this "What are they eating?" diagram as a tool for organizing my thoughts and laying out the shape and size, specific movements, profile, and appearance of the food item I plan on matching.

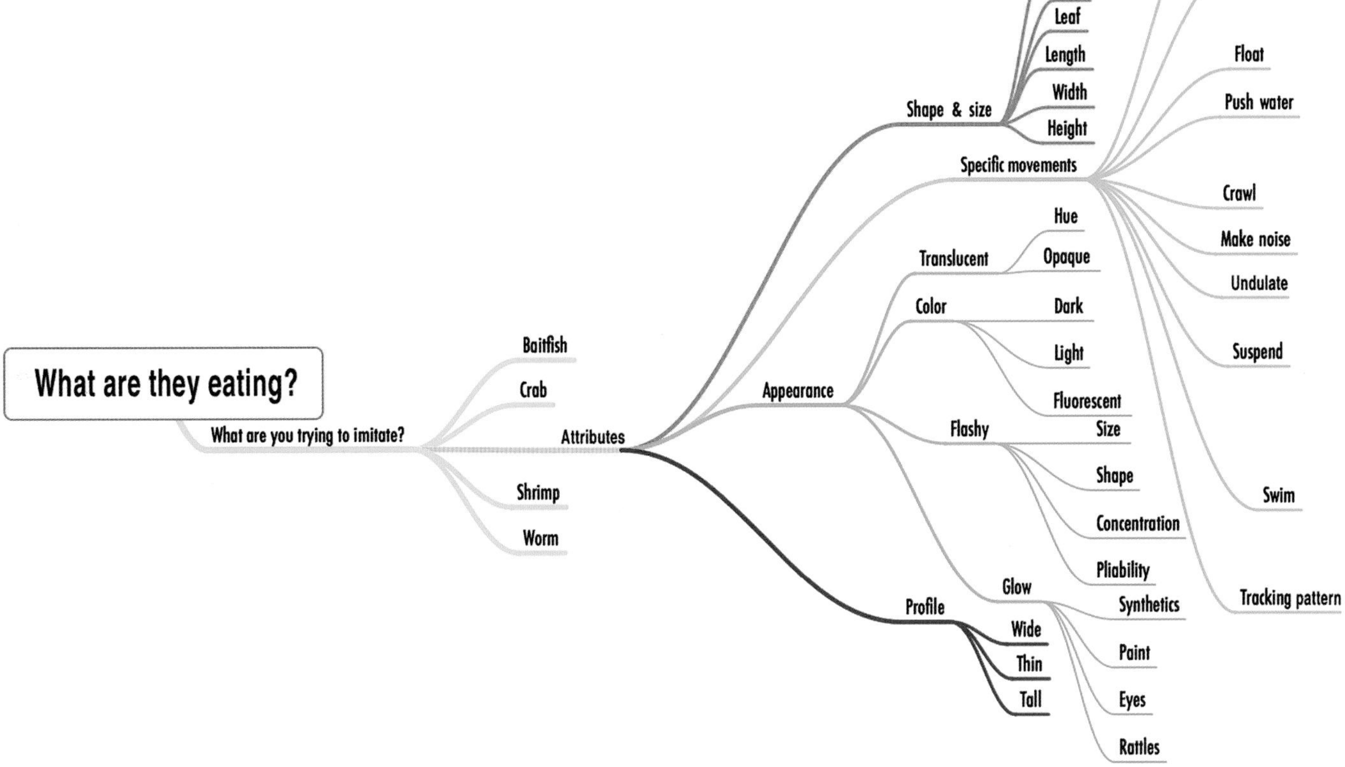


Once I have a clear picture of how the food looks and acts, then I can select materials to design a fly with the same characteristics. I need to consider a lot more than just color.

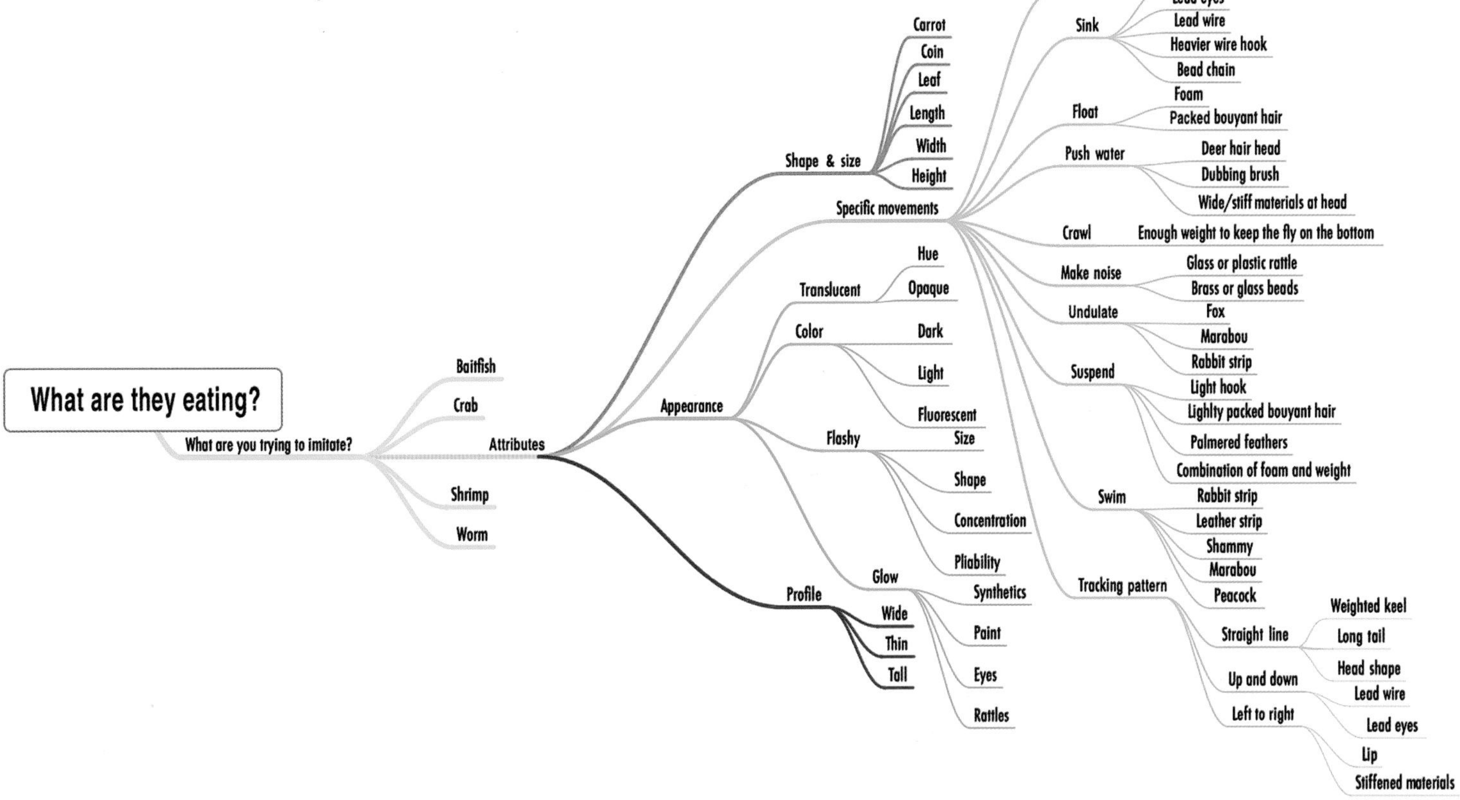

dyed a custom color for a specific situation or fish. For those fly tiers who are not quite as sick yet, there is an endless array of choices and colors available online and at your local fly shop, but determining which ones to choose and why can sometimes be a little tricky. Setting color aside, here are a few examples of materials that can be used to emulate a specific movement or characteristic. The more materials you test, the better you will become at judging how they will act in the water. You don't need to use this exercise every time you sit down at the vise, but it is a useful way to organize your thoughts as you test new materials and tweak patterns.

The next question is "Where are they eating it?" I use the same organization process here as well. Determining where the fish are looking for food and keeping your fly in that section of the water column is critical. It is much easier to get the attention of a fish with his head in the grass, feeding on the bottom, with a sinking fly than it is to get him to stop what he is doing and look up.

If fish are crushing bait on the surface, the fly may need to create a disturbance or a noise to get their attention. If there is a lot of grass or debris in the water or the fly needs to be fished tight to the mangroves, a weedguard is a must. Each step in this process has a set of questions and answers that leads me to a list of materials or another set of questions and answers that help me determine what material to choose based on the environmental conditions and where the fish are eating.

As you continue down the rabbit hole of Q&A, you will find that several materials might accomplish the action or attribute you desire or the answer to the question may be a combination of a few materials. The purpose of all the questions is to make you think through the materials you choose and why. Learning to accurately read feeding fish and the environment they are in takes time on the water. Developing and selecting the right patterns for each situation is the next step, and it just takes a little pragmatic thinking.

## Durability, Castability, and Fishability

There is no denying that a large part of creating productive patterns is learning how to read the surroundings and the environmental cues presented in the area you are fishing.

After determining where in the water column the fish are feeding and what the conditions are, we continue to expand on the "Where are they eating?" diagram in order to select the proper materials to ensure our fly gets to the fish. Hook color, weedguards, and weights may all need to be considered, depending on the fishing situation.

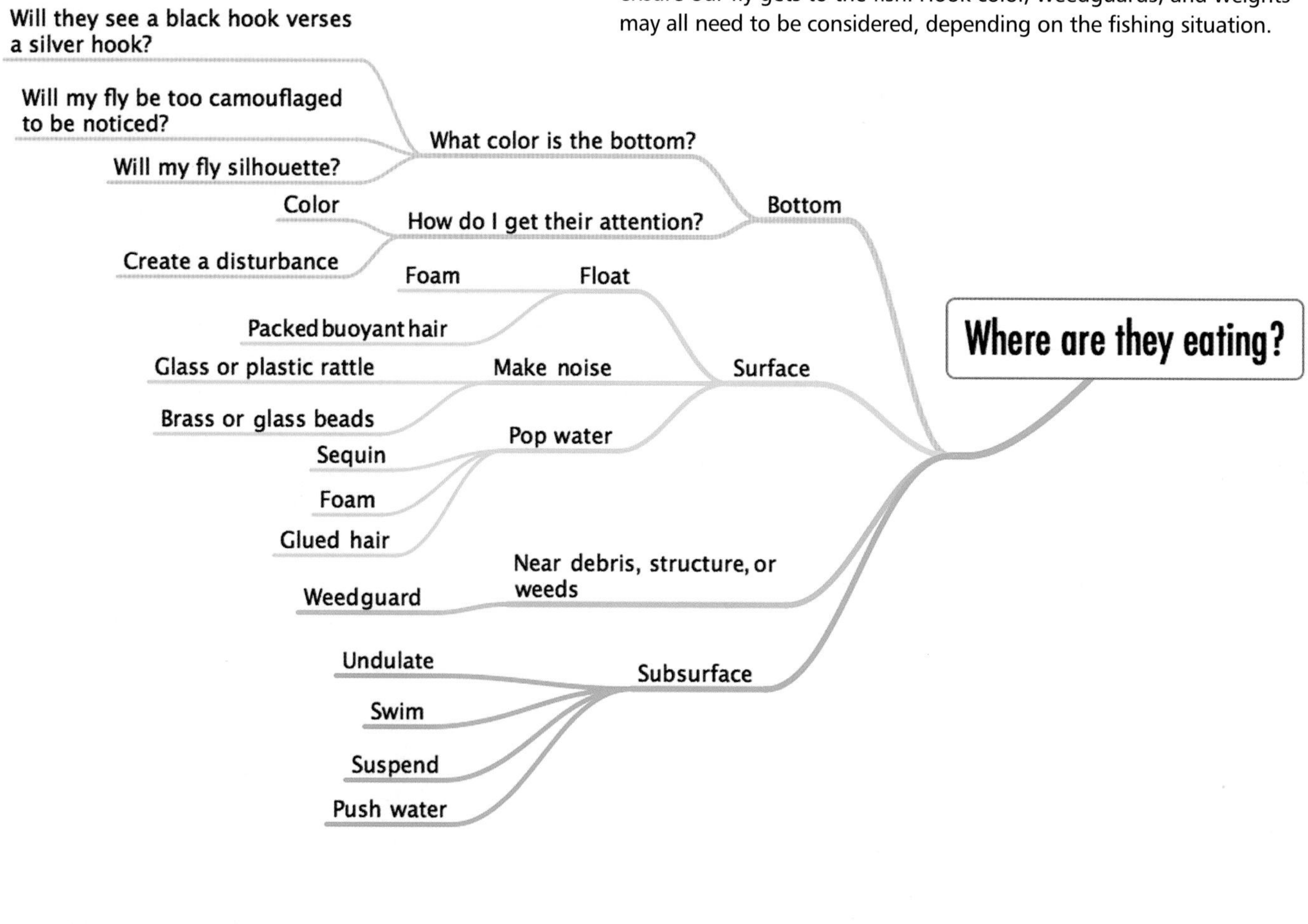

Familiarizing yourself with the available materials and knowing their qualities and characteristics is the other big piece of the puzzle. Honing the skills you need, however, does not happen overnight. Mastering the ability to interpret all this information and apply it to pattern development may take the better portion of a lifetime. A good way to fast-track your understanding of how this all works is to study patterns that have a proven track record of catching fish. These flies do a great job of mimicking a prey item and its specific movement. Understanding where the fly was intended to be fished, what factors led the designer to choose the materials he did, and why the pattern has evolved helps to give you the whole picture. The collection of information, stories, and interviews at the end of the book gives you a peek into the heads of some innovative tiers. Studying how they think and create new patterns gives you an insider's perspective, valuable insight, and hopefully encouragement to create your own unique patterns.

A few "abilities" that flies need to have to catch fish are sometimes overlooked during the creative process. I admit I have created some real train wrecks that cast like trash can lids or disintegrate with the first round of false casts, but that's how you learn. Spot-on realistic flies and extremely delicate shadow-box flies that will never touch the water have their place, but if your aim is to wrestle fish, then you need to take a few more things into consideration.

I use this "Where are they eating?" diagram as a tool for organizing my thoughts and laying out the shape and size, specific movements, profile, and appearance of the food item I plan on matching.

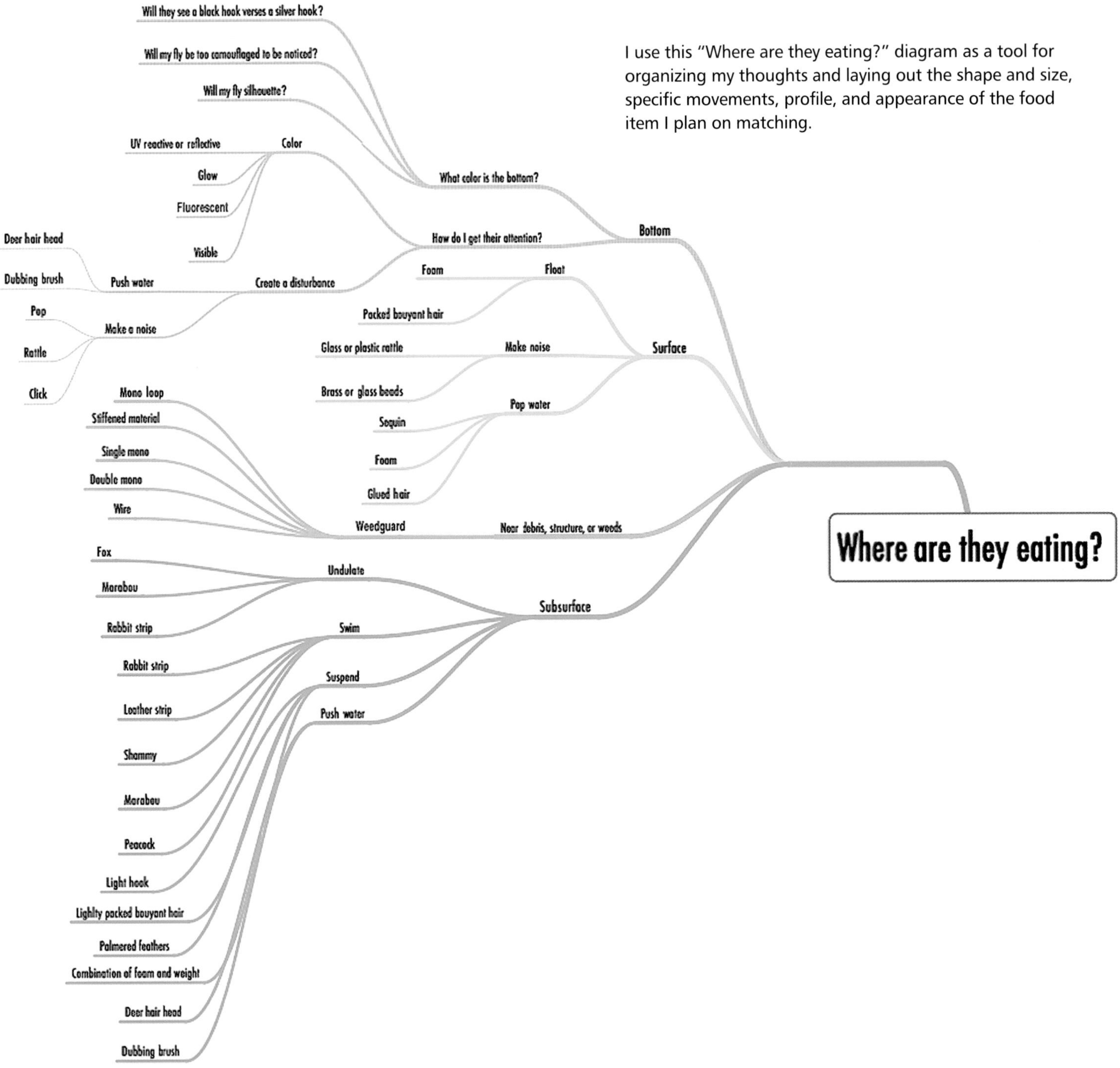

### Durability

Durability is pretty self-explanatory. Will my once beautiful fly resemble cat vomit after catching one or two fish? Toothy critters like mackerel and barracuda have a tendency to destroy anything you put in front of them, but you can make your flies more durable–if not bomb proof–with certain materials and techniques. Synthetic materials are far more durable than natural ones, and countless glues, epoxies, and acrylics give your flies a longer life span. I often palmer materials through a bead of glue applied along the entire hook shank, or twist a natural material with a Kevlar thread before palmering to increase the longevity of the fly. Heat shrink tubing can also be used to protect the head and thread wraps of your flies, especially if you are fishing with a wire leader.

### Castability

"Castability" is a term I use for the fly's aerodynamics. If you are making 60-foot casts to super-spooky fish, you need a fly that casts like a dream and floats to the water's surface like a whisper. Behemoth popping corks or dime-size lead eyes are not going to be high on your list of materials to work with. The size of the fly you need to catch fish can often dictate the size of line you need to carry and turn over the fly, which in turn affects the size of rod you are fishing with. I won't get into line and rod recommendations in this book. Simply put, you need to tie with materials that allow the fly to be cast easily at great distances.

### Fishability

"Fishability" refers to the fly's performance in the water when it is retrieved. Does it foul, spin, or not track correctly in the water? If so, what could you alter to make it perform better or more reliably? Oftentimes you can achieve the same look but improve a fly's fishabilty by changing a material, removing the weedguard, or trimming the fly slightly. More on this in the test and tweak portion of the book.

# CHAPTER 2 Overlooked Aspects of Fly Design

The most fundamental components of a fly, like the hook or the thread, often play the most significant role in determining its ability to catch fish. Overlooking or underestimating the importance of selecting these basic items may not be aesthetically critical, but all it takes is one missed opportunity or losing the fish of a lifetime and you may change your mind.

## Thread

When it comes to selecting thread, unfortunately color is often the only factor that novice tiers think about. Ought and denier are the two classifications for measuring the diameter or tensile strength of thread. Both are quite simple to grasp if you remember that the scales are opposite each other. The term "denier" refers to the number or count of fibers that makes up the thread. The higher the denier number is, the more fibers it has, so the stronger or thicker it will be. For example, a 100-denier thread has about half the diameter and strength of a 210-denier thread.

Thread classified with the ought system is the exact opposite; the lower the number before the ought, the stronger and thicker the thread will be. Thread that is 1/0 is stronger than 6/0. If you can't remember the difference, the easiest way to determine the size of the thread is to compare them side by side.

The standard size for thread on most saltwater flies is 210-denier or 3/0 thread, but in my opinion this is overkill.

*Above:* Salinity, current, your leader, or any number of other factors can affect how your fly falls through the water. Sometimes a minor adjustment in the sink rate of a fly is all you need to make your fly appear more natural and turn on the bite. I like to tie identical flies with different-size bead-chain eyes for different situations.

Inexperienced tiers tend to gravitate toward the stronger threads because they are much more forgiving if you accidently nick them with the point of the hook or apply a little too much pressure. The downside of the added strength is that novice tiers have a tendency to add a few extra wraps with each additional material. The excessive thread builds up in a hurry, even if you flatten your thread, making flies tremendously bulky and hard to manage. The more wraps you add in an effort to fix or even out the problem areas, the worse it gets. The thread is slippery, and the extra wraps slide out of place. All of this can be frustrating for new tiers.

I recommend going down in thread size whenever possible. You may break off a little more at first, but you will get better at controlling thread pressure and your flies will look tidier. It is also a good habit to start counting the number of thread wraps you make. Counting them will make you more aware of how many you are using and make your flies more uniform. Three to five well-placed turns is more than enough to secure the vast majority of materials.

## Choosing the Right Hook

While you are thinking about where the fish are eating and what materials to use, you also need to take into consideration what hook to start with. I consider four factors when determining what hook to build my fly on: shank length, wire, gap, and color.

### Shank Length

When it comes to toothy fish like mackerel or barracuda, a hook with a long shank is perfect for keeping the leader away from razor-sharp teeth. It is also the perfect platform for spinning deer hair for large topwater patterns or high tying materials to build a wide profile. Conversely, the added length of the hook shank can be a disadvantage when you are fighting fish. Highly acrobatic fish like tarpon jump and shake their heads while trying to free themselves, and the longer shank gives them added leverage to pry the point of the hook free. One alternative for creating extra-large flies without increasing the length of the hook shank is to create your patterns on a plastic or metal tube. This requires a special vise and different types of tubing and styles of brass heads for tube flies.

### Wire

Visibility, durability, penetration, and sink rate are the major factors to consider when choosing the thickness of the wire. Some fish have acute vision and are more cognizant of the presence of a hook, making both wire and color key considerations. A thinner wire is far less noticeable, and sometimes can make the difference between a strike and a refusal.

Durability is obviously important; you need a hook with enough backbone to hold up to the size fish you are going after. Hooks that are 2 and 3x provide extra strength for horsing the most obstinate heavyweights. Happy accidents occur and you may catch a species you were not fishing for, so I err on the hefty side if the situation allows. There is nothing worse than losing a bruiser and pulling back a straightened hook. Keep in mind, though, the heavier the wire is, the more difficult setting the hook becomes. This is especially important when your goal is fish with extremely tough or bony mouths like tarpon.

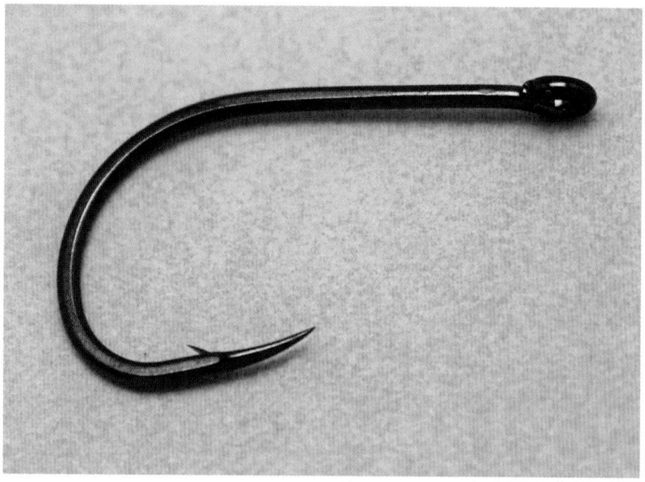

Shank length, wire, gap, and color are important factors to consider when choosing a hook.

The last factor to consider when it comes to selecting a hook is sink rate. The larger the wire, the more weight you are adding to the fly and the more rapidly the fly will sink. It may not be a deal killer; however, it is good to be aware of so you can adjust the materials you add to the fly accordingly to achieve the desired outcome.

### Gap

The distance between the point of the hook and the shank is called the gap. This distance determines how much of the fish the hook can grab onto. The bend or curved portion of the hook also acts like a keel on a sailboat and keeps the fly balanced and tracking true. A hook with a larger gap or bend has more wire or surface area for the water to push against. The extra wire adds additional weight to the bottom of the fly as well.

Materials that are bulky and do not compress well, like foam or deer hair, have a tendency to take up more of the gap space, so it is important to choose a hook with a wider gap when you are using these types of materials. If you do not have enough of the hook gap open, the fish will strike the fly and you will not be able to set the hook, or even worse you will hook just enough to keep them on for a minute or so until they come unbuttoned.

Bigger is not always better, though; hooks with smaller gaps are easier for fish to get into their mouths and are far less noticeable in clear water. There is a fine line between too much and too little gap, so a little on-the-water testing may be needed to come up with the perfect hook for your patterns.

### Color

The color of the hook is more important when you are fishing in situations where it will stand out. A black hook has a tendency to silhouette over white sand, and fish will notice it much more in clear water than they will a silver hook. Pelagic fish with very sharp eyesight like tuna are sensitive to hook size and color. Conversely, a black hook will blend in much better in dark or stained water than a bright silver hook. Blood red and many other color choices are also available. Whether you want your hook to blend in with the materials or stand out like bleeding gills, there are numerous options available.

Whatever hook you decide on, bend down the barb not only for the sake of the fish, but for your safety and the safety of everyone around you. I have taught thousands of people how to tie flies, and I emphasize removing the barb at every one of my classes. I can honestly say I take the pliers to 99 percent of the flies I tie right on the bench, but one fly I tied moments before hitting the beach and forgot. I have been stuck several times and up until that time I was lucky enough not to have buried it past the barb so the hook slipped right out. Not that one, though. Unlike the old 34007s you had to take the file to, today's hooks like the Gamakatsu SC 15 2/0 are strong, sharp, and difficult to remove from human flesh. I know the loop of mono or fly line trick for removing hooks, but that only works if you have both hands free and if the hook is not stuck in a location that bends when you yank on it. I was fishing alone, and I can tell you from experience that the physical and financial pain of spending several hours in the ER is far worse than the possibility of losing a fish. Accidents happen. Get in the habit of bending down the barbs before you get on the water.

## Shining a Light on UV Materials

In an attempt to bring some clarity to the muddy waters of fly-tying materials, and although I have no formal scientific training in this topic, I have spent a lot of time researching ultraviolet (UV) materials and the hubbub surrounding them. I have had some trial and error with my treasure trove of materials on the flats, and between that experimentation and my research, I'll try to explain what fish might be seeing.

UV reflective materials do not react under a UV light. This means that particles of light in the UV spectrum that hit the material will be reflected and become more visible to predators that can see UV light. If no light is present, then there is no UV light either. If there is no UV light, then there is no UV reflection from the materials.

If birds, fish, and insects can see UV light, and humans cannot, materials that claim to be UV reflective cannot be tested with a blue light or a UV light since they simply reflect UV light, which we cannot see.

Most but not all feathers are UV reflective. Some feathers reflect more UV light than others, such as jungle cock, peacock, and iridescent exotic bird feathers. However, birds in the ostrich family, owls, and hummingbirds have no UV reflective feathers at all. Bright-colored plumage

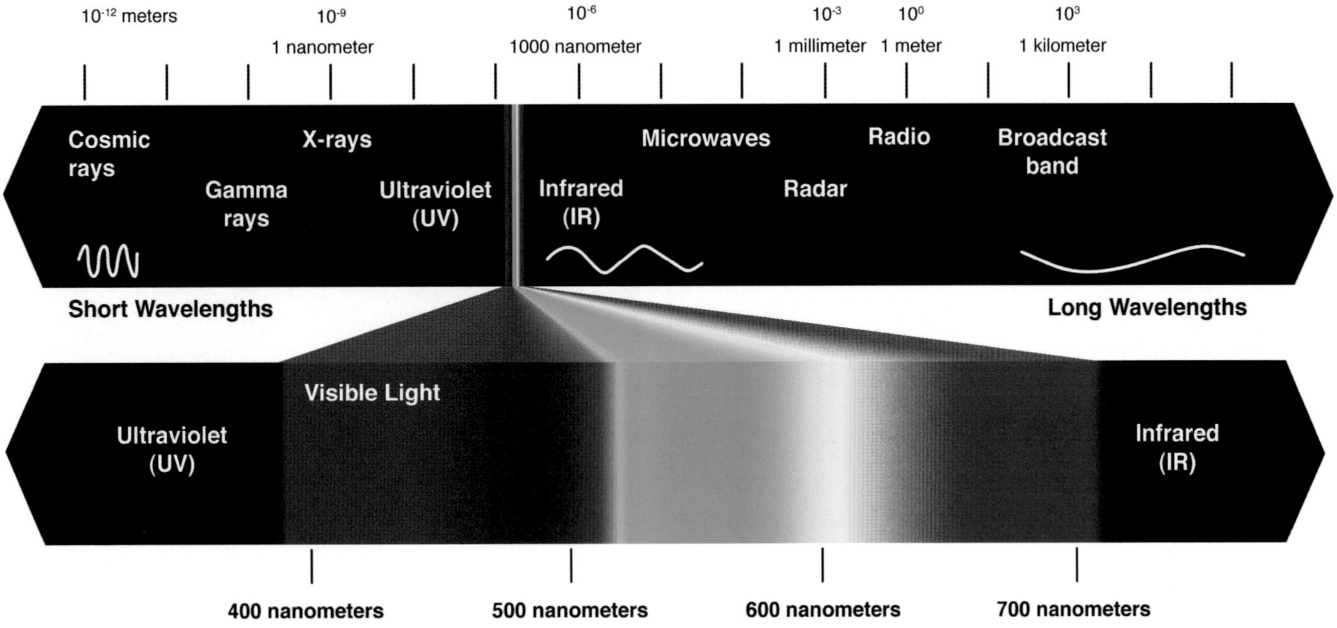


The visible spectrum shown in the colored portion of this diagram illustrates what is visible or can be detected by the human eye. Shorter wavelengths of light such as ultraviolet or (UV) light are not visible to humans and can only be seen by birds, insects, and fish.

This UV pearl Krystal Flash has a purplish blue hue and is noticeably different than standard pearl Krystal Flash, but since the human eye cannot see UV light, there is no way of determining if it actually reflects UV light particles.

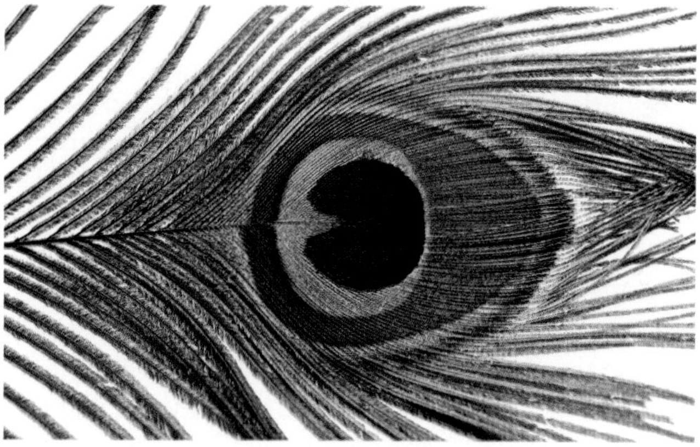

Peacock feathers are known for their iridescent qualities and are used as a fly-tying material in both freshwater and saltwater patterns. They are brightly colored feathers and are an excellent example of a UV reflective material.

and UV reflection may play a role in how these birds interact or communicate, especially when it comes to choosing a mate. UV reflective materials call attention to your fly against a dark non-UV reflective background and may trigger a strike. UV reflectivity matters most in low-light situations and at long distances in any direction, not just down. The farther away the materials can be seen, the better your chances are of attracting fish.

White or lighter colored feathers are highly UV reflective, while darker or black feathers reflect far less UV light. White has the highest UV reflectivity, followed by blue, yellow, green, red, brown, and then black. Highly reflective UV colors like fluorescents are not typically found in nature, but they work well to get the attention of fish.

So what are you seeing when materials light up in the dark when you shine a UV light on them? These are UV

Colors like chartreuse and hot pink are automatically UV reactive and can be seen at a great distance underwater. They have proven to be productive colors for a number of species and have become standard choices for most saltwater attractor patterns.

Most but not all feathers are UV reflective, and the color of the plumage plays a large role. White feathers are highly UV reflective while darker or black feathers are less reflective or not reflective at all. The color white has the highest UV reflectivity, then blue, yellow, green, red, brown, and black.

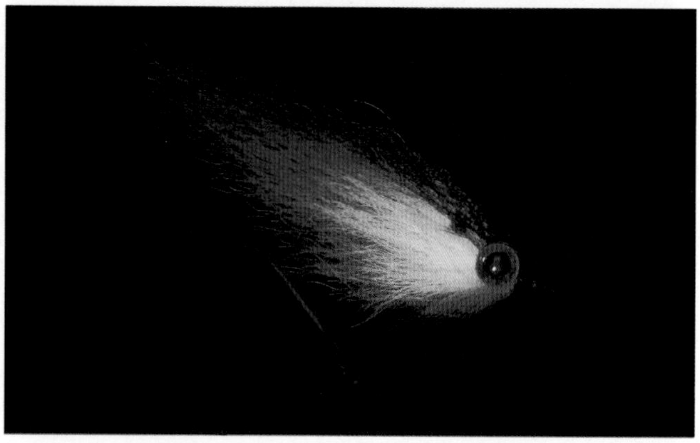

Shining a UV light on this yak hair baitfish pattern causes it to shine brightly, illustrating just how UV reactive white yak hair is. UV reflectivity matters most in low light situations, and at long distances in any direction, not just down. The further away it can be seen, the better your chances are of attracting fish.

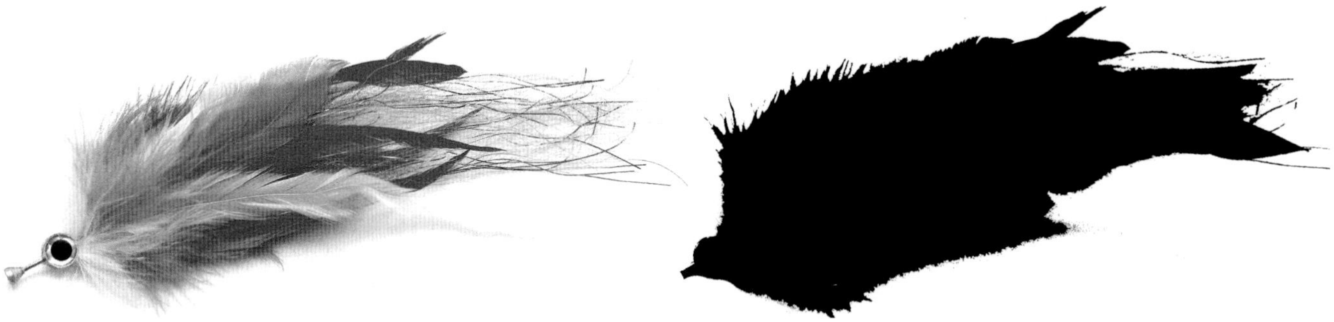

Although brightly colored flies can be seen at greater distances in lower light conditions, a dark fly that silhouettes against a light background can be just as eye-catching. Since blood is thought to look black underwater to fish, black flies may be interpreted as a hemorrhaging baitfish and an easy meal.

reactive materials. UV reactive materials shine, radiate, incandesce, or fluoresce when you hit them with a UV light. Typically this means they have been dyed with UV reactive dyes. Highly UV reactive materials can be checked with a UV light. They gather light and fluoresce or luminesce in the dark. Materials that appear fluorescent in daylight absorb UV and reflect, or radiate, with a brighter intensity.

One theory why highly UV reactive colors like chartreuse are so effective is that in some way they mimic blood in the water. However, blood does not react to UV light in the same way as UV reactive colors do. Many popular crime shows on TV portray blood as glowing when exposed to a UV light, but this is simply not true. In order for blood to glow, it needs to be treated with a reactive chemical, which makes the blood glow in the dark briefly even without a UV or black light. When exposed to UV light, blood absorbs the light but does not fluoresce; instead it appears black.

If a hemorrhaging baitfish appears black underwater, its image is a silhouette against a light background. Since most mortally injured fish float to the top eventually, its dark shape contrasts sharply against the brighter, sunlit backdrop. A silhouette is easily seen underwater at great distances, especially in stained or dark water. Again, the more visible a fly is, the better.

Each color fades and eventually appears gray at a different depth. UV light penetrates deeper in the water column than visible light does, so UV reflective or reactive materials are visible at greater distances. The colors of the visible light spectrum are gradually absorbed, depending on the color and clarity of the water. Colors with the highest energy, like red, orange, and yellow, disappear or dissolve to gray first and cannot be seen as you get deeper or farther away. This is important when selecting a fly or choosing the colors of materials for tying your next pattern. Not only do you need to take into consideration the color of prey you are trying to

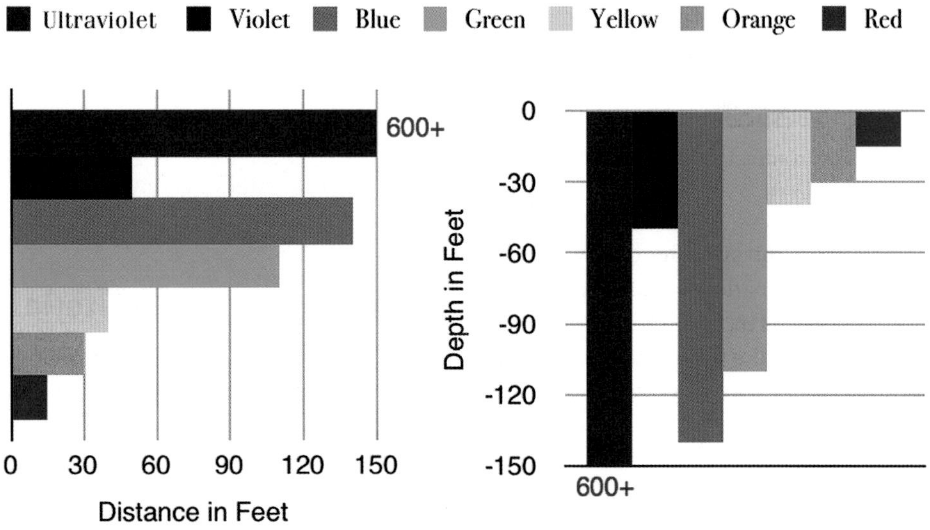


If you have spent any time scuba diving, you have probably noticed that some colors become less vibrant and eventually appear gray the deeper you go. This is because visible light can only penetrate so far in any direction, depending on the clarity of the water. This chart shows the estimated distance that visible and ultraviolet light can penetrate.

In order to give you an idea of how colors dissolve at greater depth, here is an example of the perceived color of a red fly at 0 to 10 feet.

As the fly sinks down 10 to 20 feet below the water's surface, its vibrant red color becomes dull and muted.

At 20 to 30 feet, the fly appears completely gray.

emulate, but you also need to consider the clarity of the water, the light conditions, and the depth that you will be fishing in. All these factors may affect how the fish sees the fly and ultimately how productive the fly is at attracting fish.

Visibility is much better in clear water than it is in cloudy, dark, or stained water. Clear water allows light, both visible and UV, to penetrate much more efficiently. The brighter the light, the better and farther away colors can be seen. Absence of light due to dark or stained water, time of day, or depth, reduces the depth and distance that a color can be seen. That is why on cloudy days, flies that have high contrast or a strong silhouette typically produce

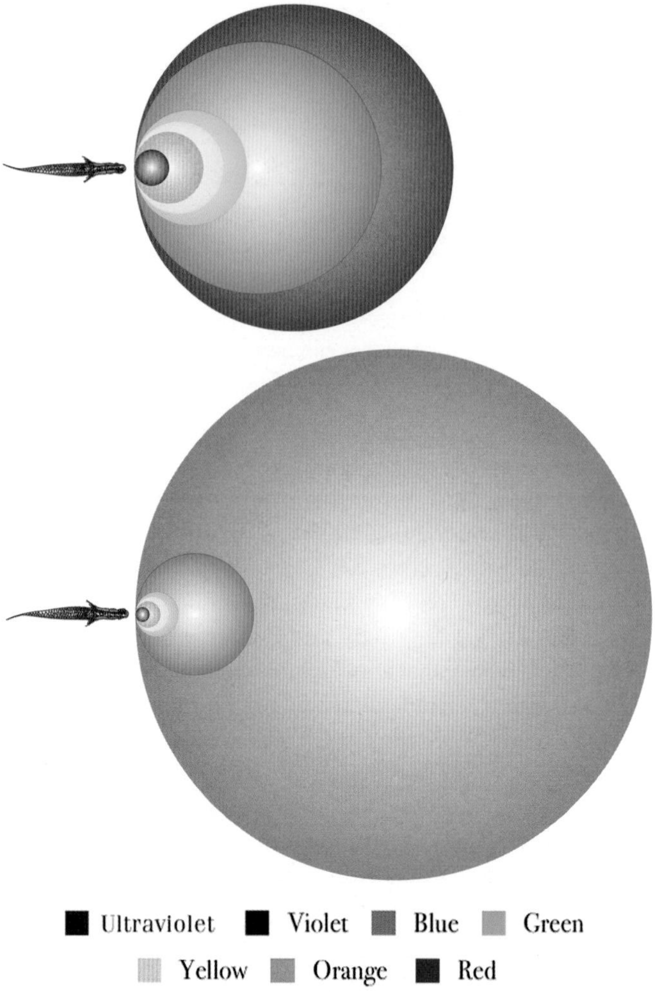


This scale diagram illustrates the relationship between the estimated size of visible color range and the estimated size of visible and UV color range. Each sphere represents the distance at which that color is no longer visible underwater. The largest sphere represents UV light, which is estimated to be visible at more than six times the distance of colors in the visible spectrum.

better than a specific color of fly . . . which explains the old rule "Bright colors on bright days, dark colors on dark days." It is a matter of getting something in front of the fish that can clearly be seen.

## Glow-in-the-Dark Materials

Glow-in-the-dark or fluorescent materials absorb short wavelengths of light like UV and immediately release them as long wavelengths of visible light, often in a slightly different color. Phosphorescent materials glow in the dark as well. They absorb and reemit light similarly to fluorescent materials, but they reemit the light slower. Once charged with light, these materials reemit or glow for a long time.

Fluorescence is the emission of light by a substance that has absorbed light. Luminescence is the emission of light by a substance not resulting from heat. Bioluminescence is the production and emission of light by a living organism. All of these properties increase visibility in lower light conditions.

Common sense tells you that flies that can be clearly seen by fish usually have a better chance of being eaten. Two ways of making your flies easier to see with the color you select are to create attractor patterns and patterns that silhouette.

Attractor patterns use bright-colored materials to get a fish's attention. Chartreuse, hot pink, and flame orange don't specifically represent any prey item found in nature. Selecting unnaturally bright colors causes the fly to stick out and be seen from a much greater distance. Just like the colors used to protect road workers or hunters in the woods, they draw your eyes, and make you aware that something is there no matter how thick the cover is. Once the fish is cued in on the fly, the fly's action will determine if it gets eaten or not.

Contrasting color combinations work in much the same way. The classic saltwater color combinations of red and white, or red and yellow, can be found in nature and represent a wounded prey. The color red is typically found on the front of the fly to mimic a baitfish that has been struck. If you have ever pulled back a white bait that has been hit by a snook or tarpon, you have noticed it takes on a pinkish hue, and more often than not the gills are bleeding or the eyes are filled with blood and bulging. At close distances the red appears red underwater, but at 20 feet the color starts to fade to gray or black. If blood is actually UV reactive and appears dark gray or black underwater, using the color red in your flies would work on a number of different levels, and be effective at both close distances and farther away as an attractor and a silhouette.

Dark color combinations like purple and black or red and black also have a proven track record in salt water. Fish like snook and tarpon have an upward-facing morphology, meaning their eyes are positioned more toward the top of their heads. They primarily feed looking forward or up. I think that if one of these fish is eating during the middle of the day, they are looking up at their prey and into the sun. This would make most objects that were not completely translucent appear black. A black or dark silhouette is far easier to see than a light-colored object.

I discovered this myself while watching bait swim around a green underwater snook light. Because the bait is backlit, the larger ones appeared black. If a fish is looking up at a bait on the surface, I think the majority of the time on a bright day the bait looks black.

Think about trying to catch a baseball while looking directly into the sun. The white ball disappears at some point and becomes black when it is directly backlit. It is very difficult to follow the ball afterward, because your eyes need to adjust and light colors are harder to see. If the ball was black, you would lose it for a second, but it would be easier to get your eyes on before and after passing through the

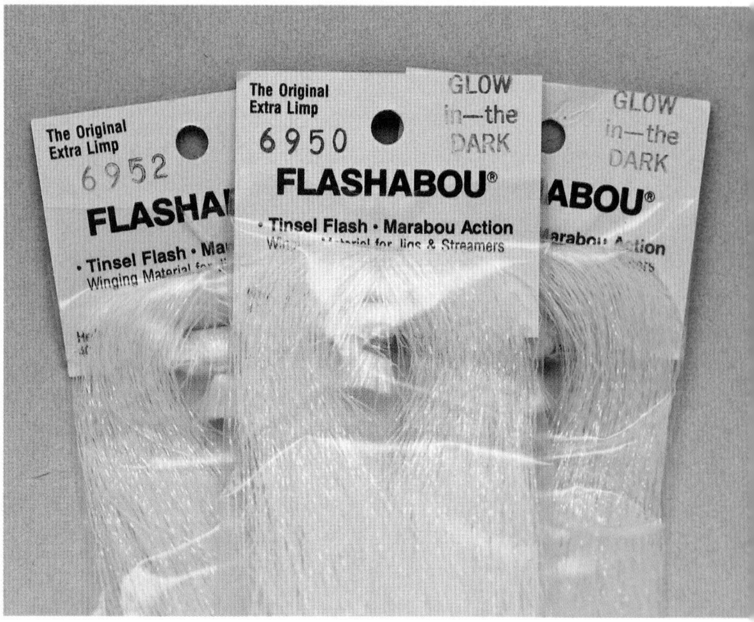


In ordinary daylight, glow-in-the-dark materials like this Flashabou appear cloudy or dull compared to similar synthetic materials. However, their fluorescent luminosity is an unmistakable attractant in the darkness.

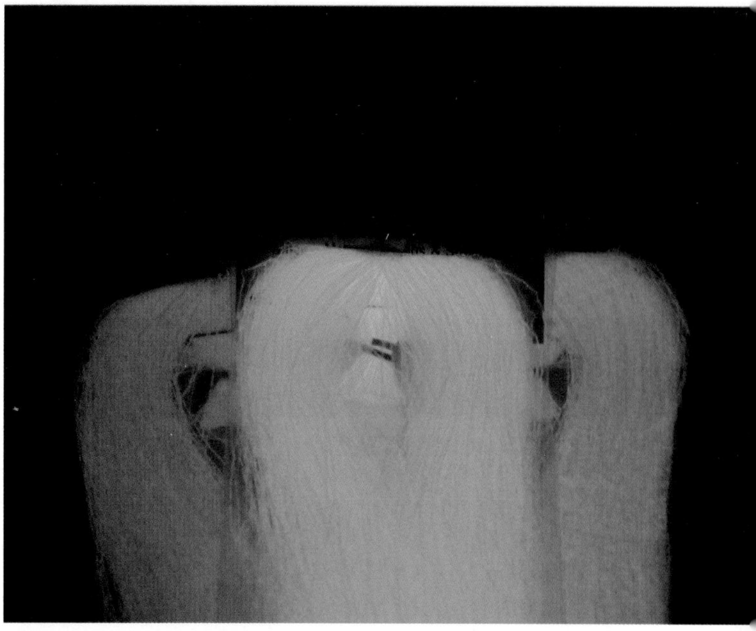

Oftentimes glow-in-the-dark materials like those above appear a slightly different color in the dark then they do in the light. Phosphorescent materials glow in the dark as well. Once charged with light, these materials reemit or glow for a long period of time.

bright spot. I would guess that is the reason that Enrico Puglisi's black and purple Peanut Butter Bunker pattern has been fished at one time by every tarpon guide in Florida and why for years Black Death was one of the most productive tarpon patterns.

I think the real takeaway is to maximize the visibility of your fly using whatever means or material you can. Analyzing the given fishing conditions, and understanding what colors or types of materials may be seen more clearly, is a good place to start. Whether or not the fish is in the mood to eat what it sees is a entirely different puzzle.

Sometimes it's not what the fish sees but what they "think" they see. Oftentimes more sparsely tied patterns or patterns comprised of translucent materials are the best choice. This is especially true in estuaries with extremely clear water, where the majority of the organisms are almost completely void of color and blend in so well they almost disappear.

## Test and Tweak

What you see in the vise is often very different from what you get once the fly touches water. More often than not with new creations, your expectations for how a fly will look in the water or act when fished will not be met without a few adjustments. Testing and tweaking your creations is an important step to producing productive patterns.

It is easy to determine how fast a certain-size prey item descends through the water column. All you need is a fish tank or clear container. With a few simple calculations, you can determine the average sink rate and use that information to create flies that act more natural in the water. I tested this theory with shrimp of several different sizes in order to determine their average sink rate.

| Prey Item | Average Sink Rate in Feet/Seconds |
|---|---|
| 2.5-inch shrimp | 1 foot every 7 seconds |
| 3.5-inch shrimp | 1 foot every 6 seconds |
| 4.5-inch shrimp | 1 foot every 5 seconds |

This table shows how fast different-size shrimp descend through the water. If you are throwing a 3½-inch shrimp fly, it must sink at the same rate as a live shrimp would if you want it to look natural. Depending on the hook and materials you choose, you may need to alter the weight slightly to accomplish this.

### Sink Rate

One of the most overlooked attributes of a fly is its sink rate. In order for your fly to mimic the intended prey item, it needs to sink at the same speed to look natural. A fly that moves too fast through the water column is often a red flag to skeptical fish, and an indignant refusal usually follows.

Testing your patterns in a pool or tank is a good way to analyze how they will perform before making adjustments to their weight or buoyancy. Whenever possible, time how long the item you are trying to emulate takes to sink. This information will help you determine which materials are best suited to match the hatch. You do not need a stopwatch or a yardstick to determine if your fly is sinking too fast or not fast enough. You simply need to know how deep the water is, and you can count how long a particular prey item takes to hit the bottom. Select a fly that moves at the same speed, or adjust your pattern accordingly. The important thing is for the fly to look natural as it falls to the bottom. You know you have cracked the code when you start getting strikes on the drop. Oftentimes a slightly longer pause than usual will trigger the strike. If there is too much weight, the fly will not move with the natural flow of the water.

It is a good idea to tie proven patterns with varying amounts of weight as well as in different sizes to match the profile of what the fish are eating. Oftentimes the size and shape of the fly is correct, but the fish don't take it because it falls faster or slower than what they are eating. Going up or down a size in weighted eyes makes the difference between a strike and a pass.

A general knowledge of size and sink rates of typical prey items will help in the pattern development process. Above are a few examples of sink rates for different sizes of shrimp.

While increasing the size of the lead wire, bead-chain eyes, or dumbbell eyes is an obvious choice for increasing the sink rate, oftentimes minor adjustments can be achieved by changing the type of hook or switching from a mono to a fluorocarbon leader.

CHAPTER 3

# Fixing Flies

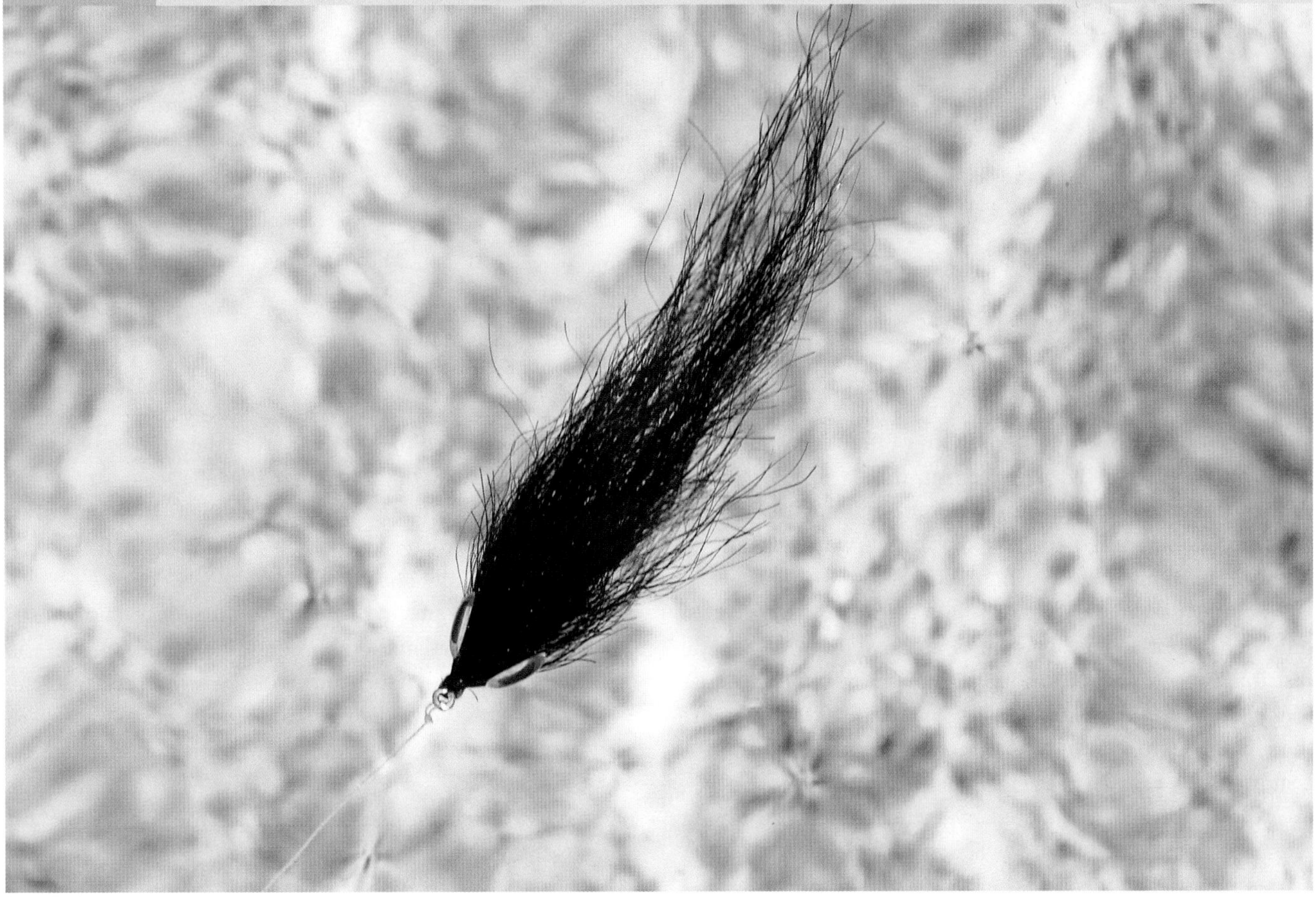

After you spend a considerable amount of time and effort behind the vise creating a masterpiece, the last thing you want to see is a fly that does not do what you expect it to when it gets wet. There is nothing more frustrating than a fly that tracks on its side when it is retrieved or spins like a corkscrew with each strip. If your fly does not sink or rides upside down, you can sometimes attribute that to the choice of materials, but also where on the fly the materials are applied or the techniques you used to tie it. Fortunately the vast majority of these faults can be corrected on the water with a little bit of know-how, and the ones that can't can certainly be avoided.

Flies tied with materials that trap air have a tendency to float or have trouble breaking through the surface of the water without several strips, which can move them out of position. This is a real problem when you are casting to cruising fish and you're timing your cast so the fly intercepts the fish at a certain depth in the water column. Adding more weight or increasing the hook size in this situation may affect the presentation or performance of the fly.

Flies tied with natural materials like deer, yak, rabbit, or fox hair take longer to become saturated with water, but they eventually do after a few minutes of fishing. Synthetic materials shed water with each false cast, so you may need to increase the weight of the fly or reduce the amount of material to offset the buoyancy of the trapped air.

To solve the buoyancy problem, hold your fly underwater for a few minutes and work the trapped air bubbles out of the materials to save you a lot of frustration and missed opportunities. If the fly still will not sink, trimming small

*Above:* An easy way to determine if your fly is tracking correctly is to compare the eyes. If the eyes are glued on evenly, you should not be able to see more of one eye than the other.

**Problem:** Fly floats

**Solution:** Massage the air out of the material while holding the fly underwater, or trim it.

amounts of material from the bottom of the fly around the hook point will usually be enough to fix the problem. Although I have not gone to this extreme yet, I have heard of fishermen who soak their flies in a Tupperware container full of water hours before using them.

Spinning flies are another common problem, with several different culprits. Flies that spin often have an imbalanced distribution of material on one side or on the bottom half (belly) of the fly. You should always have equal amounts on the left and right side of the hook, and less material on the bottom (belly) portion of the fly then the top (back) of the fly.

Exposing the gap of the hook by reducing a small amount of material on the belly of fly will often be enough to stabilize a spinning fly. The place on the fly where you trim material from is important, and will affect the way the fly tracks in the water. Reducing the material from the bottom of the fly will ensure that you do not change the balance or resistance on one side of the fly and make it spin. Start by removing a small amount of material from the bottom of the fly (belly), and this will usually correct the problem.

If the fly still wants to turn to one side, it is usually due to uneven amounts of material on one side of the fly. Wet the fly, hold it with one hand, and give it a good flick with the other hand–this will usually separate the material enough to expose uneven material. Remove uneven materials a little at a time. Don't just start hacking away! Micro adjustments can make a big difference, depending on the size, shape, and weight of the hook.

You may need to adjust a sparsely tied faltering fly on the water, where trimming is not an option. You can't simply

**Problem:** Fly spins

**Solution:** Reduce amount of material on the bottom of the fly.

## Tying the Two-Turn Loop Knot

Start with a simple overhand knot, leaving a tag end of 2 to 3 inches. Pass the tag end through the eye of the hook.

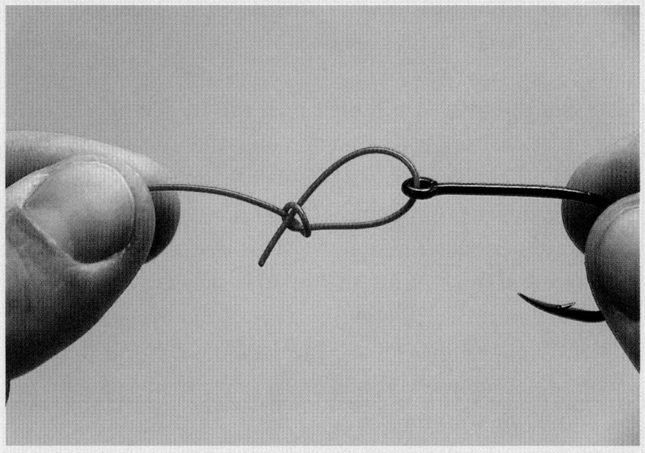

Next pass the tag end through the center of the overhand knot.

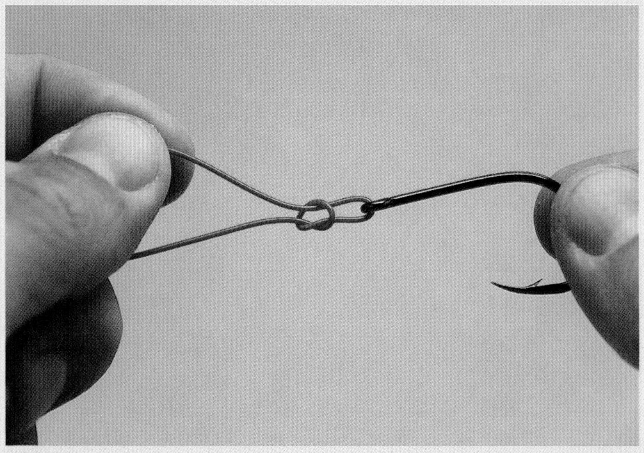

Pinch the tag end with your left hand and adjust the length of the loop between the eye of the hook and the knot to about a quarter of an inch. Keep the overhand knot open enough to pass the line back through to finish the knot, so do not pull it tight.

Make two to three turns around the main line with the tag end.

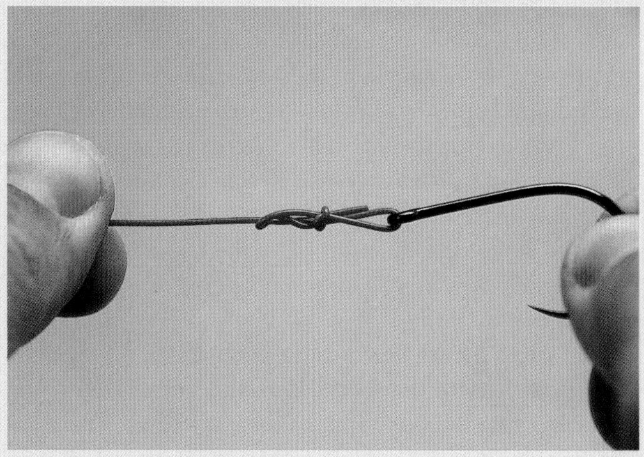

Pass the tag end back through the overhand knot, and pull the tag end, snugging the loops.

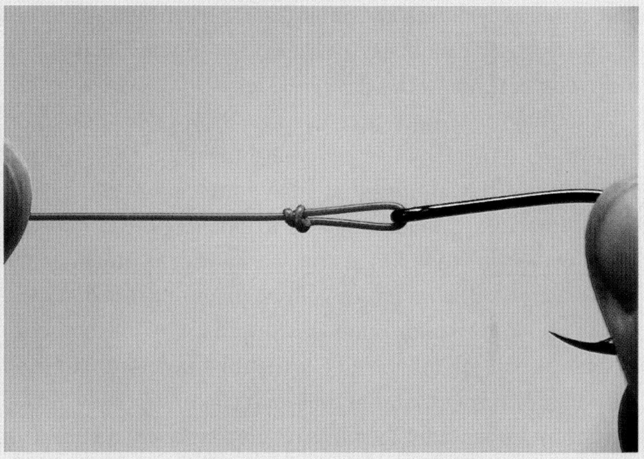

Pull tight and seat the knot. Trim the tag end as close as possible so it does not snag grass or other debris in the water.

Red wire is a great alternative to lead when you need a little extra keel weight. It's never a bad idea to insinuate blood or gills at the head of a baitfish pattern.

select a different size or style of hook to add weight to the bend of the hook. Wrapping a few turns of lead or stainless steel wire around the bend of the hook will often correct a faltering fly. You can experiment with the gauge of lead or stainless steel wire and number of wraps to see what works best depending on the size of the fly and weight of the hook. Use a dot of epoxy or UV adhesive to secure the wraps in place and increase the durability. The extra weight will act like a keel on a boat and keep the fly tracking true. The small amount of space occupied by the coils of wire will not impede the gap or the effectiveness of the hook. You can use red wire to represent gills instead of adding accent material to the throat of the fly.

The knot you use to attach the fly to the bite tippet can also affect the way the fly tracks in the water. The wrong knot can cause the fly to spin or track sideways. There are dozens of knot books on the market, and every one has an opinion on which knot is the best for a given situation. All I can tell you is pick one or two that you are comfortable tying and confident with. Experiment tying them with different pound test, and practice tying them a lot so you can tie them in low light, if not in the dark.

The majority of my time is spent fishing for snook and redfish, so typically I use anywhere from 20- to 40-pound bite tippet. I have found that I have the best results with a fixed loop connection as opposed to cinching the knot down to the eye of the hook. Imparting the fly with as much lifelike motion as possible increases your chances of success. My favorite knot is a two-turn non-slip loop. I know that some instructions call for four or five turns for maximum strength with lighter tippet material, but with the heavier fluorocarbon or monofilament, the turns seat far more efficiently with only two. I wet the knot with saliva, and use my pliers or the loop of my scissors to hold the hook for extra leverage while cinching the knot. Once it is as tight as I can get it, I trim the tag end flush with the knot. I am far more confident with a knot that is firmly seated than one that has more turns for "maximum strength." Until I start losing flies and pulling back pigtail leaders, this is the knot I'm using and recommend for the back bay.

More common culprits that can cause your fly to spin are poorly aligned eyes or weedguards. Before you break out your scissors and start chopping away, take a closer look at the head of the fly. Dumbbell and bead-chain eyes have a nasty habit of loosening up no matter how many figure-eight wraps you tie, and not even superglue can hold up to being bounced off the hull of the boat. Weedguards can easily bend or twist, so check and adjust them frequently. Even the best tied flies that use lead eyes or weedguards are susceptible to some slippage over time. Misaligned eyes or a twisted weedguard can alter the action of the fly, so check them routinely. A light layer of UV acrylic over the entire head is a quick fix.

Large baitfish patterns call for larger eyes, most of which have a tendency to protrude slightly from the side of the fly. If they are not glued on in proper alignment, this imbalance can cause a real headache. When you glue on dome eyes, make sure to check that the eyes are aligned both vertically and horizontally.

While the glue is still wet, turn the fly facing you and make sure that the eyes are even and one eye is not higher than the other. This is often why large baitfish flies track on their side or start spinning. I like to squeeze the eyes so they tip inward or angle slightly toward the eye of the hook. Next take a look at the fly from the top to make sure that one eye is not farther forward than the other. If the eyes have dried on the fly out of alignment, your best bet is to cut them off and glue on a new set. This is much easier than trying to correct the fly by trimming it.

Not only should the eyes be equidistant from the eye of the hook, but they should also be the same distance from the shank of the hook and canted at the same angle. Try not to squeeze the fly too much and flatten its natural shape.

## Fixing Flies That Foul

There seems to be a direct correlation between materials that really move and look great in the water and the propensity to become fouled. Rabbit strips, fox, Finnish raccoon, or any material that is used in a strip with the hide still attached gets waterlogged and tends to wrap itself around the bend of the hook. This is also the case with soft or weblike feathers like marabou and ostrich or thin, pliable synthetic fibers. If you stiffen the materials too much in an effort to stop them from fouling, you take away their lifelike movements in the water. Depending on the type of material you intend to use, there are a number of techniques you can use to cut down on fouling and keep the material's natural movement in the water. In the photos, bright orange fly line was used in place of monofilament in order to illustrate the techniques more clearly.

### *Mono Loop through the Material*

This technique is best for larger flies. Since the mono loop actually passes through the leathery hide, this technique really only works well with thick cut or Magnum Zonker Strips. Puncturing the strip with a bodkin weakens the strip, and the thinner cut Zonker Strips have a tendency to break off at the hole.

### *Mono Loop underneath the Material*

This technique works well with thinner Zonker Strips that cannot be punctured. The loop helps to keep the material from wrapping around the hook, but is far more effective when used in tandem with a stiffer material base or material collar. Do not make the loop too long or it will lose some of its effectiveness. A loop about a quarter of an inch long is ideal.

## *Flexible Adhesives and Acrylics*

Small amounts of flexible adhesives or acrylics can be used on a variety of materials to slightly stiffen a small portion closest to the hook. This limits the lifelike movement of the material, so use as little as possible to get the job done. Add a mono post for extra support with longer materials. Some adhesives like superglue cause the material to become brittle over time and will cause it to break where the glue ends and the untreated material begins. Experiment and test the durability before tying up a bunch of flies using this technique.

## *Double the Material*

Another effective way to keep Zonker Strips from fouling is to double the material at the tie-in point. Flies like Scott Sanchez's Double Bunny have two Zonker Strips glued together skin to skin. The fur comes alive when submersed, but even if you use a flexible glue to attach the two pieces, you lose some of the material's natural tendency to serpentine when stripped through the water. By gluing a short piece of the same material skin to skin with a flexible glue such as Tear Mender, you can maintain the snakelike motion of the Zonker Strip and reduce its tendency to wrap around the bend of the hook.

## *Material Platform*

Stiffer material like deer hair or synthetic fibers can be used to create a material platform that will prop up or support softer materials. This technique works well on smaller patterns or when the tail material is not completely flexible and has some support structure of its own, like the quill of a feather. Gather a bunch of the stiffer material the diameter of a wooden matchstick. It is just enough to stop the material from sagging down and wrapping around the bend of the hook.

### *Material Collar*

A material collar is the best tying technique when you need to contain longer, extremely pliable materials. Use this technique when you don't want to limit a material's swimming motion in the water but simply confine the material at the tie-in point so it is unable to double over or wrap around any part of the fly. Stiff hair, like deer or moose, work exceptionally well for this.

### *Stiffened Material Spine*

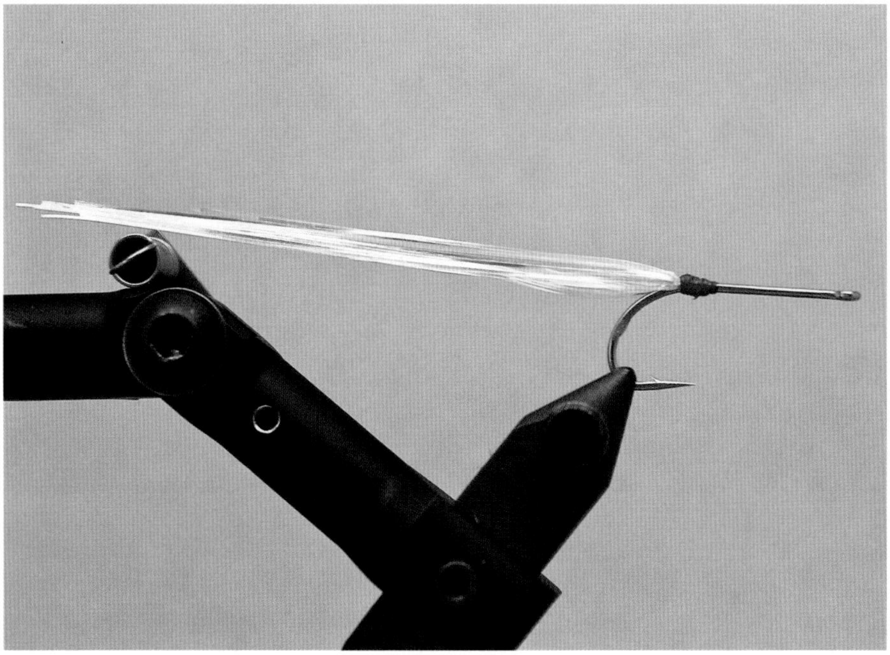

I first saw this technique used to make weedguards out of deer hair and then later in Dave Skok's long and flexible Mush Mouth. For flies that call for long, thin synthetic fibers, this is the way to go! Coat a matchstick-size gather of fibers with Clear Cure Goo Tack Free Flex, Softex, or similar flexible adhesive. The stiffer core or spine of the fly works to keep the shape of the fly, while the rest of the untreated fibers are free to undulate in the water. This technique is very effective for maintaining the realistic translucent qualities of synthetic fibers.

# CHAPTER 4 Tying Tips and Color Considerations

When talking to a child, you may describe the squirrel hanging off the birdfeeder as gray with a white belly, or the tiny minnows darting around the piles of the dock as silver, but the reality is that nothing found in nature is only one or two colors. On closer inspection, you will find that the vast majority of creatures with fur or fins are adorned with countless variations of dark and light colors, helping them blend in to their environments and ultimately keep them from becoming prey. Aquatic species often have vertical or horizontal stripes or adapt camouflage based on the color of the bottom or the water to conceal them from predators above and below.

If you want to produce believable imitations of these elaborately painted organisms, then you need to apply the same attributes to your flies. Reproducing convincing colors and patterns can be tricky, but with the right materials, tools, and techniques you should be able dupe the pickiest of predators.

*Above:* It's no secret that my favorite material to use for tying large baitfish patterns is yak hair. The key to getting consistent uniformity is to count out the fibers you are going to use. This may sound a bit extreme, but if you try to work with too much, it becomes difficult to manipulate and tie down, leaving large bumps on the hook shank. Counting out the fibers not only ensures that you don't have some flies tied heavy and some sparse, but that you will end up with the right color blend.

## Thread Control

Although thread diameter seems like a minuscule thing, the size and shape of your thread can make a big difference in the way your flies look and fish. Heavier, stronger threads with multiple filaments or higher denier are common when creating larger, more durable saltwater flies. Whether you need to flatten or condense the fibers will depend on the intended use and desired outcome. The majority of thread comes to you already twisted and condensed from the factory. If you let the thread hang freely from the hook, the bobbin holder will begin to spin counterclockwise, the opposite direction of the twist in the threads, decompressing or flattening the filaments of the thread.

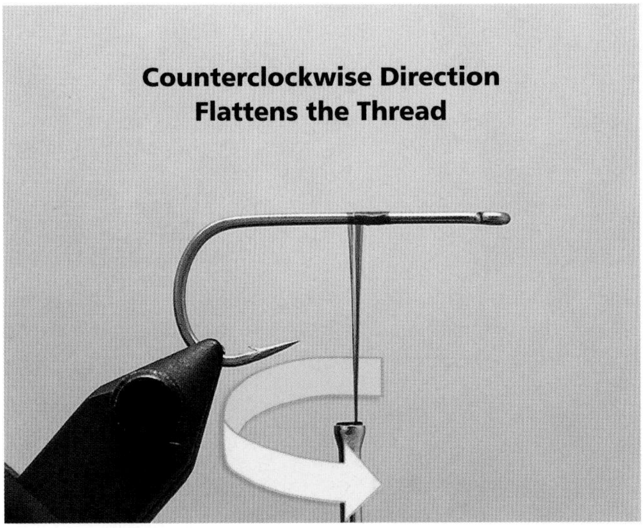


Spinning the bobbin counterclockwise flattens the thread and makes it far easier to work with for the vast majority of tying applications. If you are a right-handed tier wrapping away from yourself, you are actually spinning the bobbin clockwise and compressing the thread tighter and tighter with each turn. By spinning the bobbin holder counterclockwise, you remove the accumulated twists, resulting in a flattened thread. Left-handed tiers should do the opposite and spin the bobbin holder clockwise.

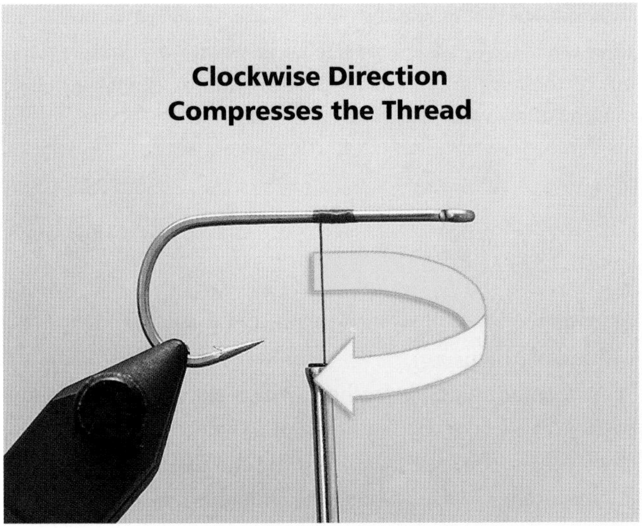


A compressed thread, or one that is twisted clockwise, is useful in tight places like a crowded eye. The twisted thread tends to curl back on itself when you release tension slightly from the bobbin, and you can loop it over the hood eye, securing your tension wraps with a simple half hitch.

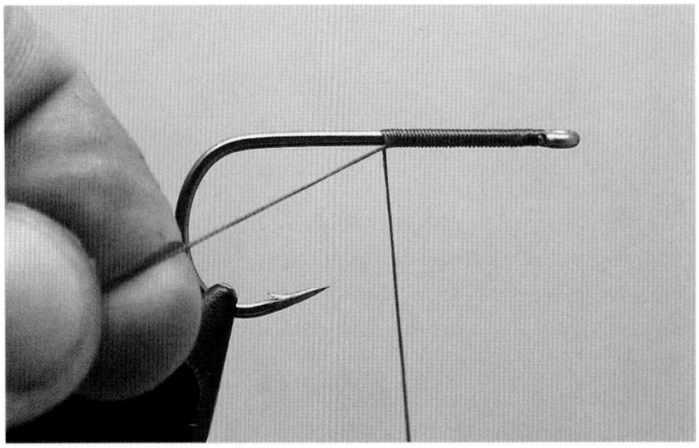

When attaching your thread to the hook, a compressed, clockwise-spun thread can also be used to cover the hook shank with neatly stacked wraps. By holding tension on the tag end of the thread, it can be used as a guide or a rail to slide and tightly stack each progressive wrap.

A flattened thread is critical for creating a thread bump, thread dam, or building up the head of a tarpon fly. A wide flat base of thread allows you to stack layer upon layer of thread without sacrificing hook shank and securing materials from slipping forward or spinning. A flattened thread also has more surface area than a compressed thread; therefore, it does not cut into delicate or brittle materials or break as easily since it is not under as much tension. The wider profile is more efficient at gathering and containing slippery materials like squirrel hair. Splitting a flattened thread allows you to sandwich a material in order to create a simple dubbing loop.

## Selecting and Working with Natural Materials

Although there are hundreds of different synthetic materials on the market today, don't forget about natural materials when stocking up on materials. Fur, hair, and feathers are the original saltwater tying materials, and they make up the bulk of elements used to create the vast majority of popular patterns. Three fundamental fly-tying components for saltwater patterns are feathers, bucktail, and rabbit Zonker Strips. Alone and in concert, these three elements are used to create countless fly patterns. They are easy to find in an assortment of natural or dyed colors. These basic materials are a must for all saltwater fly tiers. However, not all natural materials are the same, and there are a few things to look for and several to avoid when shopping.

## Bobbin Half Hitch

**A compressed or clockwise-twisted thread is useful for making a bobbin half hitch in tight places like a crowded eye and when spinning deer hair. A right-handed tier wrapping away from him- or herself is actually spinning the bobbin clockwise and compressing the thread tighter and tighter with each turn. (Left-handed tiers spin the bobbin counterclockwise.)**

**The twisted thread wants to curl back onto itself when the tension is released slightly from the bobbin, and it can be looped over the hook eye. Secure the tensioned wraps with a simple half hitch.**

**By applying a simple half hitch after each bunch of spun deer hair, you ensure that the fly will not come unraveled if you accidentally break the thread.**

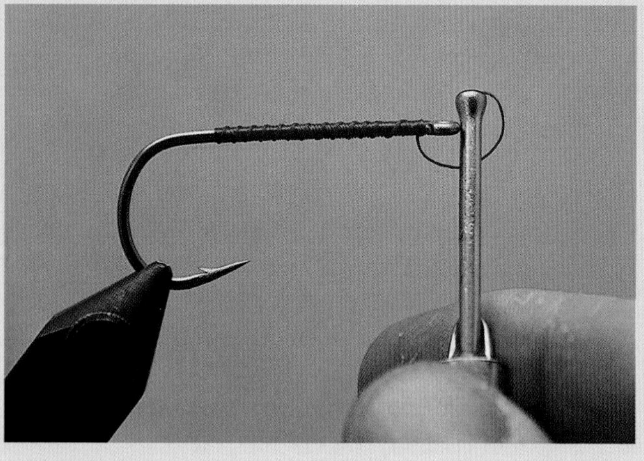

Compress your thread by spinning for one or two seconds. When you take the tension off the tread by moving the bobbin toward the hook shank, the thread should start to curl and form a loop. If it does not, give it a few more twists. If the thread bunches up in a ball, you need to spin it in the opposite direction to remove a few twists.

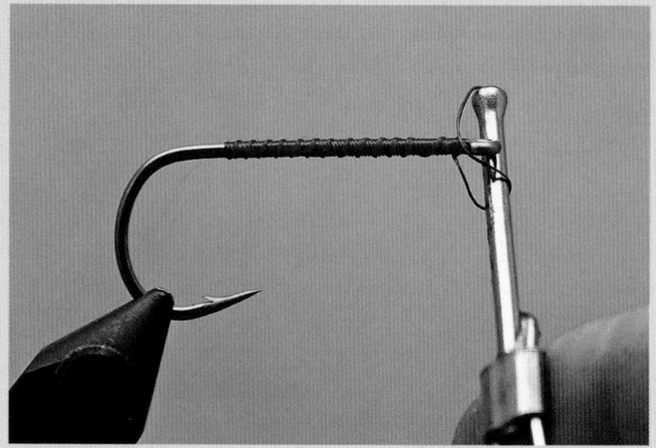

Once the loop forms, pass the loop over the eye of the hook. I like to shorten the thread to about one inch so I can use the tip of the bodkin to control the loop.

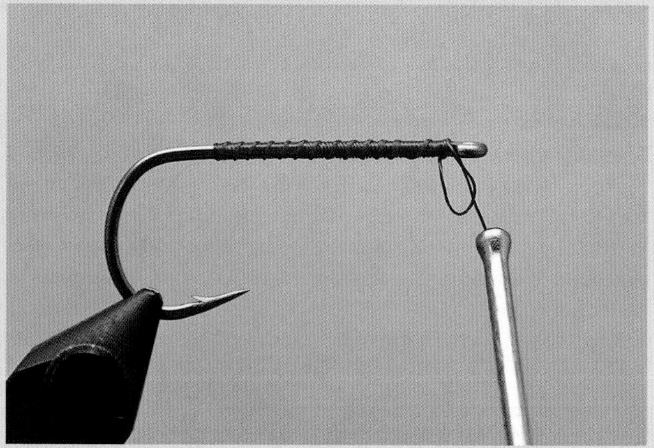

After the loop is placed over the eye of the hook, pull the bodkin out of the loop and cinch the half hitch down tight by pulling the bodkin toward you.

### Feathers

Feathers come in a lot of different shapes, sizes, variants, and colors, but let's avoid getting into the terminology of specific types of feathers and stay with the basics. Saltwater rooster or cock capes are typically what you find on the shelf at your local saltwater fly shop and are what I like for the majority of patterns. The rooster cape is larger than the hen, and they are usually more readily available. I typically tie on a range of hooks between size 4 and 1/0, so I look for a cape that is wider with the highest concentration of feathers in the 2- to 5-inch range. I don't use too many feathers on the cape shorter than that, so I try to avoid capes with a long neck section. The middle third of the cape is what you will mostly be using.

When shopping for feathers, whenever possible open the package and take the feathers out so you can inspect them closely. Flex the cape back, fanning the feathers. The feathers should be clean, not oily, and should not have any greasy fat spots. The feathers should also be straight without kinks or sharp bends in them. Feathers at the far left and right sides of the cape will have some curvature, and that's OK, but for the most part the feathers on the center of the cape should be straight.

Be sure to look closely at the tips, barbs, and stems of the feathers as well. You don't want feathers with broken tips or twisted, crooked, or bent or brittle stems. Older feathers have a tendency to become brittle and are easily broken when palmered. Bent tips are pretty common–this happens a lot when a natural material is larger than average and is too long for the packaging, but it is stuffed in at an angle to make it fit. Although many of these problems can be corrected by soaking and steaming, it is better to avoid the headaches if possible. Larger capes may contain more fly-tying fodder, but bigger is not necessarily better. The quality of the materials is far more important than the quantity.

Typically, feather physiology is explained or compared and contrasted with freshwater or trout flies in mind. Capes are categorized or graded by the size or number of flies that can be tied, and hackle length is king. Volumes of information have been produced focusing on selecting the right feathers for Prince Nymphs or Elk Hair Caddis, but if you're looking to apply that information to creating superior saltwater flies, and aren't really concerned about matching the barbs to the hook gap, you're pretty much left to fend for yourself with the sharks.

The terms "saddle" and "cape" or "neck" both refer to the area on the body where the feathers are located. Both hens and roosters have saddles and capes. The cape is the section of feathers that range in different sizes from the bird's head to the top of its back. The smallest feathers are found at the top of the cape where it is skinny; this is where the bird's head was. These feathers are pretty small, but they can be used on small bonefish flies or as claws for permit flies.

When shopping for feathers, whenever possible open the package and take the feathers out so you can inspect them closely. Flex the cape back, fanning the feathers.

As you follow the cape down the back of the bird, the feathers become wider, larger, and more webby. Cape hackles have a shorter, wider, more robust look in the water, and are better for creating flies with wider profiles. Chinese or Indian capes are simply capes imported from China or India.

The saddle is the section of feathers found on the back below the cape. Saddle hackles are usually long and have thinner rachis or stems. This makes them easy to palmer and gives them a slim profile and more movement in the water. Strung saddle hackles are feathers from the saddle that are sorted to matching size and length.

# Light-Curing Acrylics

No matter how careful I was with epoxy, whenever I used it, everything on my bench ended up tacky except for the spot I was trying to cover. It always yellowed and never seemed to cure properly. The smell was not exactly pleasing and rarely, if ever, did I get the full five-minute curing time to apply the stuff. That being said, I still have my modified rod turners/epoxy wheel. It is fully equipped with five foam disks and able to accommodate dozens of globbed up flies at once, but I am glad those days are over.

Thanks to their clarity, durability, quick curing times, and odorless attributes, UV-curing acrylics have been used in dentistry for more than three decades. At first, questions concerning safety kept UV-curing acrylics out of the fly-tying world, until the early 1980s when the products were modified to cure using blue or visible spectrum lights. Tuffleye was the first safe, light-curing acrylic marketed to fly tiers, and it claimed to be the fix-all for all of epoxy's shortcomings. It was quickly made popular by Atlantic fly tier Bob Popovics. His ultra-realistic patterns and innovative techniques proved to be very productive and were all the rage in fly-fishing magazines from coast to coast.

Although Tuffleye was head and shoulders above two-part epoxy for curing time, it had a different set of problems. Most noticeable was its tendency to crack or shatter, its tacky finish and yellow hue, and its exorbitant price. Clear Cure Goo was the next big name to emerge, and the company offered a number of much cheaper alternatives that remedied the yellowing and durability issues. Plus Clear Cure Goo uses chemicals made in the United States. This was key to ensuring that no fillers are added to the material that could yellow, brown, or shatter. However, you still had to finish your flies with an alcohol wipe, hand sanitizer, or a topcoat of Sally Hanson in order to remove the tacky finish even though Clear Cure Goo uses the UV light spectrum to cure its products.

Both Tuffleye and Clear Cure Goo have continued to enhance their products over the years, as well as offer a number of new tack-free or flexible variations. Although Tuffleye and Clear Cure Goo were among the first, several companies currently offer light-curing products, all boasting different and unique attributes for fly tying. Another exciting innovation is Loon's new line of UV paints, which provide an entirely new medium for fly tiers to create with.

With all these new products available, I have gone back through many of my old patterns and have begun experimenting with different brands to see which ones work the best for a given job.

My go-to products five years ago were oftentimes the only one available. After researching and experimenting with as many light-curing products as I could find, I created this product matrix to help clearly illustrate each product's attributes and abilities.

As you experiment with these products, make sure you never look directly into the curing light. I know they are assumed to be perfectly safe, but after a few hours of tying and using the light, my eyes and my stomach feel a little funny. If you're going to cure hundreds of flies, I recommend wearing UV-filtering and blue-light-filtering glasses. I find the amber-tinted ones the dentist wears work the best.

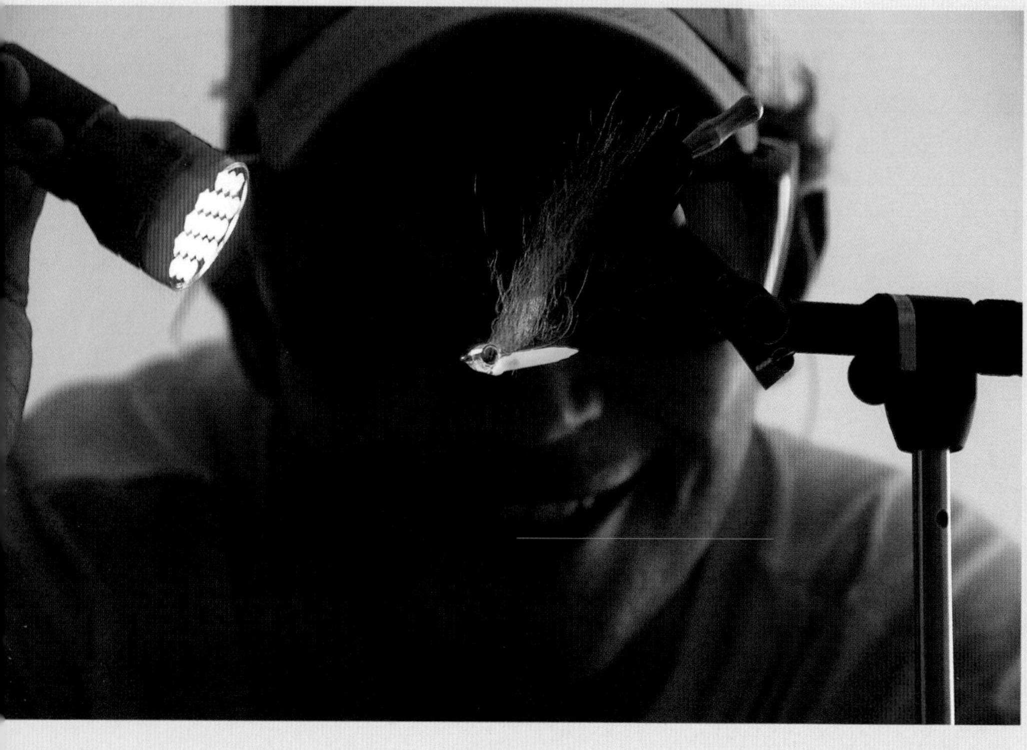

The numerous types of UV-cured acrylics on the market today provide a faster, easier, and cleaner alternative to epoxy. There are countless varieties available with varying thicknesses, finishes, flexibility, and colors. I know they are assumed to be perfectly safe, but if you're going to cure hundreds of flies, I recommend wearing UV-filtering and blue-light-filtering glasses. I wear amber-tined fitovers that my dentist gave me, but if you don't have a buddy who's a dentist, you can purchase them online.

| Product | Viscosity | Cure time (seconds) | Tack-free surface | Color after curing | Pliability | Applicator | Intended/best usage of product |
|---|---|---|---|---|---|---|---|
| Clear Cure Goo Fleck | thick | 7–10 | no | pearlescent fleck | hard | syringe | accent flash for heads or lateral lines |
| Clear Cure Goo Flexible | thick | 15–20 | no | clear | flexible | syringe | substitute for Softex or silicone, chewy consistency |
| Clear Cure Goo Hydro | very thin | 5–10 | yes | clear | hard | brush, squeeze bottle, tips | top coat for other materials, coating poppers |
| Clear Cure Goo Thick | very thick | 7–10 | no | clear | hard | syringe | larger profile flies, drip free, affords you time and control |
| Clear Cure Goo Thin | thin | 7–10 | no | clear | hard | syringe, squeeze bottle | penetrates deeper into larger patterns, round heads, smoother finishes |
| Clear Cure Goo Brushable | very thin | 7–10 | no | clear | hard | brush | top coat for other materials, coating poppers |
| Clear Cure Goo Tack Free | very thick | 15–20 | yes | clear | hard | brush, syringe | larger profile flies, drip free, affords you time and control, no need for alcohol or top coat |
| Clear Cure Goo Tack Free Flex | very thick | 20–30 | yes | clear | hard | brush, syringe | Charlie's Air Heads, Hollow Flies, Mushmouth, Chewy, or flexible flies, no need for alcohol or top coat |
| RIO Knot Sealer | thin | 20+ | no | clear | hard | wide-tip squeeze bottle | leader connections, smaller flies, deep penetrating, smooth and round heads |
| Loon UV Knot Sense | thin | 10–15 | no | clear | flexible | squeeze bottle | leader connections, smaller flies, deep penetrating, smooth and round heads |
| Loon UV Paint | very thin | 10–15 | no | yellow, orange, red | hard | squeeze bottle | colored eyes, accents |
| Loon UV Clear Fly Finish | very thin | 10–15 | no | clear | flexible | squeeze bottle | top coat for other materials, coating poppers |
| Bug Bond Original | very thin | 3–5 | yes | clear | hard | brush, squeeze bottle | smaller flies, deep penetrating, smooth and round heads |
| Bug Bond Light | very thin | 3–5 | yes | clear | flexible | brush, squeeze bottle | very small flies, deep penetrating, smooth and round heads |
| Tuffleye Core | thick | 10–20 | no | clear | hard | syringe | larger profile flies, drip free, affords you time and control |

The saddle is the section of feathers found on the back below the cape. Saddle hackles are usually long and have thinner rachis or stems. This makes them easy to palmer and gives them a slim profile and more movement in the water.

Saddle hackles are typically about the same size, whereas feathers found on a full cape vary much more in size. This uniformity results in a narrow range of sizes on any given saddle, so if you are tying trout flies, this restricts the range of flies that can be tied with that specific size saddle. Again, for saltwater this really doesn't matter. What you need to know is that saddle hackles are much longer, and strung saddles, which are sorted into matching sizes and lengths, are great for tying a lot of one large pattern like Deceivers. Capes have a wide range of feather sizes, so if you plan on tying lots of different patterns and sizes, they are the way to go. The majority of the feathers are 2 to 5 inches long and very wide and webby, so they are a good choice for the majority of saltwater patterns.

## Some Tips for Working with Feathers

After teaching fly tying for several years, I have come to the realization that feathers cause more confusion and frustration than any other material. For both beginning fly tiers and seasoned pros alike, keeping them secured, straight, and even on the hook is an onerous chore that can suck the fun right out of fly tying. Keeping shifty saddles from rolling can be difficult and maddening, but with a little know-how, you can avoid the annoyance.

*Tip:* You can rejuvenate bent or matted feathers by steaming them. I have piles of old feathers that I have been able to successfully revive by first washing them with Dawn dish soap and then steaming them. Steaming also works wonders for softening stiff or brittle feather shafts before palmering, or fluffing deer hair bass bugs before trimming them to shape as well.

If you are using really webby feathers, you can trim a section of the quill, but make sure you leave some of the barbs attached to the stem of the feather. Although you won't have a large volume of barbs left attached, this added width will provide more surface area and help to keep the feather from sliding out of place or spinning when you apply thread pressure.

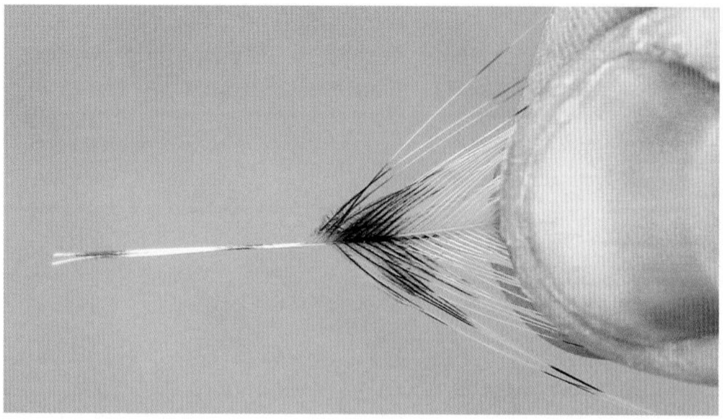

Beginners often strip away a section of barbs from the quill in order to make it easier to see their wraps when tying in single or multiple feathers. This exposes the bare quill or rachis of the feather. Depending on what type of feather is being used, the round or triangular quill of the feather is cinched down against other round feathers and a round surface of the hook, and you guessed it . . . the feathers roll every which way. Keeping those barbules on the quill is crucial to securing the feathers in the position they were intended.

Some instruction recommends you create a small gap or opening between the barbs for a clean tie-in point, but I do not advise this technique. Even stroking back a few of the barbules to create a small gap can cause problems. When you are working with feathers, you need to make sure your thread is flat. There are situations when you want to use a tightly twisted or compressed thread, but this is definitely not one of them.

Your best bet is to fold back all the barbules and make your wraps on top. Even though they are slender, the extra bulk will help to fill in all the tiny gaps and make the bundle more stable. Think of barbs like filler that can be compressed against the hook for added stability.

Once you have the tips of your feathers lined up, you can apply a small amount of glue to keep them from moving when you are tying them in. The glue will also help keep the feathers from rolling and keep them on top of the hook as you secure them. However, some types of glue become hard and brittle and tend to glob up your flies, so test a few and see which one works best for you.

If you are tying a fly with splayed hackles (like a classic Keys tarpon pattern), start the thread on the hook and create a small bump of thread. Flattening the thread and then making several consecutive wraps on top of each other will do this. The bump will help separate the feathers.

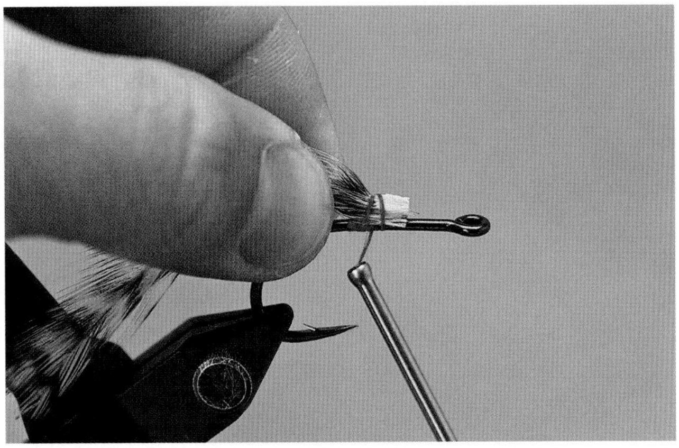

Match the tips of each pair first, and then match up the two pairs to one another and tie in all four at the same time. To secure the feathers, start with two loose wraps around the feathers and then cinch down the feathers by pulling your thread up.

The direction and amount of thread pressure you apply is important when it comes to controlling the material and achieving the desired result. By pulling up, you are applying pressure on the bottom of the hook shank and pinching the thread against the underside of the hook, which forces the feather up and secures it tightly on the top of the hook, instead of rolling it to the far side of the hook. You can see that the sides and bottom of the hook are clearly exposed here, and the feather did not shift or roll at all.

Inexperienced and even some intermediate tiers have a tendency to use the same amount of thread pressure for every wrap or only apply pressure to the thread while it is going away from their body. This causes the materials to roll or shift to the far side of the hook. If you want your materials to stay on top of the hook, you need to apply thread pressure up to pinch the thread against the underside of the hook shank and force the materials up. Once the feathers have been cinched down, make four or five tighter wraps to secure them.

A dead giveaway to a poorly tied fly or an inexperienced tier is mismatched hackles. Lining up the tips of the feathers is essential not only for aesthetic reasons, but also for the fly to track correctly in the water.

Most flies have two pairs of matched feathers, one on either side of the fly. If one pair of feathers is longer than the other, the fly will have more water resistance on that side and most likely will track on its side or spin.

"Marrying the hackles" refers to placing the concave or undersides of the feathers together. Another common term for this technique is "praying hands." When wet, all the feathers come together and look as one.

The opposite of praying hands is splayed hackle. This means that the feathers are lined up at the tips and tied onto the hook so the convex sides of the feathers are facing each other. When wet, the two pairs of feathers separate and appear to kick when stripped. This technique is often used for crab claws or on Keys-style tarpon flies.

Tented hackles are married hackles that are slightly opened at the bottom and touching at the top, to create a tent shape. This technique is often used to emulate the V-shaped back of a bait-fish. When wet, the two pairs of hackles swim as one and create a wider, more cylindrical profile. Jonny King uses this technique when tying his Kinky Muddler patterns.

When choosing feathers from the cape, try to choose like sizes. Don't pair one wide, webby feather with a thin, skinny feather.

Try to keep all of the feathers as uniform as possible. Length is less important since you will line up the feathers at the tips, but they should be nearly identical in width and taper. It is also important to choose feathers that have similar shapes at the points.

If you hold the cape in your hands skin down, you will notice that the feathers naturally curve to follow the bird's body. Feathers around the sides of the cape typically have more curvature than the ones in the middle of the cape, and the majority curve in one of two directions.

Feathers from the far left side of the cape curve or cup down and to the left and the opposite is true for the right side of the cape. If you are marrying the two pairs of feathers, pick feathers from the left side of the cape that curve to the left for your pair closest to you, and feathers from the right side of the cape that curve right for the far pair. That way both pairs of feathers curve slightly downward when married together.

## Folding Hackles by Hand

I have seen several different ways to fold a hackle in preparation for palmering, but they all give the same result. What you want is a higher concentration or density of barbs in order to reduce the number of turns you need to make a collar. When you palmer an unfolded feather, no matter how careful you are, you inevitably trap a few of the barbs with each forward wrap. By folding all of the barbs onto one side of the quill, you can wrap it without trapping the barbs under consecutive wraps. This technique is especially handy on smaller flies where you can only make one or two turns or where materials and tying space are tight, such as when you tie a post or are crammed against the hook eye. You can use a block of foam, wood, or cardboard to fold the barbs. Cut a slit in the piece of foam and pull the feathers through the slit. Tying the tip of the feather down and gently running the edge of your scissors over it as if you were a curling piece ribbon will also do the job; however, the technique I am about to show you does not require any extra tools.

Practice on larger feathers with thicker quills to start. Once you get the hang of it, you will find that this technique works on pretty much any feather, even marabou. It may take you one or two tries at first, but stick with it; you will use this skill a lot.

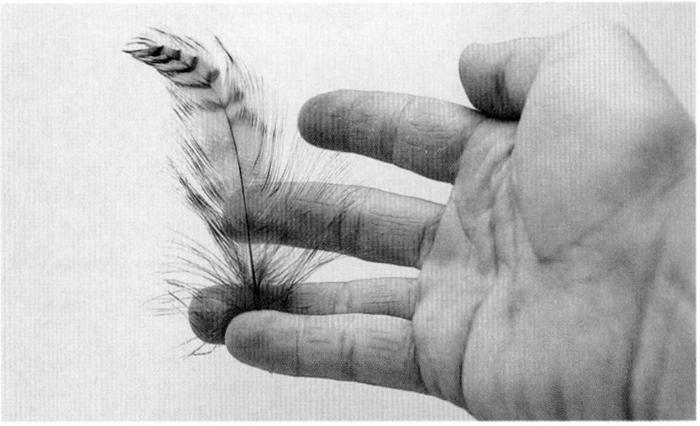

Start with the convex side of the feather facing you and pinch the feather between the pinky finger and ring finger of your dominant hand.

Pinch the tip of the feather with your opposite hand and stretch the feather tight.

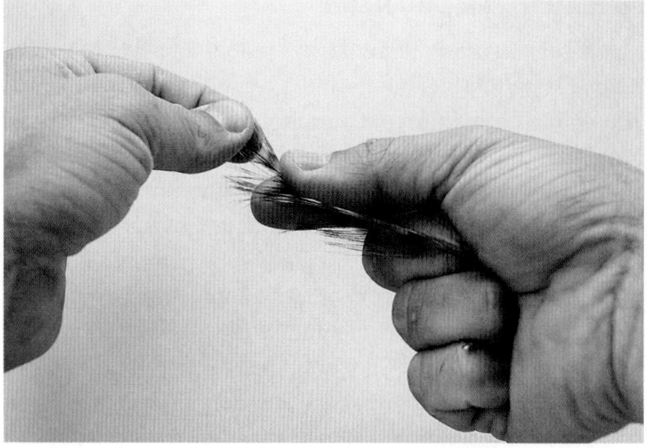

Place your index finger and thumb on your dominant hand together. The feather will slide between these two fingers, forcing all the barbules away from you.

Stretch the feather tight and begin sliding your pinched index finger and thumb down from the tip of the feather. Pulling the tip of the feather up with your left hand, continue sliding your index finger and thumb down the length of the quill.

Roll your wrist down and away from you to fold over the bottom of the feather. Once all the barbules are folded over, smooth them in place with one or two more strokes.

## Bucktail

The balance of rigidity and flexibility is what makes bucktail such an effective fly-tying material. It is perfect for creating very large yet virtually weightless flies. These flies tend to push a large volume of water and move with a lifelike undulation when stripped. When wet, the supple hairs become slightly opaque and naturally take on a tapered teardrop shape, perfectly emulating that of a baitfish.

The lion's share of saltwater fly patterns call for long, wavy, wiry hairs. The added texture and thickness of crimped hair is pivotal in creating flies that are larger and have wider profiles. The crinkly hairs force the water to travel around the strands in a more irregular path, pushing significantly more water in an inconsistent fashion as the fly is stripped. These abnormal vibrations and waves are more detectable to fish genetically programmed to seek out the erratic behavior of a wounded baitfish.

You will find that the top two-thirds of the majority of bucktails contain the highest concentration of long, stiff hair. The hair found in this portion of the tail contains much less underfur as well. Always try to cut the hair as close to the skin as possible to avoid damaging the hair underneath.

Flies produced with straight hair do not act the same in the water. Water moves past and around straight hair in a smooth and even path, with less resistance. For this reason they often sink faster, and they do not move as much water when they are stripped. I am only aware of one saltwater pattern that specifically calls for extra-straight deer hair: Joe Mahler's Straw Boss. The bullet-shaped head created by reverse tying extra-long deer hair secures a stiff wing tied perpendicular to the hook shank. The action of the fly is derived not from forward motion like most patterns but a rhythmic, back-and-forth swinging motion as the fly flutters to the bottom. For that reason, straight hair is far more effective in letting the fly fall without added resistance.

When purchasing your bucktails, examine their undersides. The tanned skin should be flat, not curled or kinked. Avoid tails that are bent or twisted; look for the straightest materials possible. This is important because the hair follows the direction of the skin and becomes twisted and unusable if it is packaged with deep bends. This is an easy flaw to look for, so take the time to flip the tail over, and don't just grab one off the shelf in the color you want.

Oftentimes you will find bucktail that is too long for the packaging it is being sold in, and the tail is bent in order to make it fit. Try to avoid these tails, but if the skin looks good, the color is right, and the hair is the texture you are looking for, go for it. Minor bends can be corrected by soaking or steaming the tails.

If you are ordering natural materials (bucktials, Zonker, feathers) online, you are taking a leap of faith. You don't have a choice, and you have to take what they give you, so when it comes to natural materials like hair and feathers, I always try to buy locally where I can inspect what I'm buying. If you can, open the bag and take a close look.

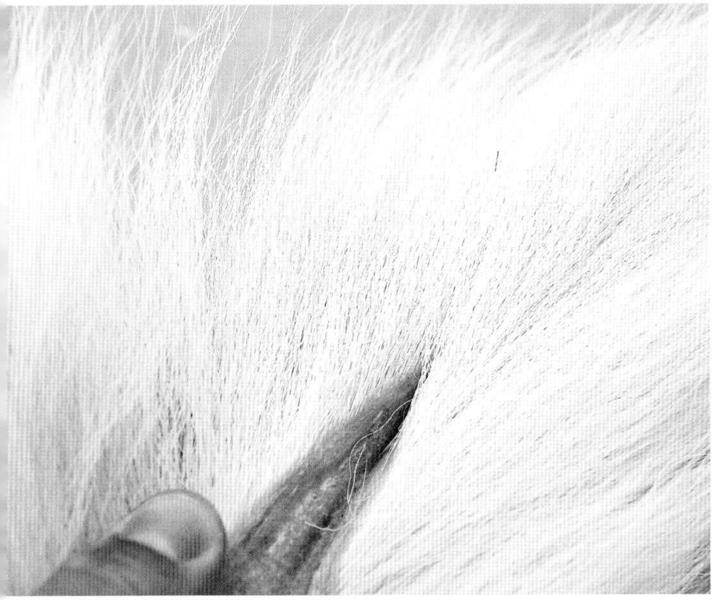

Bucktail, or the hair found on the tails of whitetail deer, has a variety of different textures, depending on the animal it is harvested from. I look for bucktails with particularly long, coarse, and wavy hairs. You can recognize the tails in the package by their broad width and fullness. Usually the bag they are in looks like it is about to explode.

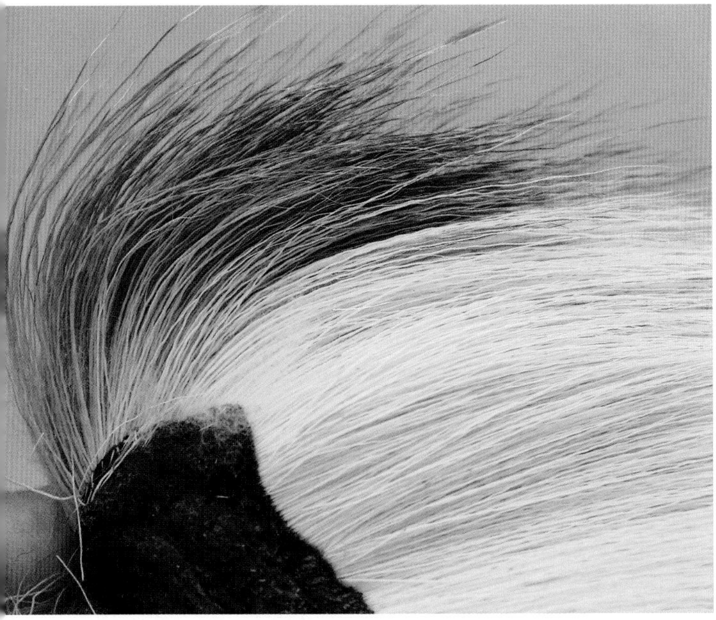

The lower third (the portion closest to the animal's rump) has shorter hairs with a spongy, hollow feel to them. This hair has a tendency to flair when you apply thread pressure, and it is intermixed with fuzzy underfur much like deer body hair. It may not be the best for streamer patterns, but it has a tendency to float and can be spun easily, making it good for deer hair heads.

## Tapering

**When you are using a material without tips like yak hair or a synthetic like EP or SF Fiber, you can cut a section so you have two flat ends. The section will contain multiple fibers or hairs that are the same length. You can make the section longer by pulling a few hairs or fibers from the ends. This will make the entire section longer and taper the ends.**

**At one end where the cut was made, pull 30 hairs out ½ inch. Of those 30 hairs you pulled away from the cut section, pull 20 of them out a little farther, and of those 20, pull 10 out a little farther. Now you have a taper at each end of the section and a longer section of materials. This is the method I use to taper materials in the step by steps in part II.**

### Zonker Strips

Zonker Strips are thinly cut strips of fur with the tanned skin still attached. They are popular for saltwater fly patterns thanks to their remarkably fishy action in the water. Soft and supple, their fur seems to come alive when submersed, and the leather strip magically snakes along as it is drawn through the water. Unlike feathers or bucktails, there are not as many pitfalls or glaring differences between the bags of materials found on the shelves of your local fly shop. However, you should be aware of some minor differences.

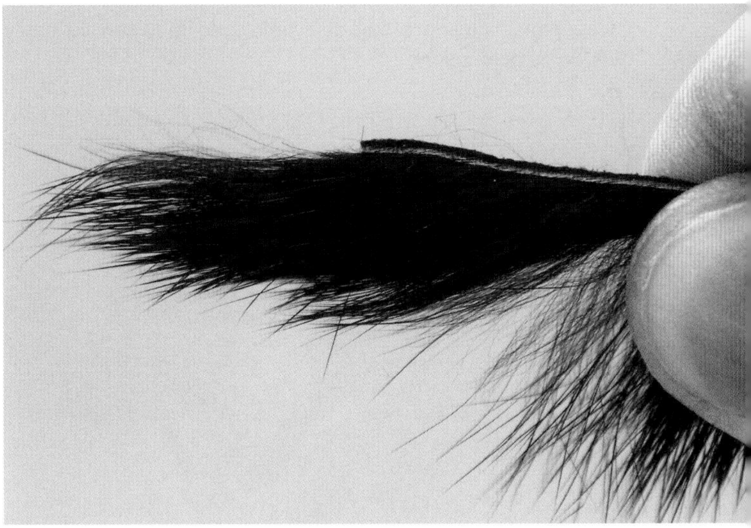

Zonker Strips are one of the most useful materials for creating lifelike swimming action in your saltwater patterns. They come in an endless assortment of colors and a variety of thicknesses and cuts.

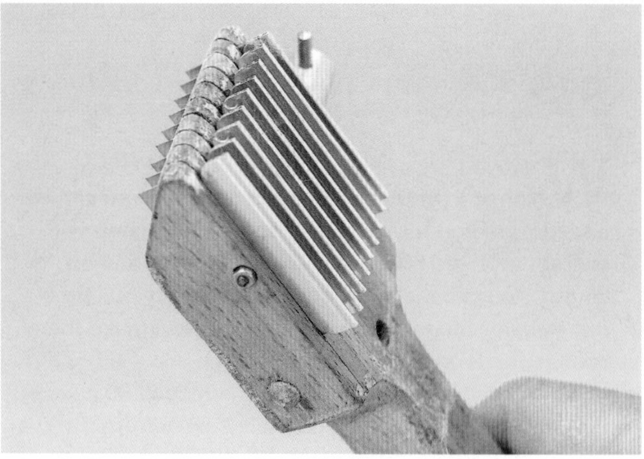

Zonker Strip cutters are fairly rudimentary tools—basically fixed razor blades spaced to the desired thickness of the cut. They are difficult to find in fly-tying shops, so most avid fly tiers fashion their own with a series of nuts, bolts, washers, and razor blades.

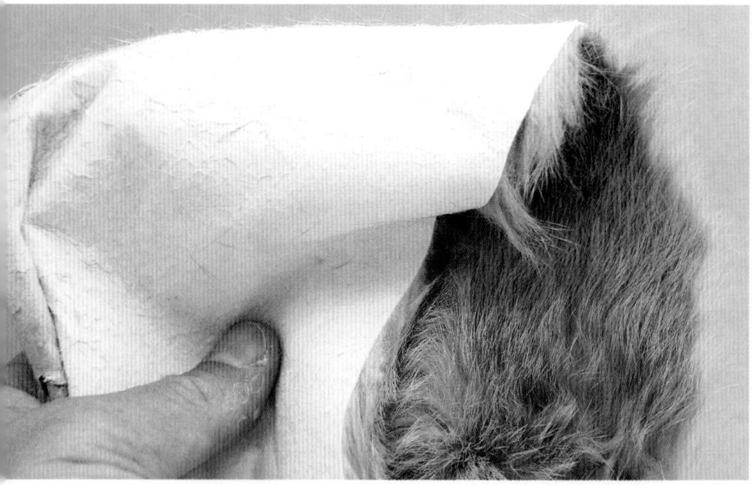

Whole rabbit pelts, if processed correctly, are relatively simple to cut yourself with a Zonker Strip cutter. Whole pelts are much cheaper than buying a bag at a time, and they can be easily dyed to custom colors.

For clean, uniform strips, press hard enough to deeply score the leather on the first pass. If you don't, you end up with a big mess when you try to cut the pelt again.

As you work more and more with Zonker-style materials, you will start to notice subtle differences in the pliability of the leather. This is due to the slight difference in the leather's thickness. When given the option to compare, I try to choose Zonker Strips with the thinnest leather possible. Although you lose some durability, the difference in action is notable, especially in the magnum-cut strips. Thicker strips hold more water and can also make a big difference in the weight of your flies when palmering around the shank of the hook.

Zonker can be purchased in a number of different thicknesses and cuts. The standard thickness is 1/8 inch, but I typically use magnum, or 1/4-inch cut, for saltwater patterns. Crosscut Zonker Strips have been cut horizontally or across the animal's body, not nose to tail. These strips are typically used for palmering and create a fluffy hair collar.

When selecting Zonker Strips, take a close look at the thickness of the hair. Older or inferior materials often have spotty or sparse hair throughout the strip. Also pay close attention to the condition of the leather strip. Avoid materials with brittle, dry, or cracked leather strips, which will break off after a few casts.

Other undesirable characteristics that should be avoided are short hairs and broken tips. The strip on the top with long, thick hair is what you are looking for. Strips with shorter hairs will still work, but they will not undulate as much in the current or have as much lifelike movement in the water when the fly is stripped.

If you are tying a lot of Zonker Strip flies, whole rabbit pelts are the way to go. In bulk they are much cheaper than buying a bag at a time, and they can be easily dyed to custom colors. The same rules of what to look for and avoid apply when buying whole pelts; however, you also need to look for thin spots and rips in the hide.

Zonker Strip cutters are pretty rudimentary tools, basically a handle embedded with razor blades spaced to the desired thickness. They are difficult to find in fly-tying shops, so most avid fly tiers fashion their own. The process of cutting the skin is a little tricky and should be approached with an abundance of caution. The easiest way I have found to cut whole pelts is to secure one end by clamping it between two boards, fur side down. Stretch the other end tight with your nondominant hand and slowly drag the razor blades across the skin with your dominant hand. Press hard enough to deeply score the leather on the first pass. If you don't, you end up with a big mess when you try to cut the pelt again. I like to separate the strips after each pass.

## Dying with Kool-Aid and Coffee

Although there are a rainbow of colors available in almost every material, I often find myself searching for a specific shade or a slightly different hue in a certain material that just doesn't exist on the shelves of my local fly shop or even online. Dying the materials at home is cheap and easy and allows me to continuously modify a material's color, taking custom creations one step further. You can produce an endless array of colors by varying the combinations and concentrations of coffee and Kool-Aid, and don't be afraid to experiment with different brands of drink mixes. I have not found a brand of drink mix that this technique will not work on, but stay away from the ones that are sweetened, and never add sugar when making the dying solution. (Sticky is not good.)

Fabric dyes give you more precise control, but they are more expensive, difficult to acquire, and usually the selection of colors is limited. The spectrum of colors offered is typically more muted as well. Kool-Aid is far more readily available, and what you see on the package is what you get. I also like the fact that there is not a lot of measuring. Two packages of Kool-Aid packs more than enough pigment punch for the majority of materials.

Here are some examples of what colors you can expect from each flavor of Kool-Aid or coffee. Two packets of Kool-Aid were used in the solution to create the colors. The more Kool-Aid you add, the more intense or concentrated the colors will be. If you don't get the color you want, simply add more Kool-Aid to the solution and reheat. As the feathers absorb the dye from the Kool-Aid, the water becomes clearer. Yellows and greens are not as concentrated as the other colors, so if you are looking for brighter versions of these colors, start with twice as much Kool-Aid. All the red flavors produce similar shades and need extra rinsing time to remove all the excess dye. The colors are remarkably permanent, and the fruity smell fades when fished.

Grape Kool-Aid dyed feathers

Berry Blue Kool-Aid dyed feathers

Lemon-Lime Kool-Aid dyed feathers

Lemonade Kool-Aid dyed feathers

Pink Lemonade Kool-Aid dyed feathers

Orange Kool-Aid dyed feathers

Piña-Pineapple Kool-Aid dyed feathers

Cherry Kool-Aid dyed feathers

Black Cherry Kool-Aid dyed feathers

Mandarina-Tangerine Kool-Aid dyed feathers

Mango Kool-Aid dyed feathers

Coffee dyed feathers

It won't take too long before you are comfortable with this process and you want to create some unique colors. It does not take a lot of Kool-Aid to alter the color significantly, so start out with half or quarter packets and add a little at a time for a stronger concentration. This is especially critical with the darker colors like reds and purples. Here are a few examples of colors that I created with a combination of Kool-Aid flavors and coffee.

Two Lemon-Lime and two Berry Blue Kool-Aid packs. The turquoise blue color is a very popular offshore color and works great for mackerel imitations.

One Orange Kool-Aid, one Black Cherry Kool-Aid, and a cup of coffee. This rusty burnt orange color is one of my favorites for redfish patterns. It is very productive in stained or dirty water.

# Dyeing Feathers

Start by washing the feathers or materials to be dyed with liquid soap. You have to remove any dirt, oil, or residue in order for the dye to penetrate the material. Rinse the material thoroughly with cool water. Heat the water in the microwave in a microwave-safe bowl or measuring cup and add the vinegar, salt, and Kool-Aid to the hot water. I like to use a Pyrex measuring cup because it is wide enough to accommodate most materials and has a handle, which is nice for working with hot liquids. For larger jobs, a 9 x 13 Pyrex lasagna pan works great. Mix all the ingredients thoroughly, making sure that the salt and the Kool-Aid are completely dissolved. If you are dying with coffee, stir in the vinegar and salt to 1½ cups of hot, strong black coffee. Add the prewashed feathers or materials to the dying solution.

Stir the feathers or materials vigorously for a minute or so, making sure that none of the feathers have stuck together and the dye has covered thoroughly. Use a spoon or chopsticks to keep the material submerged and work out any air bubbles. Microwave the dye solution and materials for 1½ minutes, and then let them steep in the solution for an additional 5 minutes to ensure that the color is permanently set in the material.

**Materials List**

1½ cup water
½ cup white vinegar
½ teaspoon salt
2 Kool-Aid packs or 1½ cups coffee

After the 5 minutes are up, strain the solution from the feathers or materials. The color is now permanent. Wash away any excess dye with soap and water, and soak the feathers in cold water for a few minutes. Change the water and continue soaking the materials until the water remains clear.

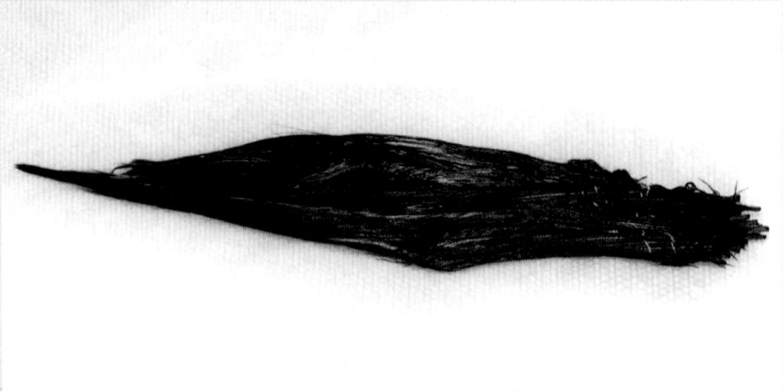

Gently pat the feathers dry with paper towels and hang them up to dry or place them on a drying rack. The drying process may take several hours, depending on the size and density of the material, but the process can be expedited with a hair dryer.

## Markering

So much you learn about catching fish is about being versatile and being able to adapt your fly to match or mimic a specific prey item in a specific situation. You might have the specific movements of a prey item down, but the appearance isn't quite right, and the fish seem to sense that. A small modification is sometimes all you need to trigger a strike. I can't think of a more versatile tool for fly tying or in-the-field alterations than permanent markers. I always try to have black, brown, red, and olive markers in my bag when I'm tying or fishing, especially if I'm traveling.

Throughout the book I have highlighted a few examples of how you can use permanent markers to customize and enhance your flies, from coloring bodies to simply coloring mono eyes with black permanent marker. Here are a few examples of other uses for permanent markers, and whether you are at your tying bench or on the flats, these techniques come in pretty handy.

In the test and tweak portion of the book, I outlined the importance of sink rate and how altering the sink rate with a different size bead-chain eye can sometimes make your fly more appealing. This works great, but not all patterns have bead-chain eyes or some other form of easily scalable weight. I often tie a number of flies that look the same but on closer inspection are weighted much differently. A few turns of lead wire can make a dramatic change in the way the fly acts in the water, and the wire can be hidden away under thread wraps and materials quite easily. One way of distinguishing your weighted flies is to mark the head of the fly with a thin band of a contrasting color. I like to use red because it gives the appearance of gills or an injured fish. Don't mark the head of your fly with a fat-tipped marker because the ink has a tendency to bleed, and more often than not the marker ends up on more than just a small portion of the head. An easy way to avoid this calamity is to mark a few inches of the thread just before whip-finishing. By applying the marker to the thread rather than the finished head of the fly, you have much more control of how much color you apply and where it goes. It is much easier to consolidate your wraps to accomplish a nice clean line, rather than to try and draw a thin line on a round shape.

The majority of bonefish flies mimic little shrimp or crustaceans that have segmented bodies. The easiest way to emulate them is by barring the wing of the fly with a marker.

When creating baitfish patterns with vertical bars or stripes, using a notecard as a guide to draw lines is an easy way to create perfectly straight lines. The card also helps to hold the material flat, so the tip of the marker does not touch unwanted areas of the fly. Dabbing the marker along the edge of the card works much better than trying to draw a line.

A series of small dots of different colors made with a fine point marker emulates the mottled look of tiny crustacean appendages. Light brown with blue and orange highlights can make a simple piece of Scud Back or latex come alive.

By applying the marker to the thread rather than finished head of the fly, you have much more control of how much color you apply and where it goes. It is much easier to consolidate your wraps to accomplish a nice clean line, rather than to try and draw a thin line on a round shape.

When barring the wing of small bonefish flies, start with a thin line on the far side. The color will bleed through the material enough to act as a guide for the line on the side closest to you. For larger bars, push the tip of the marker directly into the center of the materials and simply let the color bleed through both sides of the material.

While the fly is still in the vise, gather all the fibers of the wing material and pull the material taut. Start by pressing the marker against the material on the side away from you and hold it still until the ink bleeds through the material and can be easily seen. Mark the side closest to you where you can see the ink has bled through, and your bars will always match on both sides of the fly. This is much easier than leaning over the vise or craning your neck to line up the marks on the far side.

Frequently when I am traveling or just fishing someplace new, I tie up a few 4- to 5-inch baitfish patterns in all white and pack a few extra colors of marker instead of hauling dozens of different colors and sizes of flies. I trim and mark up the white flies depending on the size and color of bait in the area I am fishing. Most of the time when the fish are turned on, it's for a narrow window of time and you don't have time to sit down and whip up a new fly. Packing your vise and a variety of materials for half a day of fishing is a real pain, so bring a variety of blank canvas baitfish, shrimp, and crab patterns that can be easily altered on the water.

I like being able to adjust my fly immediately on the water, and a few extra markers don't take up much room, whether I am wading or fishing from a boat. Tie up and stash one all white (blank canvas) baitfish fly in your box—it might be just what you need to save an unproductive day on the water.

This is a great technique when traveling or just fishing someplace new. By tying up a few different sizes of baitfish patterns in all white and packing a few extra colors of markers, you can easily trim the white flies depending on the size and color of bait in the area. I always have a few blank canvas crab and shrimp patterns in my box as well.

## Fabric Paint Eyes

**You can create any size and color combination of eye from fabric paint. Start by shaking up your fabric paints well. If you don't, the first few eyes will be runny and the finished product will look more like bird poop than baitfish eyes. Squeeze a small amount of paint onto a paper towel and wipe any old, hardened paint away from the tip.**

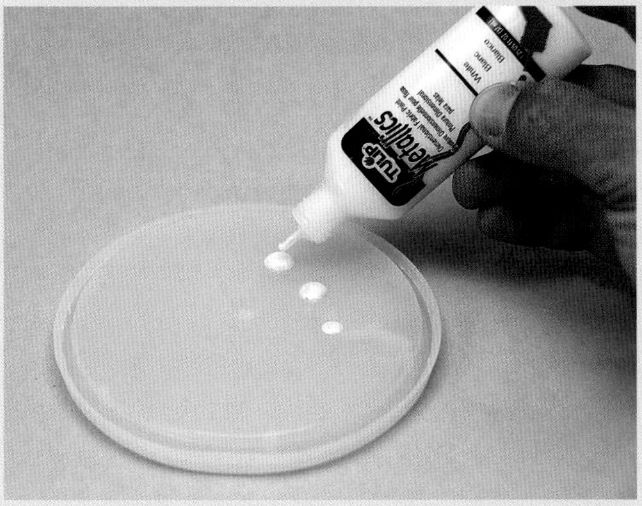

I like pearl white or a metallic color for the sclera (the whites of the eyes) and black for the pupils. Two small bottles of paint and a Tupperware lid or a piece of wax paper and you are in business. They don't take up a lot of room in your fly-tying bag, and you can fabricate loads of custom eyes in a few hours.

Using your sclera color (white), apply a dome-shaped dot of paint slightly smaller than the size you desire. Dip the tip of the paint bottle into the center of the paint, and in a circular motion work the paint outward. This will even out the depth of the paint at the edges. If you don't do this, the eyes tend to be very thick and take a long time to dry.

Place a single drop of the pupil color (black), in the center of the white. Do not worry if it sticks up slightly. As the paint dries, it will meld in to the white seamlessly.

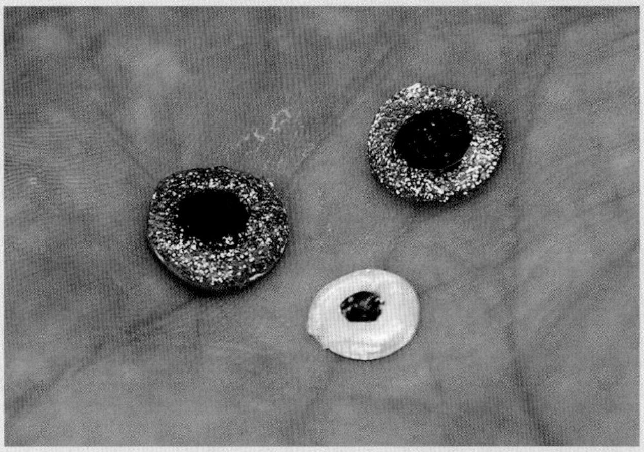

Once the paint dries thoroughly, the eyes will simply peel from the Tupperware lid. The paint can easily be trimmed with scissors if needed to round out the shape.

### Creating Dubbing Brushes

A dubbing brush is really just a customized pipe cleaner. Instead of a synthetic core like chenille, the two wires that make up the core sandwich a variety of different materials that can be palmered around the hook shank. By customizing your own brushes, you can match the other materials you are tying with exactly, as well as blend several colors, providing you with more lifelike patterns. Adding rubber legs and alternating colors makes tying crustacean patterns much easier and more uniform. Palmering the desired materials is much faster than stacking multiple colors in place, and it cuts down on the number of steps, which is extremely useful when you want to tie a dozen or so of the same pattern.

Your choice of materials is endless, but softer, thinner materials spin better without bunching up between the wires. Natural materials like marabou, rabbit, and fox trimmed from the skin are excellent choices. Softer synthetics like Antron, Puglisi, Steve Farrar's Flash Blend, or Neer Hair work much better than stiffer nylon or plastic materials. Blending different colors of materials, flash, and rubber legs makes for more realistic flies.

Several different machines have been designed specifically for making dubbing brushes quickly and easily. They all have the same basic parts and are simple to make. The stainless steel wire that holds the material is first attached to a hook that spins and captures the material. This machine uses a variable speed motor, but the same outcome could be achieved with a cup hook in a cordless drill. The wire is looped around another hook, and as the wires twist and tighten, the tension is slowly reduced with a spring. If you are using a cordless drill, reduce the tension so the wire does not break by moving your hands as the wire compresses.

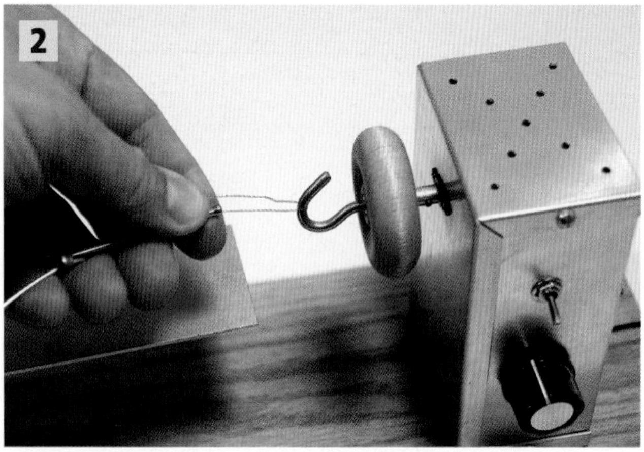

To start, make a loop with the stainless steel wire and hold the two legs together. You do not need a lot of wire—about an inch will be enough to lock the loop around the hook with a series of 10 to 15 wraps.

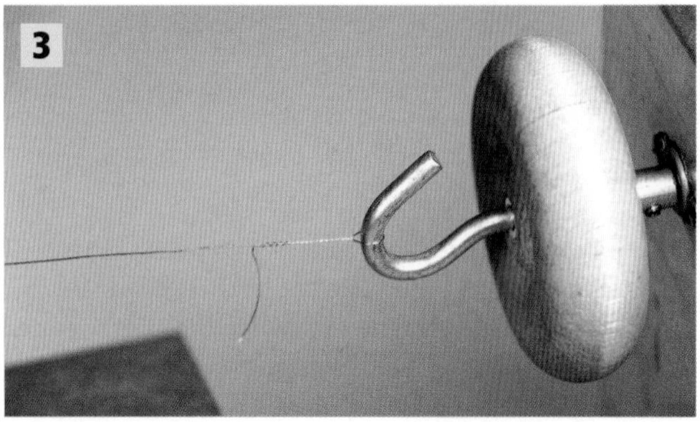

Once the wire is secure to the hook, remove the tag end by working it back and forth until it breaks. If you cut it with scissors or pliers, it will leave a sharp edge.

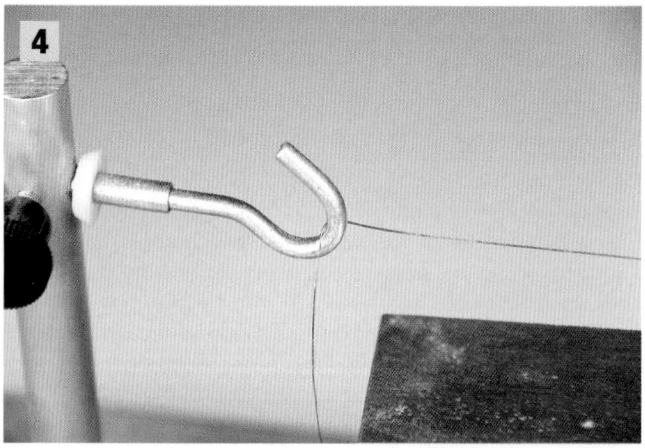

Stretch your wire around the stationary hook and let the wire bobbin hang freely.

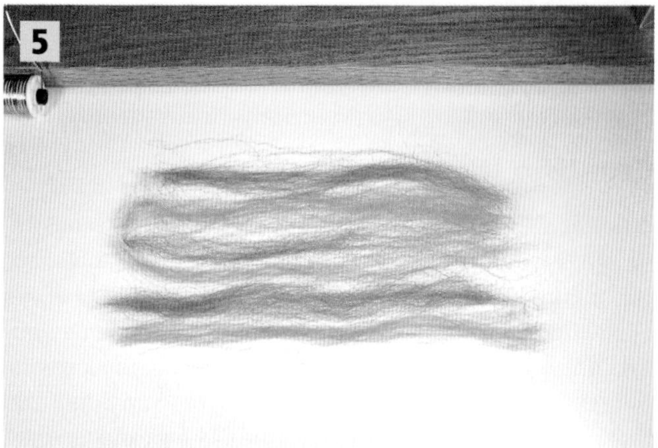

Lay out the materials to be used in the brush in pencil-size pieces and blend them together.

Here is how the wire should look stretched between the two hooks. Raise the metal tray up to the wire. This will act as a platform to lay the materials on. If you are not using a dubbing brush machine, use something you can remove when you start to spin the materials. A thick book works well.

Cut the combined materials into pieces. The longer the pieces, the wider the brush will be. One-inch pieces work well for the vast majority of my dubbing brushes.

Lay the materials on top of the wire that is resting on the tray. Try to center the materials on the wire as best as you can. If the materials are too far off-center, they will be pushed out of the loop when you start to spin the wires together. The closer your materials are to center, the more even your cylinder will be.

Trim your flash and whatever other materials you wish to add to the bush into 1-inch pieces, and spread them evenly on top. Again, do your best to keep all the materials centered on the wire.

When you are done adding materials, carefully stretch the wire across the top of all the materials back to the spinning hook where you started to wrap the wire around the hook. All the materials should be sandwiched in the middle of the wire loop.

Keep tension on the wire and turn on the spinning motor for 1 or 2 seconds to spin the hook. If you are using a drill and a cup hook, in the low setting, slowly squeeze the trigger for a couple of seconds or 10 to 15 wraps. This will lock the wires together. Cut away the wire bobbin and slowly start spinning the brush. As the wires spin together and the materials become locked in place, carefully lower the tray and increase the speed.

The brush is done when all the materials are squeezed tightly between the wires and fluff up. Pick out any trapped fibers with a dog brush or comb. Sometimes the wire breaks from the tension, but if not, cut the wire free from the hooks.

Remove the completed dubbing brush from the twister.

## Spinning Krystal Flash

Evenly dispersing flash throughout a fly is one of the hallmarks of a well-tied fly. It is relatively simple to tie in flash along with other synthetic materials to achieve a uniform and realistic look throughout the body of the fly. It is far more difficult to do when you are trying to create a cylindrical shape such as a finger mullet and finish the fly's head with the same material. The fastest and easiest way to accomplish this, in my opinion, is with a dubbing brush. You can blend multiple colors of a material, as heavy or sparsely as you wish, and with a few quick wraps you are done. The same material you created the body of the fly with is now uniformly palmered around the hook and ready to be trimmed to its final shape.

What about deer hair mullet or Muddler patterns? Some materials do not look natural or may not lay properly on the hook if you use a dubbing brush. If you try to weave a dubbing brush through deer hair, the results are usually marginal at best, and the look of the fly is poor to say the least. The wire at the core of the dubbing brush can also alter the buoyancy of the fly, depending on the size of the hook and the number of wraps. Fortunately due to the coarse nature of the deer hair, you can easily blend other finer materials such as Krystal Flash or other flashy materials with it while spinning. This will allow you to maintain the same materials throughout the fly and evenly disperse the flash throughout the spun head.

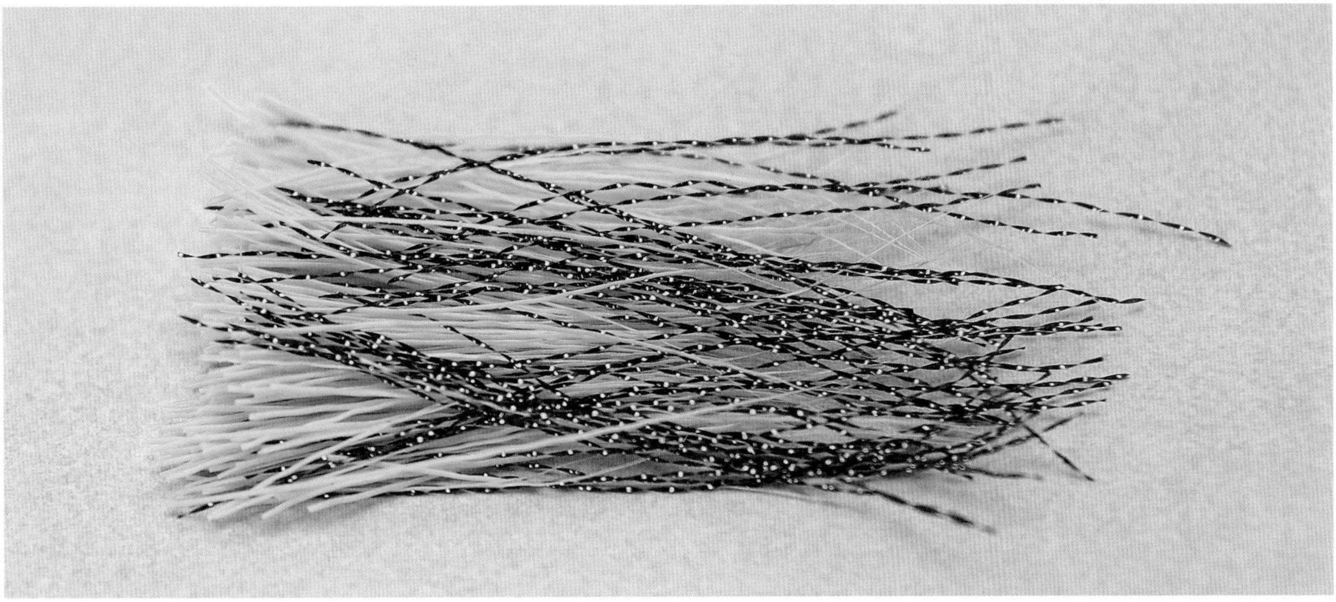

Trim a pencil-size bunch of deer hair and press it flat on your tying bench. Spread it out in a thin layer, being careful to keep the tips and butts of the hair lined up. Trim the desired amount of flash, slightly longer than the deer hair, and mix it into the pile. Stack the deer hair and Krystal Flash together, lining up the butts of the deer hair and the ends of the Krystal Flash.

Make two loose wraps around the bunch and work the materials around the hook. This will help disperse the flash and hair evenly.

Snug up the loose wraps until the hair begins to flair, and then work the bundle with your fingertips, dispersing it evenly around the shank of the hook.

Tighten the two loose wraps by pulling straight down. This will spin the deer hair and Krystal Flash around the shank of the hook evenly. Make two more wraps around the bunch to lock it in place.

This technique also works well for spinning in peacock herl.

PART II

# 14 Flies

## Designing and Tying Winning Flies

CHAPTER 5

# The Cannibal Series of Flies

The Sanibel Cannibal is a large, translucent baitfish imitation that is meant to emulate the 3- to 5-inch fish that dart in and out of the shallow surf. These long, cylindrical baitfish are void of almost all color except for a very slight tan-gray hue. The Sanibel Cannibal is tied in a similar fashion as Enrico Puglisi's Peanut Butter Bunker or Jonny King's Kinky Muddler to create a more realistic profile. The pattern uses yak hair mostly for its translucent qualities, but also because its length and wiry texture allows you to create larger flies. The natural fibers are great for blending because the strands of hair can be counted easily. This allows you to create flies that are more uniform in color and fullness. The coarse hair becomes supple when wet and has a lifelike quality when stripped.

If you take a close look, you will find that nothing in nature is just one color. Even in super-clear water, when most species are void of color, on closer inspection it is quite difficult to describe the variety of perfectly blended pearlescent hues. Although they are often faint, they seem to appear when the sun hits them just right. Taking that into consideration, when I am fishing in clear-water situations with lots of visibility I try to make my flies look as realistic as possible. Learning to blend multiple colors and create true-to-life patterns is the key to closing the deal. Blending materials evenly so you can tie more uniform and more lifelike patterns can

*Above:* The flies in the Cannibal series are 3- to 5-inch translucent imitations meant to emulate the demure baitfish that dart in and out of the shallow surf. Each of the three variations is tied with a precise blend of colored yak hair, and each is designed for different water conditions: the Sanibel for clear water, the Captiva for green or turquoise conditions, and the Caloosahatchee for stained or brackish water. The sparse, yet full body, proper trimming, and careful color mix produces a realistic profile that is a dead ringer for baitfish.

A couple of years ago while chasing snook on the beaches of Sanibel Island, I carelessly stepped on my fly line, and unfortunately I was holding the fly in my hand at the time . . . The result was a trip to the emergency room. I thought the name "The Sanibel Cannibal" was fitting for this pattern since it was as though the fly's Gamakatsu 2/0 hook was gnawing on my finger due to the excruciating pain of several failed attempts to remove it with the barb still intact. All of the flies in this series are tied with saltwater yak hair using the same techniques. Only slight variations in color differentiate the Captiva Cannibal (top), Caloosahatchie Cannibal (center), and Sanibel Cannibal (bottom).

be a little tricky, but with a little patience and practice it will become second nature.

You can blend many different kinds of fibers, from synthetics to bucktail. My favorite material to use for large baitfish patterns is yak hair. It's not as good on smaller baitfish ($1\frac{1}{2}$-inch patterns), but I tend to reach for natural materials over synthetic materials whenever possible. If they are not available, Puglisi or SF Fiber are my second choices, and more times than not my first choice on the smaller flies. I like yak hair because it is just a touch thicker and stiffer than most synthetics when it is dry, but quickly softens when it saturates with water. Yak hair's long natural fibers are somewhat translucent, and the lighter colors react to UV light well. It comes in a variety of colors, and most importantly it is easy to separate individual fibers from the bunch and they blend well. The problem with yak hair is if you try to work with too

I caught this pretty snook cruising in about a foot of water off the shore of Captiva Island. A few short strips with a large Captiva Cannibal fly was enough to close the deal.

It was my lunch break and I only had an hour to fish, so I grabbed my 9-weight from the truck, threw on a sand-colored shirt and buff, and headed for the beach. I saw this bruiser coming fast from about 20 yards away, so I made a quick cast to get the line out of the rod and then a second cast to place the fly a few feet in front of her. A long slow strip and a tip waggle brought the Sanibel Cannibal to life. She gobbled the fly up and after a brief wrestling match, we posed for a couple of shots and I headed back to the office with a smile from ear to ear.

If you look closely, you can see the Caloosahatchee Cannibal hanging out of this stocky redfish's mouth. It's no coincidence that I caught him in the Caloosahatchee River.

Here I am with another summer snook that fell prey to the Sanibel Cannibal.

much of it at once, it becomes difficult to manipulate and tie down without leaving large bumps on the hook shank.

I start with a base color or the color I see the most when I look at the bait I am trying to mimic. For most baitfish, that color will be white or a cream color and that color will end up being more than two-thirds of the fly. I then select two or three accent colors. These colors are typically found on the back or sides of the baitfish.

If you are looking at a baitfish or a picture of bait and you squint your eyes, you will lose focus on the detail of the fish and only be able to see basic colors. That is how I like to think about what accent colors I pick. Whatever color I see the most of first, for that split second, is what my first accent color is. It is usually a light shade of tan, gray, blue, or green. Looking at the color of the water you are fishing in helps to narrow it down. The second accent color is usually the darkest color found on the highest part of the back: dark green, blue, or black. The colors blend naturally from light to dark, from belly to back, camouflaging the fish from predators above and below.

After you select the colors, you have to determine the quantities of each. Depending on what type of materials you select, you need to devise a system of measuring quantities exactly so you can reproduce the blend if you run out of materials halfway through, or if you simply want to create a number of uniform flies. This is why yak hair works so well for large baitfish patterns: you can easily count the number of colored strands you want to blend in advance and lay them out in neat piles before you start tying.

My first pile is the base color, and I start with 80 strands of white yak hair. The base color makes up the majority of the fly's belly and midsection. This sounds like a lot of material, but it's really not. I used to blend the flash in as well, but a lot of it fell out while I was tapering the material, so now I apply flash between stages of yak hair.

The second pile is made up of 80 strands as well, but is broken down into 50 strands of white, 20 strands of a lighter accent color, and 10 strands of the darkest color. If I am using three accent colors, I adjust the blend according to the concentration of colors I am trying to mimic. A little bit goes a long way, so as a rule of thumb I do not go over 30 strands of color no matter what the combination is.

Once I count out the strands of the colored yak hair for the back of the baitfish fly, I lay them on the pile of 50 white strands, making sure to spread them out evenly. If I have little pockets of color in the pile, I shuffle the fibers around until I have an evenly blended pile.

## Building a Better Baitfish

1

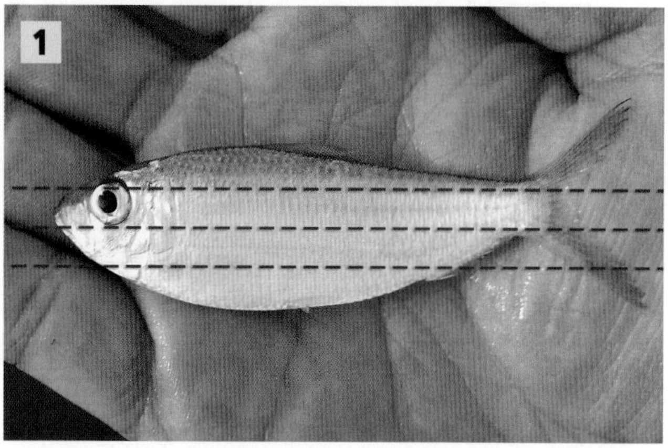

For all my baitfish patterns, the ratio of color to white is about 25/75 (30 colored strands to 130 white strands). If you were to cut a baitfish into four lengthwise pieces, the ratio of color to white would be about the same.

2

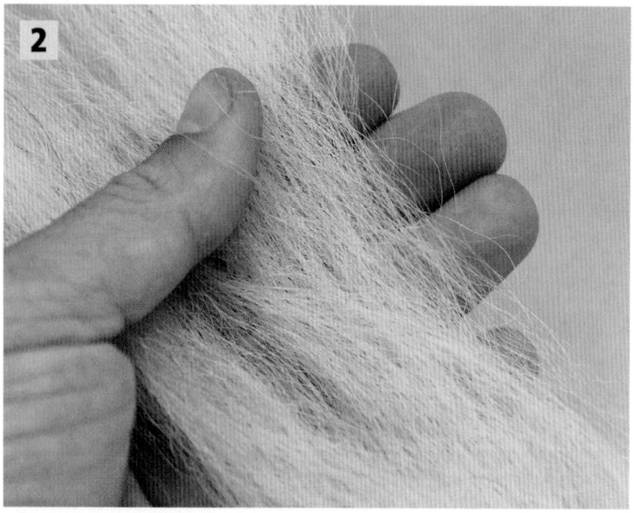

White yak hair is the base of all my Cannibal series of baitfish patterns and makes up about 75 percent of each fly's materials, depending on the baitfish I am trying to emulate. In order to avoid lumpy flies and tie more uniform-looking flies, I count and lay out the fibers I will be using before I start tying. This ensures that I don't have some flies tied heavy and some sparse, and also allows me to really hone in and perfect my favorite blends of colors.

3

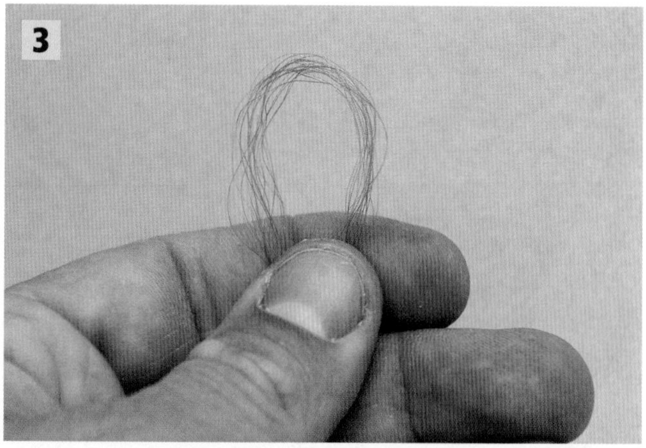

The first accent color and most predominant color for most of the baitfish patterns I tie is tan.

4

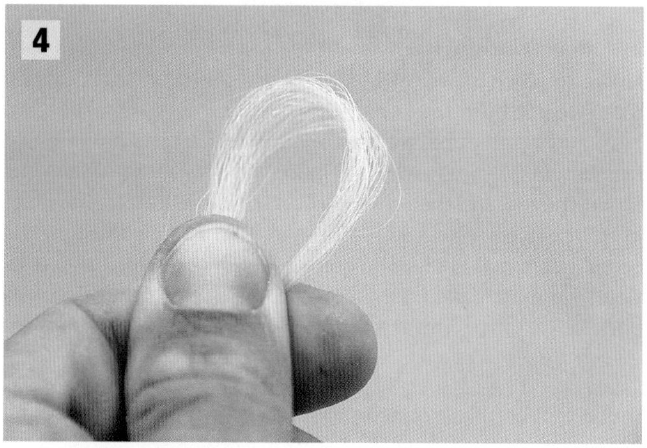

Eighty strands of white yak hair are used for the belly portion of the batifish pattern.

5

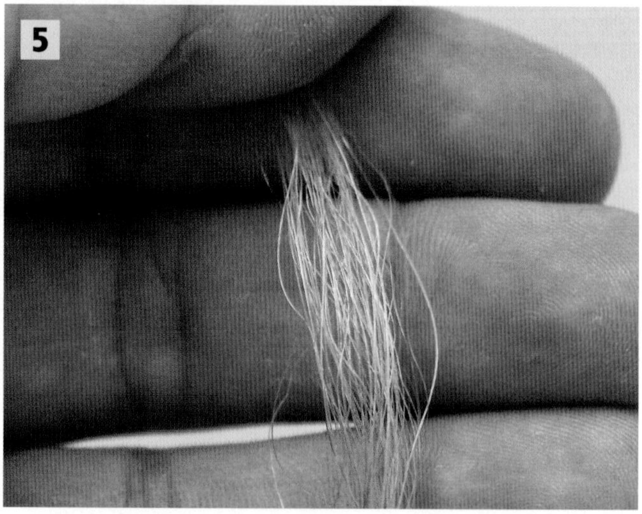

The colored portion (back) of the fly is a blend of two or three colors, primarily white with one or two accent colors.

### Sanibel Cannibal (Clear Water)

**Hook:** #2/0 Gamakatsu SC-15
**Thread:** 4-pound mono
**Belly:** White saltwater yak hair and pearl Wing N' Flash
**Back:** White, gray, and tan saltwater yak hair, silver Wing N' Flash
**Eyes:** 8 mm clear doll eyes with post

For the belly portion of the fly, use two bundles of 80 strands of white saltwater yak hair and pearl Wing N' Flash.

For the back color, blend 50 strands of white saltwater yak hair, 20 strands of gray saltwater yak hair, 10 strands of tan saltwater yak hair, and silver Wing N' Flash.

## Tying the Sanibel Cannibal

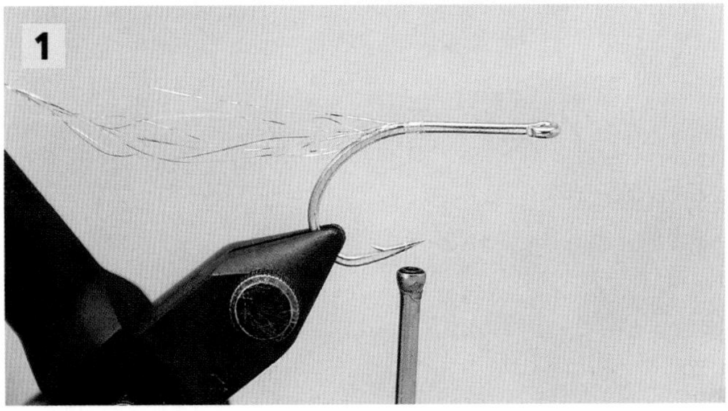


Start your mono thread at the point of the hook (8 to 10 wraps is enough to secure it). I like to use a 2/0 Gamakatsu SC-15 hook. I prefer the 2/0 because it is a very sturdy and sharp hook that gets the yak hair down a little faster when casting to cruising snook.

Tie in a few strands of Wing N' Flash, making sure it sticks out 4 or 5 inches past the bend of the hook. Advance your mono in front of all your previous wraps.

Cut a 4½-inch piece of the white (belly color). I like to measure it from the tip of my middle finger to the first line on my palm, so all my flies have a uniform length and shape.

Taper each of the ends until it is between 7½ and 8 inches (see page 35).

Tie in the tapered piece at the middle with eight turns, wrapping backward.

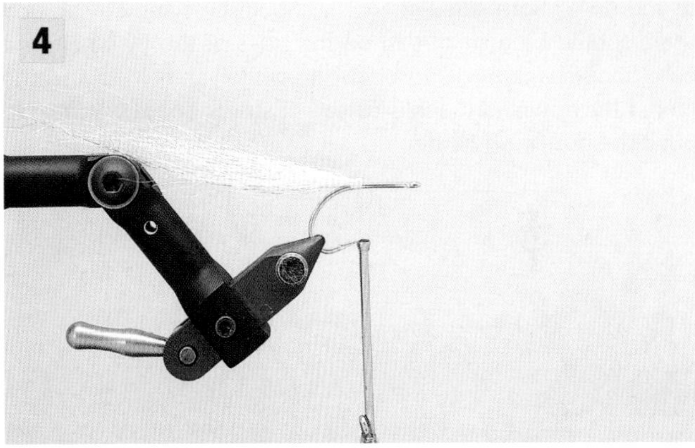


Fold back the forward-facing half and tie it down on top of the rear-facing half. Secure by wrapping forward with eight wraps. I do this to position my mono for tying down the folded back half of the material so I do not have to make a large jump with the mono over the bend. It enables me to wrap forward without doubling up my wraps and gives me a cleaner, sleek look and makes for smoother transition from the top of the material down to the hook shank. The mono is round and slippery and wraps have a tendency to slide off bulky materials.

Cut another piece of white saltwater yak hair about 3½ inches long (about the length of your middle finger) and taper both ends until it reaches 6½ to 7 inches in length. On the side of the hook closest to you, tie in the piece below the other materials and angle it slightly downward. Make eight turns, stacking your wraps behind the previous wraps and pushing them forward.

Fold the forward-facing half under the hook shank and back on top of itself. Secure it with eight forward wraps on the far side of the hook. Both sides of the fly should be symmetrical, and there should be a small gap on the sides of the fly where the bare hook shank peeks through the white yak hair. Laying the hair at the downward angle instead of straight back will start to build the profile of the fly.

Cut a $4\frac{1}{2}$-inch piece (about the length from your middle finger to the middle of your palm) of the color-blended bundle and taper each of the ends until it is between $7\frac{1}{2}$ and 8 inches. Tie in the tapered piece on top of the hook shank and in front of the other materials at its middle point. Secure the bundle with eight turns, wrapping backward.

Fold back the forward-facing half and tie it down on top of the rear-facing half. Secure by wrapping forward with eight wraps.

On the underside of the hook shank in front of the previously applied materials, add a pinch of pearl Wing N' Flash. It does not need to be much longer than 1 or 2 inches because it will be trimmed after the fly is complete.

Next cut a 3-inch section (about as long as your index finger) of white yak hair and divide it into two bundles, one for each side of the hook. Taper each piece until it is roughly 6 inches. Tie in the first piece on the near side of the hook so that it is slightly longer toward the tail of the fly. This piece fills the material gap and hides the exposed hook.

Fold the forward-facing half of the bundle back on itself and angle down to cover the gap of the hook. Repeat on the other side of the hook.

Cut another piece of color-blended yak hair 3½ inches long (about as long as your middle finger) and taper both ends until it reaches 6½ to 7 inches in length. On the top of the hook in front of the other materials, tie in the section at its middle, securing it with eight turns and stacking your wraps behind the previous wraps and pushing them forward.

Fold the forward-facing half back, but this time instead of securing it directly on top of itself, position the material in a V shape to create shoulders or width. Each half of the back colored material should be angling slightly wider than the first tail piece.

Add another pinch of pearl Wing N' Flash to the belly of the fly and advance the mono slightly.

Cut a 2½-inch piece of white yak hair (about the length of the first two segments of your middle finger) and taper it slightly. Tie it in on the underside of the fly so that the forward-facing half is slightly shorter. Fold the forward-facing half back directly onto itself and secure it with eight turns. Turn the fly over in the vise and use your thumbnail to disperse the material evenly around the bottom and sides of the hook. This will help cover any spots where the hook is exposed.

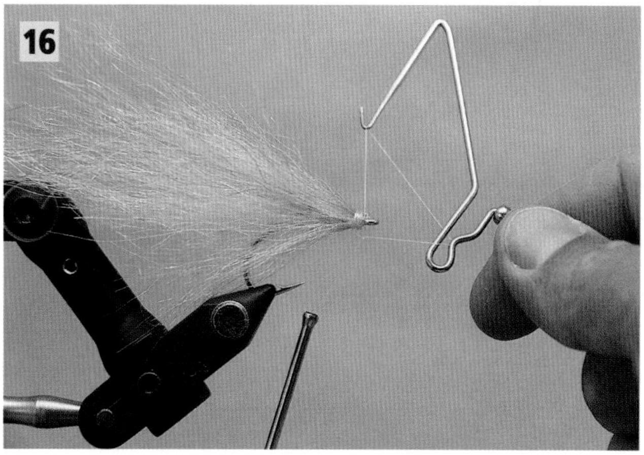

Cut a 3-inch section (about the length of your index finger) of the color-blended yak hair and taper it to approximately 6 inches. Apply this piece in the same V fashion as the previously applied back piece. Whip-finish two or three times and coat the nose of the fly with UV acrylic.

Take the fly out of the vise, and with a dog brush, comb out any tangles and blend all the colors. Comb each side of the fly to create a wide, flat leaf shape.

Put the fly back in the vise and glue on the dome eyes slightly in front of the hook point, making sure they are aligned from a top view.

Turn the fly toward you and double-check that the eyes are aligned from a forward-facing view. If the eyes are out of alignment, the fly will spin when stripped.

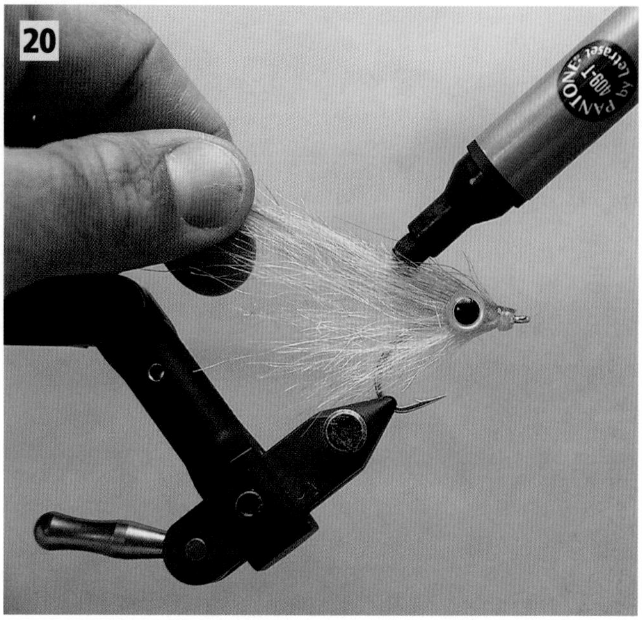


Once the eyes are completely dry (in 15 to 20 minutes), take the fly out of the vise, and with a long pair of kitchen scissors, trim the fly to the baitfish shape. Put the fly back in the vise, and with a Gray Pantone 409-T marker, paint a very thin stripe on the top of the back. Do not overdo this; you just want to add a hint of color. Two to three passes with the marker is adequate.

Completed Sanibel Cannibal

### Captiva Cannibal (Green/Turquoise Water)

**Hook:** #2/0 Gamakatsu SC-15
**Thread:** 4-pound mono
**Belly:** White saltwater yak hair
**Pearl:** Pearl Wing N' Flash
**Back:** White, gray, tan, and turquoise saltwater yak hair, silver Wing N' Flash
**Eyes:** 8 mm clear doll eyes with post

For the belly portion of the fly, make two bundles of 80 strands of white saltwater yak hair and pearl Wing N' Flash.

For the back color, blend 50 strands of white saltwater yak hair, 15 strands of gray, 10 strands of tan, 5 strands of turquoise, and silver Wing N' Flash.

### Caloosahatchee Cannibal (Stained Water)

**Hook:** #2/0 Gamakatsu SC-15
**Thread:** 4-pound mono
**Belly:** White saltwater yak hair
**Pearl:** Pearl Wing N' Flash
**Back:** White, tan, and yellow saltwater yak hair
**Eyes:** 8 mm clear doll eyes with post

For the belly portion of the fly, make two bundles of 80 strands of white saltwater yak hair with pearl Wing N' Flash.

For the back color, blend 50 strands of white saltwater yak hair, 25 strands of tan, and 5 strands of yellow.

CHAPTER 6

# Moonshiner Minnow

The Moonshiner Minnow is one of my go-to flies for early season beach fishing. It was designed to emulate the tiny minnows that congregate around snook lights and school up just off the beaches in the summer months. Snook, mackerel, and ladyfish love this fly, and you may even catch the occasional jack. If the fish are following the fly but not taking it, try a few short, popping strips with a long pause so the fly has a chance to sink.

**Moonshiner Minnow**

**Hook:** #6 or 4 TMC 811s or Daiichi 2546
**Thread:** Clear mono
**Body:** Mylar cord, clear vinyl rib
**Tail:** White marabou
**Eyes:** ⅛-inch stick-on hologram
**Collar:** Pearl Mylar cord

I started working on this pattern about eight years ago; it was originally designed for snook lights, but it ended up becoming one of my go-to flies for early season beach fishing. I had been watching those little 2-inch translucent glass minnows hover around a green snook light, and I wanted something that had a little better action than the standard all-synthetic fiber flies. I really liked fishing Capt. Greg Bowdish's Soluble Minnow pattern, but after studying those glass minnows, I noticed that they had a much wider profile at the head that tapered down to almost nothing, and only the rear half of the fish seemed to move. I wanted to come up with a pattern that had a fat head and shoulders but would really wiggle and move at the tail.

When I saw the same bait during the day on the beach, they were almost clear and all I could see was their guts and eyes, so I wanted the body to be translucent with a small pearlescent gut sack.

This pattern changed over time for both those fishing situations. A lot of people at the time were fishing Norm Zeigler's Schminnnow pattern and having a lot of luck, but I wanted something smaller with a more tapered shape for the beginning of the season when the bait was really small.

I chose marabou because it gave me a lot of movement and was still pretty translucent in the water. I played around with some synthetic fibers, but they didn't have the same movement.

I chose Mylar tubing for a few reasons. First, it was a little stiffer when I frayed it out at the back of the fly, and I needed a material collar to keep the marabou from wrapping around the bend of the hook. The Mylar tubing was also easy to palmer and created a compact little body with a pearlescent sheen. And finally I needed some bulky material at the front of the fly in order to activate the movement of the marabou. The material was easy to tie into place and then pick out afterward. When I experimented with small bunches of other flashy materials, it was a real pain trying to deal with all the unruly fibers. Originally I pulled all the fibers back and created an even collar around the shank of the hook, but I found that by doing this, the fly would have a tendency to spin. I trimmed the bottom of the fly for a while, but I found it was easier to tie the tubing off on top of the fly and then pick out the fibers. The extra drag on top of the fly helps stabilize it and keeps it tracking straight.

This fly is a great combination of translucency and movement. It has the right profile and is pretty durable. The marabou has a tendency to get beat up, but the rest of the fly can take quite a beating because the thread wraps are protected by the V rib and UV acrylic head. So you can catch a lot of fish or even a few toothy critters and it still stays together well.

I fish this fly in two different ways. At night under snook lights, try to cast it just outside the circle of light on the water. Retrieve as fast as you can with 1- or 2-inch strips. You want the fly to move fast in short, darting motions. The strike usually comes when the fly skirts the edge of the light and the fish have a chance to see it well, but only for a split second. Although sometimes you can get away with heavier leader, I have my best results with 20- or 25-pound fluorocarbon. With this lighter bite tippet, you will break off on dock piles, so make sure you have a stockpile of flies before you head out.

The other way I like to fish this fly is on the beach when the bait is very small. A long, slow strip seems to work best. Snook, mackerel, and ladyfish love this fly, and you may even catch the occasional jack. If you start to get follows but they're not taking it, try a few short, popping strips with a long pause so the fly has a chance to sink. They will usually take the fly on the drop or at the first sign of movement after the drop. You may need to incorporate a small piece of wire leader into your setup if the mackerel start breaking off.

## Tying the Moonshiner Minnow

Start the mono thread at the point of the hook or where the hook just starts to bend. Make 10 to 12 wraps and add a drop of superglue to lock the thread wraps to the shank of the hook. Tie in the marabou with 4 to 5 wraps, leaving about one hook length for the tail.

Cut a piece of Mylar cord about 1½ inches and remove the iridescent Mylar sheath. Fray one end of the Mylar cord about ¼ inch, fold the Mylar around the hook shank, and tie it down. Tie in a 4- to 5-inch piece of vinyl rib at the same point as the marabou and the Mylar tubing. Add a drop of superglue to ensure the vinyl rib does not slip when stretched during palmering. Advance your mono to the eye of the hook.

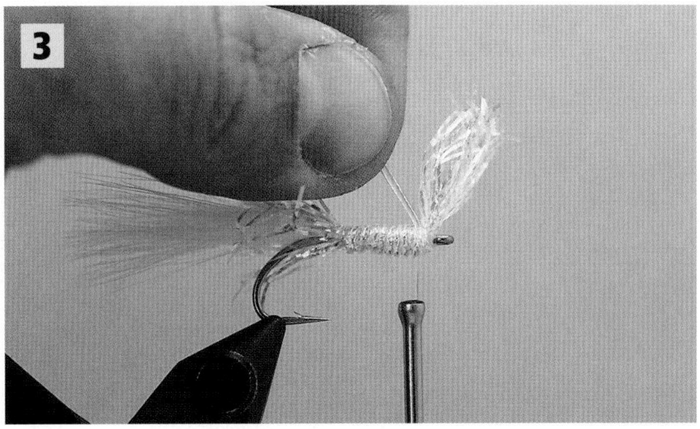


Palmer the Mylar tubing to the eye of the hook, securing the excess ½ inch of Mylar straight up. Palmer the vinyl rib over top of the Mylar tubing, stretching the vinyl to create neat, concentric wraps. Tie off the vinyl rib on top of the hook behind the tag of Mylar tubing.

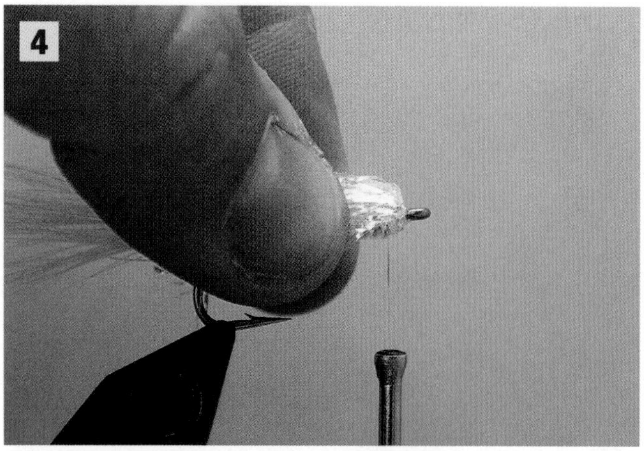

Fray the tag of Mylar tubing and fold it back, distributing it evenly around the top and sides of the hook.

Tie down the Mylar, wrapping back 10 to 15 turns. You need enough of a head to glue on the eyes. Whip-finish twice and cut away the mono. This is to ensure the slippery mono does not come undone before the epoxy or acrylic is added.

A handy trick I sometimes use with acrylic and epoxy is to fill the eye of the hook with ChapStick. This prevents any of the epoxy or acrylic from filling in the eye of the hook. Flavored or colored lip balms are easier to see and ensure the area is protected.

Glue on the eyes with a small dab of E-6000. Look at the fly from the top and from the front to ensure that the eyes are lined up with one another.

Add one or two drops of UV-curing acrylic or epoxy and spread it evenly over the eyes and the head of the fly. Try not to get too much of the product in the Mylar. While the acrylic is still wet, take a look head-on as well and check for proper alignment. Cure the product with a UV light or place on the drying wheel if using epoxy. Some UV products leave a tacky residue behind after the product is cured, which can be removed with an alcohol wipe or a coat of Hard as Nails.

Remove the ChapStick from the eye of the hook with a feather. This technique also works well if you get glue or epoxy in the hook eye before it hardens. Run the feather back and forth to clear the unwanted material.

Completed Moonshiner Minnow

CHAPTER 7

# White Noise

The White Noise is a translucent, sparsely tied impressionistic pattern designed to pique the curiosity of nearby fish in ultra-clear water. Adding UV reflective and glow-in-the-dark materials brings attention to the jigging and wobbling action of the fly.

**White Noise**

**Hook:** #1 or 2 TMC 811s or Daiichi 2546
**Thread:** 4-pound clear mono
**Body:** Steve Farrar's SF Flash Blend (white) and UV Krystal Flash (pearl)
**Eyes:** Large mono (black)
**Head:** Five-minute epoxy or UV acrylic
**Rattle:** Glow-in-the-dark plastic worm rattle

I came up with the White Noise in the summer of 2007 after fishing the beach of Captiva. The water there is extremely clear over the bleached white sand, and all the bait I encountered swimming around my feet were almost completely clear. The only way you could see them was to pick up on their eyes or key in on the little cylindrical gut pouch on the belly of the fish. It looked like it just hung off the head, and there wasn't too much else you could distinguish. Even the shrimp that some of the locals fished with seemed to be bleached. They weren't the usual tannish pink hue; they were clear. The only thing you could make out was the dark black spot (the brain) and maybe the antenna if you caught the light right.

That was the idea behind this pattern. I wanted to make a little noise to attract the fish's attention, but I did not what the fish to have much to investigate. I wanted the fly to re-

When it comes to big snook, oftentimes I find that bigger flies are better. Purple and black work well in off-color water, but when all else fails I go to all-white patterns like the White Noise.

semble food, but nothing in particular. I had not played around with too many patterns that had a rattle at the time, so I was experimenting with those. I chose the SF Flash Blend because I wanted a sparse, translucent fly that had enough weight to be hopped like a shrimp and could be easily mistaken for a number of different items on the menu. The few strands of UV Krystal Flash add another layer of attraction or represent the faint violet band of some of the local baitfish. The wobbling motion was not intended in the design, but was an added bonus that I discovered later due to the UV acrylic.

Adding the glow-in-the-dark rattles was a happy accident as well. When I found the plastic worm rattles at a tackle shop in north Florida I was excited because up until that time I could only find the glass ones, and they seemed too fragile and were a pain to tie down. I wasn't really looking at the packaging and assumed they were all the same when I grabbed every package they had off the hook. I store all my worm rattles in the same slotted tray, but I must have grabbed a bag of glow-in-the-dark ones with the others. They look similar and only vary a little in color. I was tying up a bunch of them using Rio's UV Knot product for the head. I was having a hard time curing them due to the amount of product I applied, so I left them outside in the sun to make sure they got plenty of UV light. That night when I opened my fly box it look like an NYC rave. The couple of flies I had accidently tied with glow-in-the-dark rattles had been fully charged in the sunlight and were glowing bright green. The rest is history. Other than experimenting with types of UV acrylic for the head and the glow-in-the-dark rattle, I have not changed the original pattern.

If any fly had a spectrum of reasons for its productivity, this fly is it. The UV reflective and glow-in-the-dark materials bring attention to the jigging and wobbling action of the fly. The sharp clicking sound from the rattle travels much farther underwater and helps make fish aware of its presence. The broad acrylic head moves a volume of water when stripped, and on closer inspection its translucent qualities make it hard to distinguish.

My favorite place to fish this fly is on the beach for snook in the same fashion as the Moonshiner Minnow. Long, slow strips work best, and every once in a while I throw in a tip waggle for a little added movement. However, I have had several reports from fisherman in north Florida and North Carolina who have had great luck with a chartreuse over olive variation, and a chartreuse over hot pink variation of this pattern for sea trout over heavy grass flats.

## Tying the White Noise

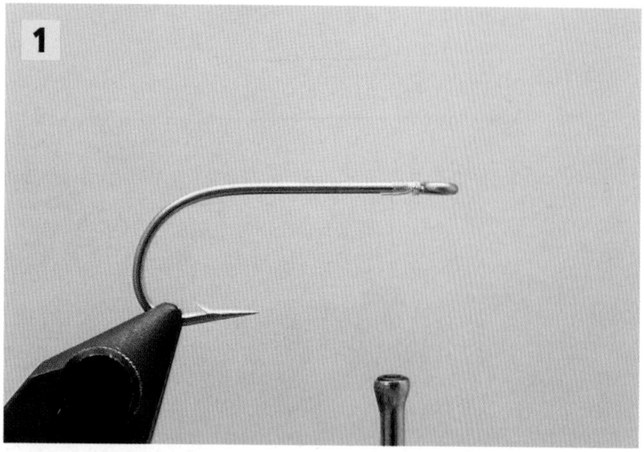


Start the mono at the eye of the hook with 10 wraps. Secure the wraps with a drop of superglue.

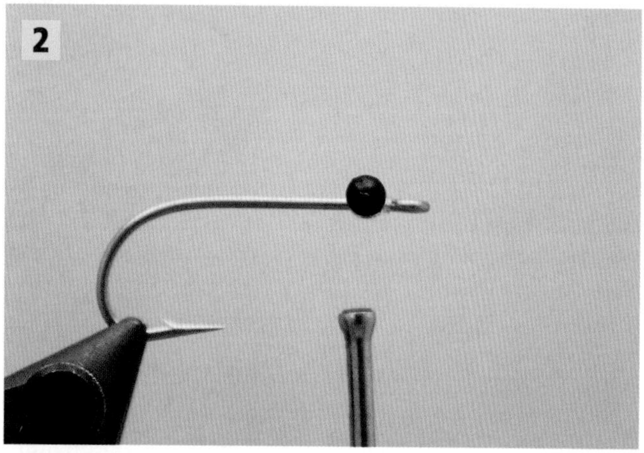


Tie in the dumbbell eyes with a series of four to five figure-eight wraps.

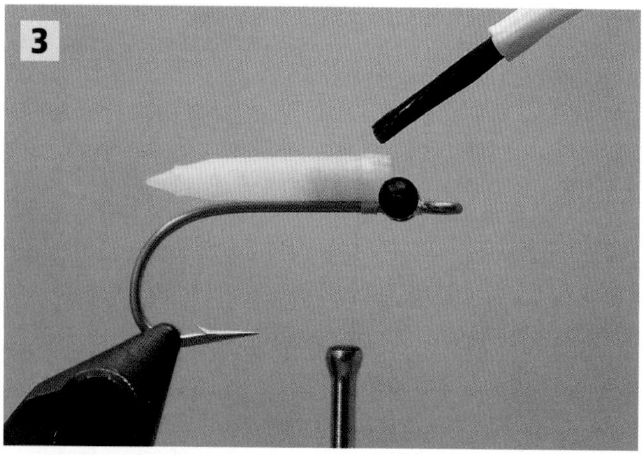


Secure the rattle directly behind the eyes with 10 to 12 wraps. Cover all the mono wraps with glue.

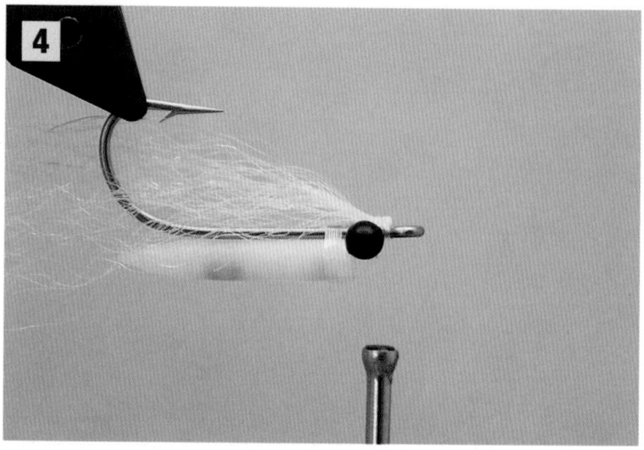


Turn the hook over (hook point up) and taper the ends and tie in a 6-inch-long bunch of SF Flash Blend in front of the mono eyes with four to five wraps.

Fold the material back on top of itself, making sure there is an even amount of material on each side of the hook.

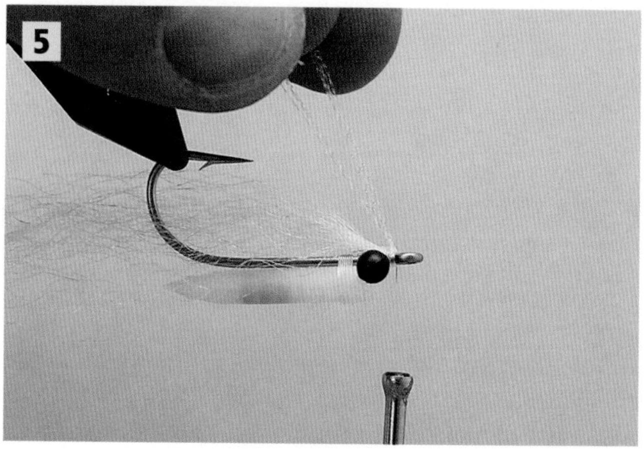


Fold four strands of UV Krystal Flash around the mono and tie in on top of the SF Flash Blend. Split the strands evenly on each side of the hook.

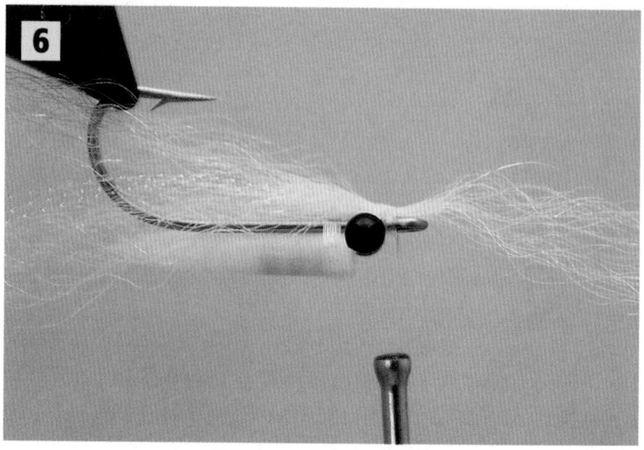


Taper the ends and tie in a second 6-inch-long bunch of SF Flash Blend on top of the first bunch and the Krystal Flash.

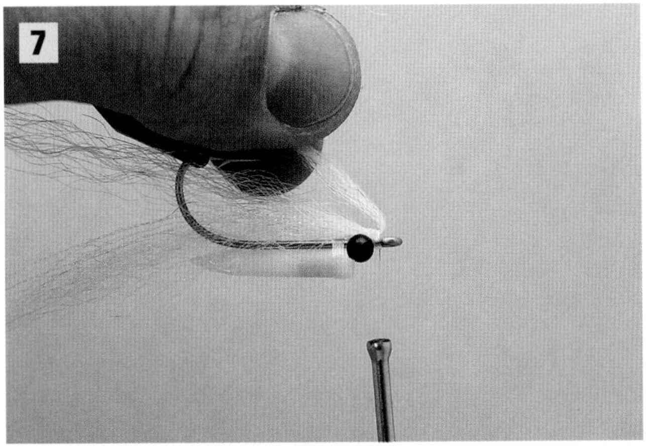


Fold the material back on top of itself, making sure there is an even amount of material on each side of the hook.

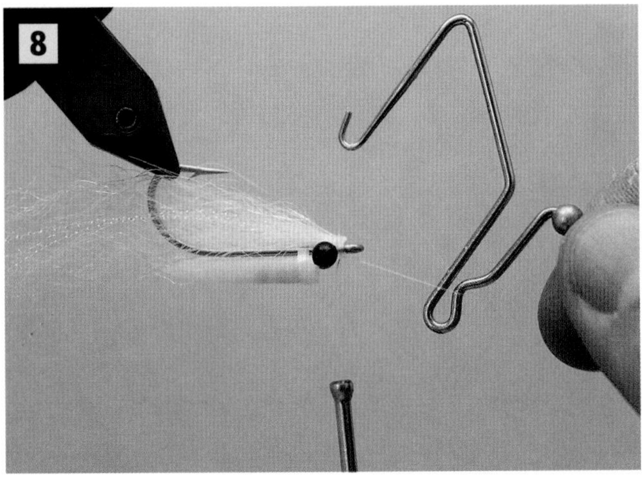


Whip-finish twice and secure the wraps with a drop of superglue.

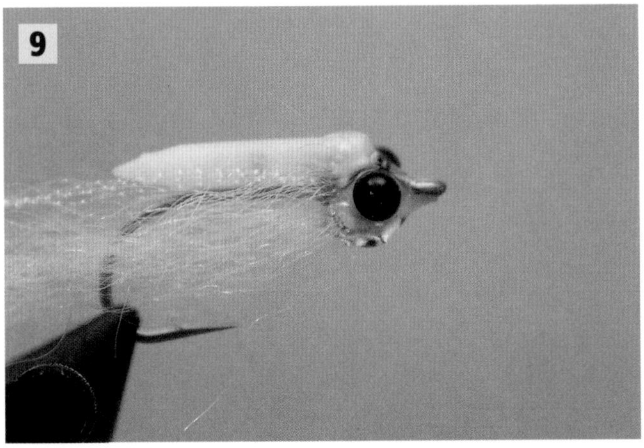


Add one or two drops of UV-curing acrylic and spread it evenly over the eyes and the head of the fly. Try not to get too much of the product in the SF Flash Blend.

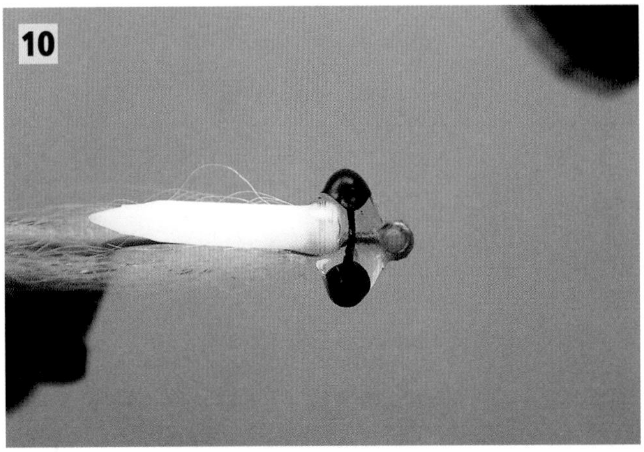


Rotate the fly in the vise or by hand until the acrylic is dispersed evenly around the rattle and eyes. Cure the acrylic with a UV light.

The majority of the acrylic should be on top of the eyes, creating a cylindrical shape and weighting the fly to ride hook up when fished.

Completed White Noise

CHAPTER 8

# Disco Shrimp

The Disco Shrimp is a top-water pattern that is a blast to fish. Although it seems small at first glance, this realistic shrimp pattern moves an excessive volume of water with each strip and makes quite a commotion on the surface. The Disco Shrimp was originally designed for mangrove snapper, and short strips with a longer than usual pause work best if snapper are what you're targeting. However, it has proven to be an effective back bay utility fly with snook, redfish, and seatrout all succumbing to the disco call.

**Disco Shrimp**

**Hook:** #1 or 2 Mustad 34011 or long shank
**Thread:** Brown Danville 210-denier
**Body:** Tan 2 mm closed-cell foam, Golden Brown Ice Dub, and red foxtail
**Eyes:** Large EP crab/shrimp (black)
**Rattle:** Plastic worm rattle
**Tail:** Two 4 mm gold sequins

My good friend Warren Weatherford, an unbelievably creative fly tier, is the type of guy who has been known to covertly trim his dog, Halloween wigs, or even his wife's sweaters in his quest for new and better fly-tying materials. Oftentimes we bring each other bizarre materials that you wouldn't necessarily find at your local fly shop and ask, "What do you think we can do with this?" Most of the time the answer is throw it away, but every once in a while we discover a gem.

Without a doubt the most versatile and useful discovery Warren and I have stumbled upon lately has been the sequin. The thin, sparkly disk, commonly associated with Vegas show girls, old ladies' shirts, and the disco era, has found a new home on the bench of fly tiers!

One of my favorite fish to catch and eat is the mangrove snapper, but they're not often thought of as a prime target for fly rodders. While fishing the mangrove shorelines of Pine Island Sound last May for snook and redfish, I was astonished by the size and number of mangrove snapper tucked up under the overhanging roots. I cast to them several times, but could not seem to coax them out from their mangrove lair.

After presenting a smorgasbord of different baitfish patterns with no luck, I made the switch to top water. The popper had to be small enough not to spook the fish and fit in the snapper's mouth, but large enough to get their attention before getting too far away from the school's stronghold. The conundrum was this: in order to make a noticeable disturbance on the surface with a small foam bug, I needed to strip the fly pretty forcefully, but after three or four strips, the popper had moved too far away from shore and out of the strike zone. The solution . . . a plastic worm rattle and a couple of sequins.

The foam shell of the shrimp protects the brittle plastic rattle as well as positioning half of the cup-shaped sequin above the water's surface at a 45-degree angle. The result is one heck of a disturbance on the surface with very little forward movement of the fly. The trifecta of the clicking rattle, sharp pop from the sequin, and a spray of water work in harmony to command the attention of any fish in the area. A mono weedguard is very helpful when casting deep underneath bushes and gives you a little leeway in your casting accuracy, allowing you to carefully fish the fly out of the foliage without getting snagged. The Disco Shrimp was originally designed for mangrove snapper, and short strips with a longer-than-usual pause work best for them. However, snook, redfish, and sea trout all succumb to the disco call. I use a floating line with a mono leader to keep the small fly afloat. A fluorocarbon leader sinks, and despite the buoyancy of the foam, it tends to pull the sequin underwater.

## Preparing the Mono Shrimp Eyes

Nothing is more realistic than mono eyes for shrimp or crab patterns. I prefer them to plastic dumbbell eyes for most if not all patterns because they are more durable. Tying two of them parallel to one another allows you to create a wider profile, and they hold up to far more abuse. The conventional way of making mono eyes is to melt mono with a lighter and color the melted ball with permanent marker. A thin coat of UV acrylic keeps the color sharp and gives the eyes a realistic, shiny translucence. Using UV paint is an even easier way to make mono eyes.

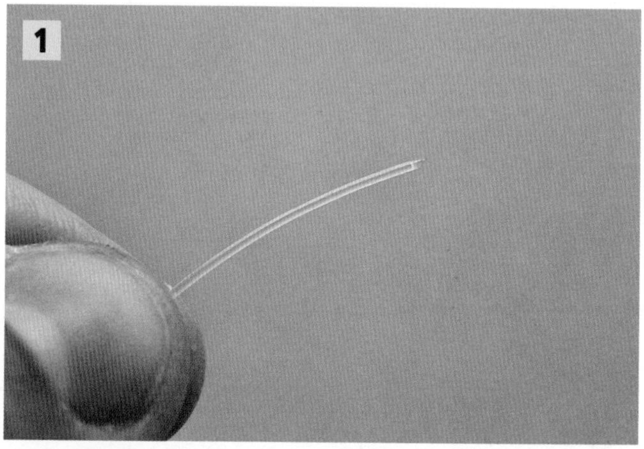

Start with a 2- to 3-inch piece of 16- to 20-pound monofilament. (Fluorocarbon does not melt as well.)

Use a lighter, and slowly pass the tip of the mono through the flame until the material starts to melt and form a ball. If the mono ignites, lightly blow out the flame, being careful not to blow the melted mono away. Be careful not to let the material burn too fast and drip. It is extremely painful and difficult to get off your skin if you are careless, so make sure you are leaning over a bench and away from your legs.

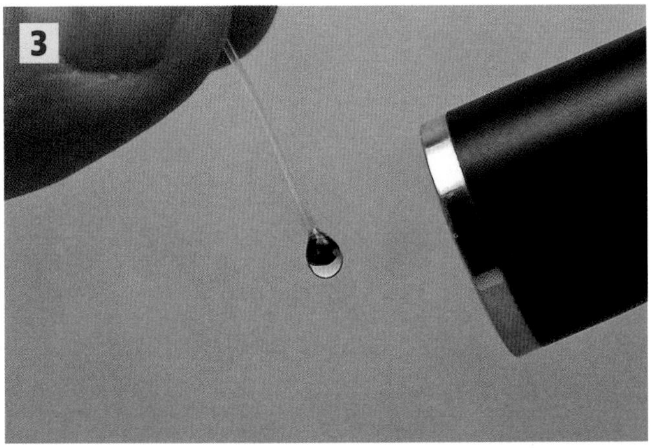


When you are happy with the size and shape of melted mono eye, let it cool and color it with a permanent marker. Add a coat of UV acrylic or epoxy for a smoother, more realistic look and greater durability.

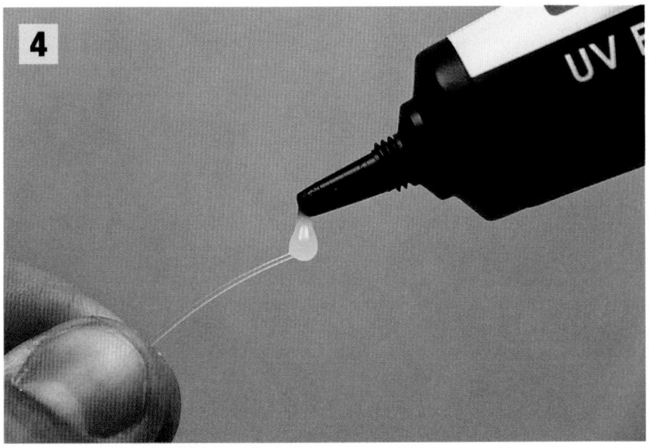


An easier and faster way of creating eyes is by using Loon's red, yellow, or orange UV paints. Simply add a drop of UV paint to the end of your mono, hang it upside down, and cure it with a UV light.

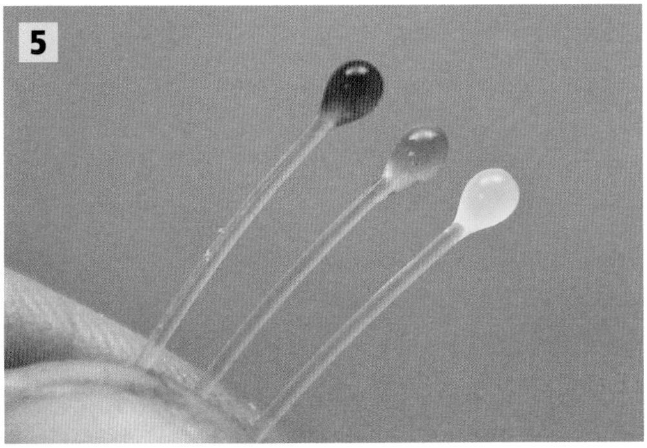


These eyes take about 30 seconds to make. There are no toxic fumes or risk of dripping hot mono on yourself, but you are limited to the three colors available right now. Clear Cure Goo offers a product called Fleck that has sparkly metal flakes mixed into the acrylic, and it's just a matter of time before manufacturers offer every color in the rainbow.

## Tying the Disco Shrimp

Bend down the hook barb and slide on the gold sequin with the convex side toward the eye of the hook. Place the hook in the vise point down, and start the thread at the point of the hook. Tie in a small tuft of fox tail fur about 1 inch long.

On top of the fox tail, tie in four legs. Fold the legs back so they point backward past the bend of the hook. I like to trim them different lengths, leaving some longer than the fox tail.

Tie in the eyes on top so that they extend slightly past the bend of the hook. Splay the eyes with a few thread wraps between them.

Tie in the rattle on top and slightly in front of the eyes, pointing forward. Tie in two doubled strands of Krystal Flash for the antenna.

Tie in another small bunch of fox to cover the rattle. Dub the thread with about 1 inch of dubbing.

Wrap forward to cover all your previous wraps.

On top of the rattle, tie in the foam with four or five overlapping wraps. It should be 2½ inches long, ¼ inch wide, and tapered to a point at one end.

Dub the thread with enough Ice Dub to make three or four turns (about an inch), and dub about ¼ inch under the foam.

When you are out of dub, tie down a segment of foam.

Repeat this process twice more, reducing the size of the segment slightly each time.

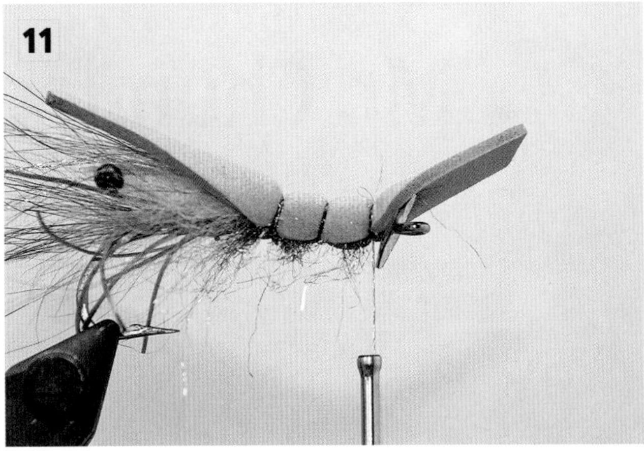

The tail of the foam should be propped up by the sequins.

Trim off the excess foam, and whip-finish behind the sequins to complete.

CHAPTER 9

# Mr. Chumlee

Mr. Chumlee is an innovative variation of a basic baitfish pattern, tied sideways on the hook in order to mimic a wounded baitfish floating on its side. The extra-long Craft Fur tail provides just enough movement to accurately mimic the intermittent wiggle of the paralyzed baitfish.

**Mr. Chumlee**

| | |
|---|---|
| **Hook:** | **#1/0 or 2/0 Gamakatsu SC12** |
| **Thread:** | **4-pound mono** |
| **Tail:** | **White Craft Fur** |
| **Belly:** | **White SF Fiber** |
| **Back:** | **Chartreuse SF Fiber and 2 mm foam** |
| **Eyes:** | **8 mm pearl dome eye** |
| **Gills:** | **Red Wing N' Flash** |

When I moved to Florida and started fishing salt water more often, I spent a lot of time with guides, soaking up as much knowledge as possible. The technique that was completely foreign to me (growing up in upstate New York and freshwater fishing my whole life) was live chumming. At first light, as soon as the sun hits the surface of the water, 4- to 5-inch pilchards or white bait come to the surface in schools. If you're lucky, the water is flat calm, and you can see the tiny splashes from their tails flicking and breaking the surface of the water. You're looking for that change in the surface of the water; it looks like a faint dimpling or shaking patch of water. A circular cast net is thrown over the school, and the baits are collected and kept in a live well. When you show up at the spot where you think the fish are and you intend to fish, the guide starts throwing handfuls of white bait overboard and if there are

It's been said that if jack crevalle would jump when hooked they would be in contention for the greatest gamefish ever. They are tremendous fighters that take a fly quite regularly. Catching them on the surface with a wounded baitfish pattern like a Mr. Chumlee just adds to the excitement.

gamefish in the area, the water usually starts to explode as the bait are driven to the surface and devoured. Once the fish start the feeding frenzy, baits are often hit but not eaten immediately and left twitching erratically near the surface half-dead. Because they are floating on their sides, they are bright white and silhouetted from above and below and become easy targets for other fish and birds.

After throwing one or two handfuls of unmolested bait, the guide usually starts squeezing a few bait or smacking the dip net full of bait on the hull of the boat to stun or disorient the pilchards or white bait, making critically injured baits. When he launches them close to mangroves, they tend to float sideways and swim in circles. Their chances of swimming to safety are nonexistent, and they become a easy meal as they flutter helplessly on the surface . . . and that is exactly what Mr. Chumlee looks like.

The extra-long Craft Fur tail gives just enough movement to mimic the intermittent wiggle from the paralyzed baitfish. The wide piece of foam on the back of the fly keeps the fly on the surface and keeps it from spinning when stripped. It also makes a wide platform to glue the materials to. This helps maintain the profile of the fly when wet. If you do not fan the material out and glue it to the foam, it has a tendency to lay back, and the fly takes on a rounder profile over time. I chose the Gamakatsu SC12 hook because it is extremely sturdy but light enough not to overpower the buoyancy of the foam. This hook has a wide gap, is extremely sharp, and has plenty of room on the shank for building up the material.

I work the fly with a series of 1-foot-long strips as if the baitfish was getting a second wind, but then I stop and let the fly float back to the surface. A series of micro strips and tip twitches gyrates the fly on the surface without moving it too far. I let the fly settle for a few seconds and then start the process over. The strike usually comes when the fly is still, so be prepared to strip-set. Trout, snook, and tarpon are all attracted to this pattern, and you never know what may be lurking below.

## Tying the Mr. Chumlee

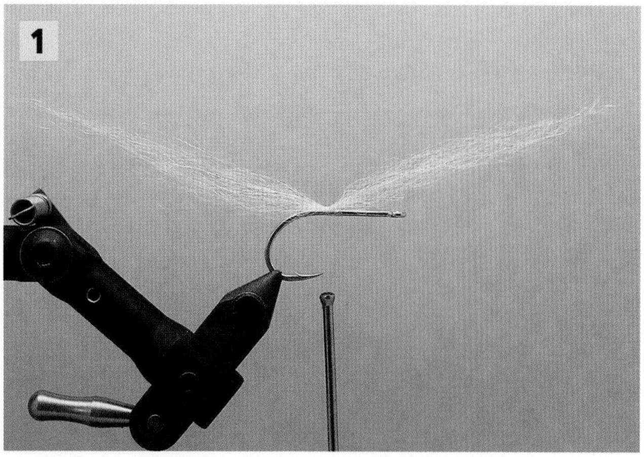


Start the mono thread in the middle of the hook and make 10 wraps. The mono should hang at the point of the hook. Take a matchstick-size bunch of white SF Fiber and cut it in half. Taper one of the sections at both ends and tie in at the middle.

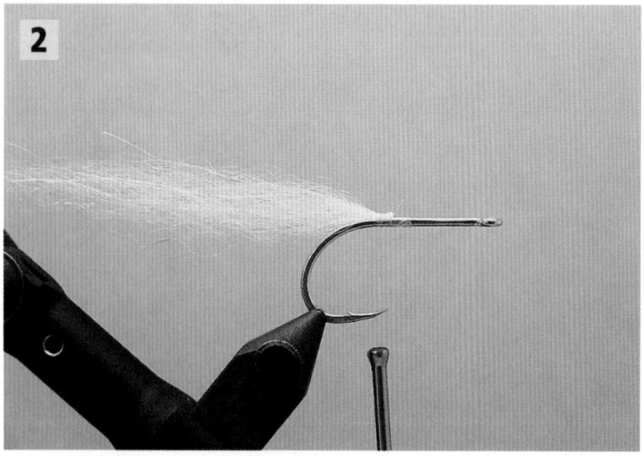


Fold the material on top of itself and secure it with four or five wraps. This mimics the lateral line on a baitfish and supports the Craft Fur and keeps it from fouling.

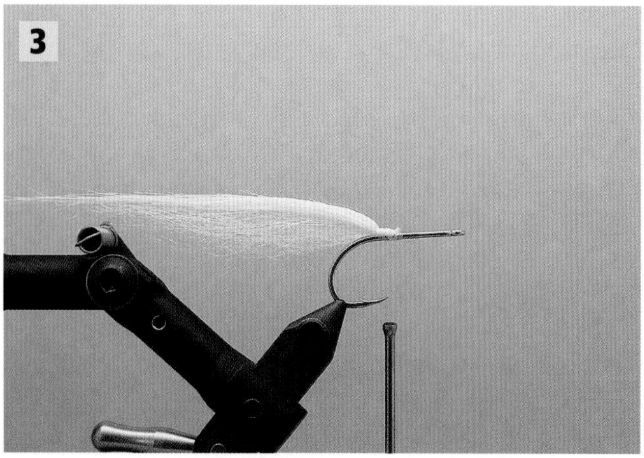


Cut a bunch of Craft Fur the width of a pencil and three times the length of the hook and remove any loose fibers or fluff. Tie in the Craft Fur three times the length of the hook with six to eight wraps.

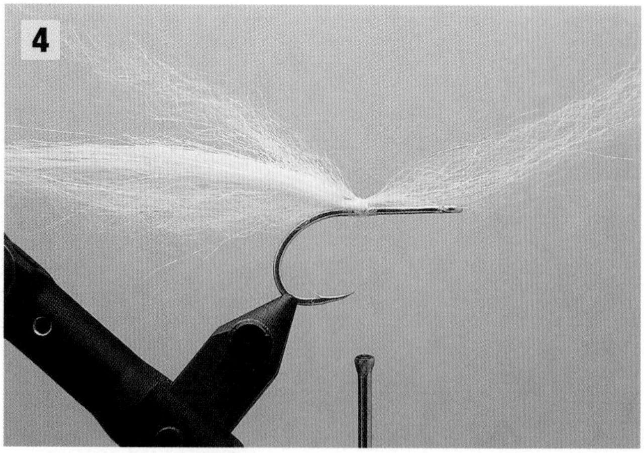


Taper the other half section of white SF Fiber at both ends and tie it in at the middle.

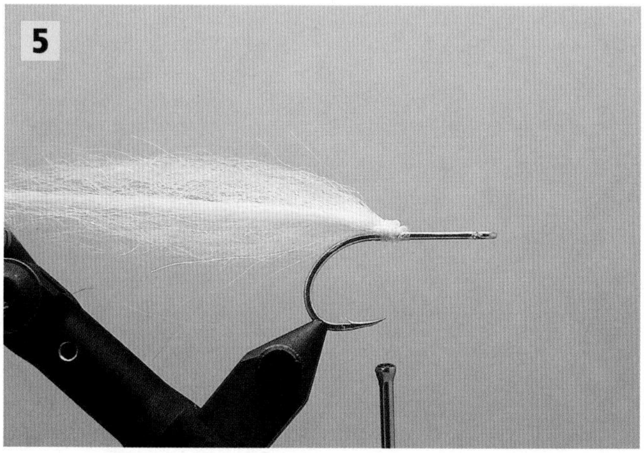


Fold the material back on itself on top of the hook and secure it with three or four wraps.

Turn the vise sideways so that the hook point is away from you and the sides of the hook are now top and bottom.

Cut a matchstick-size bunch of white SF Fiber in half and taper one of the sections at both ends. Tie it in at the middle and secure it with four or five wraps.

Fold the material back on itself on top of the hook and secure it in place with four or five wraps.

Turn the vise over so that the hook point is toward you and the sides of the hook are top and bottom. Cut a matchstick-size bunch of chartreuse SF Fiber in half and taper one of the sections at both ends. Tie it in at the middle and secure it with four or five wraps.

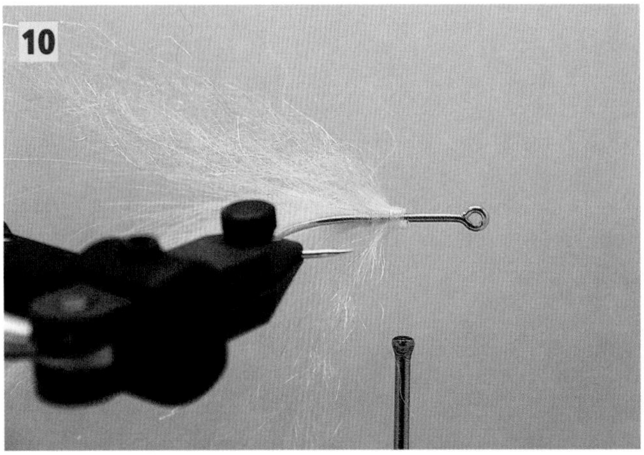


Fold the material back on itself on top of the hook and secure it in place with four or five wraps. Add a drop of Zap-A-Gap to secure all the materials and thread wraps.

Advance the mono two or three wraps so that it's in front of all the materials. Taper the remaining half of the white SF Fiber at both ends and tie it in at the middle. Secure it with four or five wraps.

Fold the material back on itself on top of the hook and secure it in place with four or five wraps. Add on drop of Zap-A-Gap to secure all the materials and thread wraps.

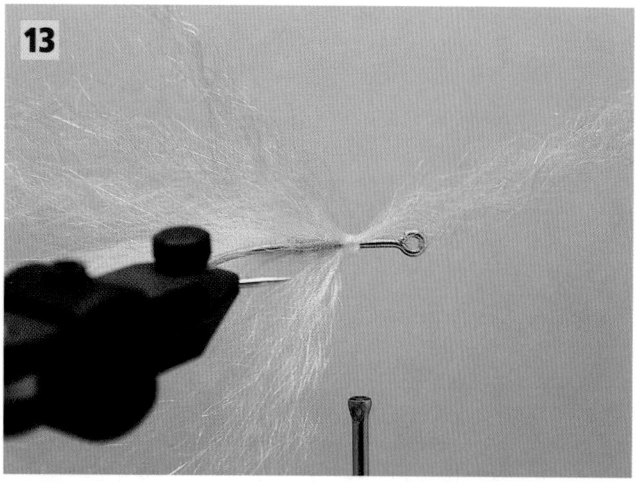

Taper the remaining half of the chartreuse SF Fiber at both ends and tie it in at the middle. Secure it with four or five wraps.

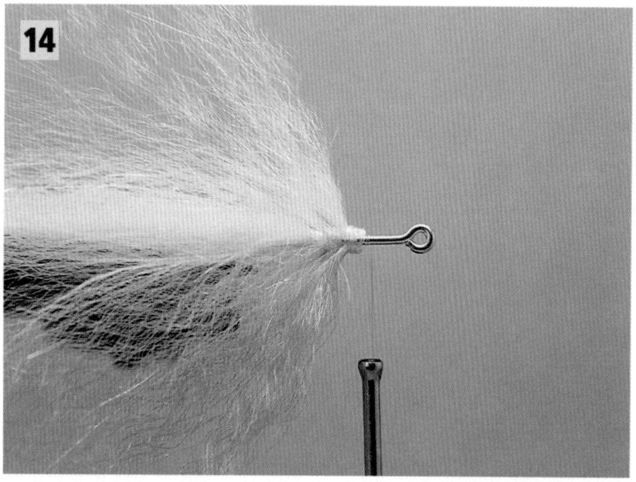

Advance the mono two to three wraps so that it's in front of the materials. Add a drop of Zap-A-Gap to secure all the materials and thread wraps.

Repeat the process two more times with consecutively shorter pieces of white SF Fiber on the belly and chartreuse SF Fiber on the back to create a tapered shape.

On the white half of the fly, tie in a 1-inch piece of red Wing N' Flash at its middle with four or five wraps. Fold it back on itself and secure it with four or five wraps. Folding the materials in half makes them is easier to secure with fewer wraps and keeps the eye of the hook clear from the tips of the materials.

Whip-finish twice and secure the wraps with a drop of Zap-A-Gap. Fan the SF Fiber out away from the hook shank in a flat leaf shape. Start from the eye of the hook and trim the SF Fiber lightly toward the tail of the fly. Be careful not to cut the Craft Fur. Slowly trim until you have a baitfish or teardrop shape.

Cut a piece of foam into a crease-fly or guitar-pick shape and glue it on top of the fly.

19

Turn the fly over and glue on one 8 mm dome eye slightly behind the eye of the hook.

How to glue on small eyes with precision without getting glue all over everything is probably the question I'm asked most, second only to what kind of glue to use for attaching dome eyes. With this technique, it's easy to position the eyes symmetrically and keep from using too much glue on the flies, but if you do end up getting glue somewhere you don't want it, don't try to fix it while it is wet. The glue dries clear and peels off the front of the eyes easily, so let the fly dry and then deal with the excess.

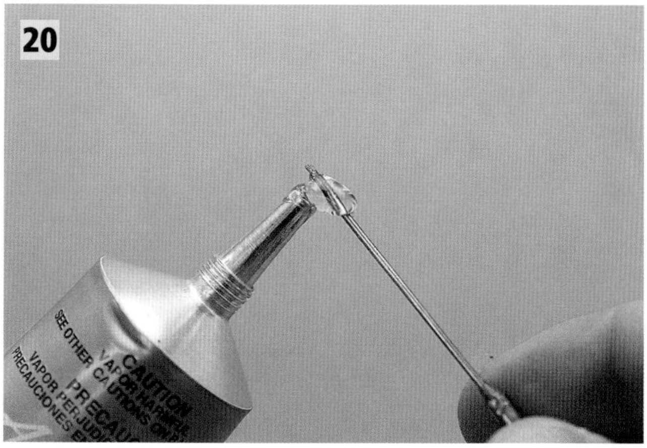


20

Using the tip of a bodkin, collect a drop of viscous glue like Goop or E-6000. The drop should be slightly smaller than the eye you are gluing.

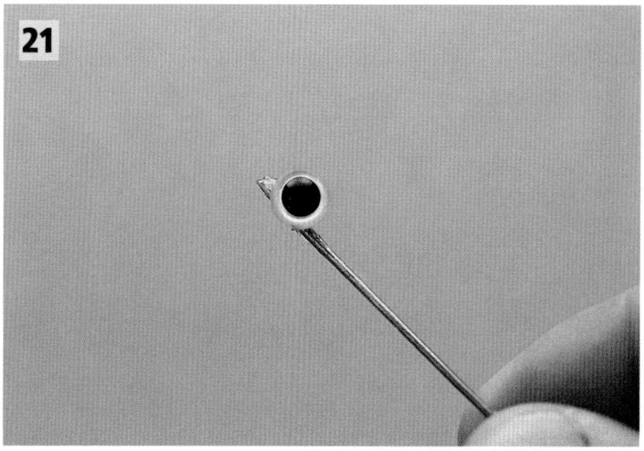

21

Remove the post of the plastic eye if necessary, and lay the eye dome side (or good side) down. Touch the back of the eye near one side with the glue-tipped bodkin. It will be tacky enough to lift and maneuver the eye into place without using your fingers.

Place the eye where you want it and spin the bodkin in your fingers to release the glue from the bodkin. Slide the bodkin out from underneath the eye away from the eye of the hook.

Press down on top of the eye with a clean finger to force the glue into the material and onto the shank of the hook to make a solid bond and keep the glue from the front of the eye, eye of the hook, or the materials.

CHAPTER 10

# Devil's Daughter

The Devil's Daughter is one of my favorite patterns for persnickety baby tarpon. The black pattern silhouettes well in low light conditions, and it's spun deer hair head effectively pushes volumes of water. Peacock herl intermingled throughout the pattern glows an orange color in dark water and works well to call attention to this small fly.

### Devil's Daughter

**Hook:** #1 or 1/0 TMC 811s or Daiichi 2546
**Thread:** Black 210-denier Danville
**Tail:** Peacock herl and black ostrich plume
**Body:** Black marabou plumes
**Head:** Black deer body hair

Casting my 9-foot rod in the tunnellike mangrove creeks was difficult at best, and sometimes the best option was to break the rod apart and only cast its top half. The black water was full of baby tarpon, and everything I threw seemed to get the middle fin! Everybody and their uncle had found and cast at these fish by now, and I'm sure that after seeing so many different patterns, a few of these fish could tie their own flies.

After experimenting with a number of different colors, shapes, and sizes, I finally realized there was nothing I had that they wanted. I had a few encouraging looks, but no takers, and anything with synthetic flash in it was disregarded immediately. Darker flies seemed to appeal to the little guys, but they just weren't convinced. I needed to create something that would move a lot of water and get their attention.

After days of trying different variations of small black or brown flies, I tried one with a few peacock herls for a tail.

It was my birthday, and my wife, Susan, and I were fishing with some close friends in the canals of Pine Island. We found a pod of happy baby tarpon and I landed a few, but Susan caught this beautiful 80-pounder and I assisted with the release.

I was amazed to find that the fly was an iridescent orange in the dark water, and within a few casts I had a miniature silver king hooked up. Since the fly's materials were sparse, I wanted to incorporate as much of the peacock herl as possible throughout. Spinning it with the deer hair worked perfectly, and it was easy to trim to shape.

Once the lightly spun deer hair head gets saturated, the fly will sink, and I usually let it hit the bottom or close to it before I start my retrieve. Aggressive, short strips with a long two- to three-second pause in between is the way to go.

## Tying the Devil's Daughter

Start the thread at the point of the hook. Tie in 10 black ostrich plumes 2½ to 3 times the hook length.

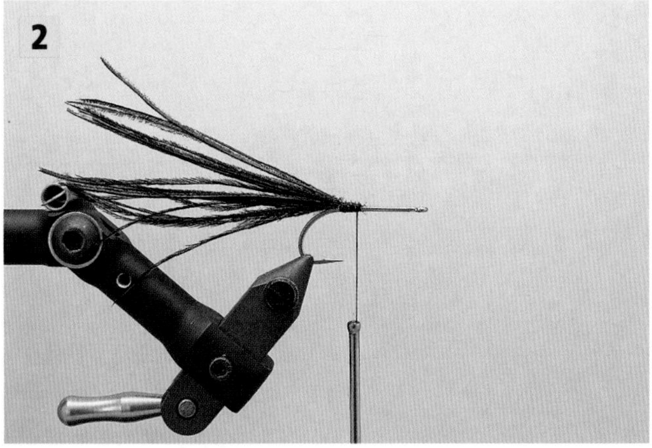


On top of the ostrich plumes, tie in six peacock herls the same length. Advance your thread slightly in front of the materials two to three wraps.

Fold the marabou in half so all the barbules are on one side and tie it in at the base of the feather. Advance your thread to the middle of the hook. Holding the tip of the feather, palmer it forward until you run out of feather and then tie it off.

Repeat the process with a second marabou plume—pull the feathers back and pack them tight. The thread should be slightly in front of the middle of the hook.

Cut a pencil-size bunch of black deer body hair and mix it with 10 to 15 peacock herls cut the same length as the hair.

Make two loose wraps around the middle of the bunch and work the hair and herl around the shank of the hook with your fingers. Pull the thread tight and spin the bunch around the hook.

Lock the bunch in place with two firm wraps and work the thread forward. Push the hair and herl back and place a couple of half hitches or a whip-finish in front. (If you break the thread, it will secure the bunch from coming apart.)

Repeat the process two or three more times until you fill the shank of the hook, lightly pushing the hair and herl back as you go. Do not pack the hair tight or the fly will float on top like a popper. The herl should be evenly dispersed among the deer hair around the shank of the hook.

When you run out of hook shank to spin hair on, with your left hand pull all the hair back away from the eye of the hook.

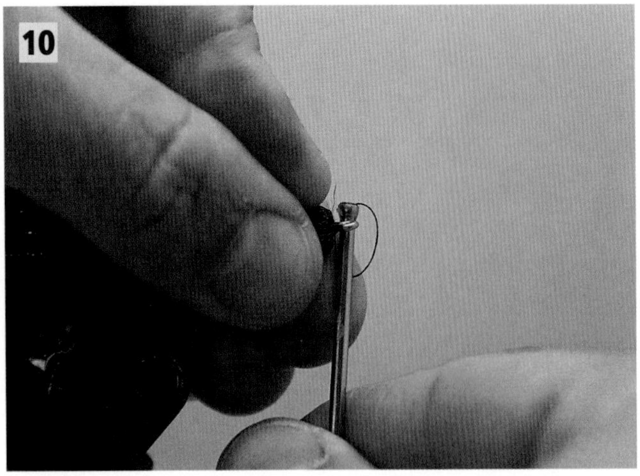


Spin the thread counterclockwise and slowly move the bobbin toward the eye of the hook. The twisted thread will want to curl back on itself when the tension is released slightly from the bobbin.

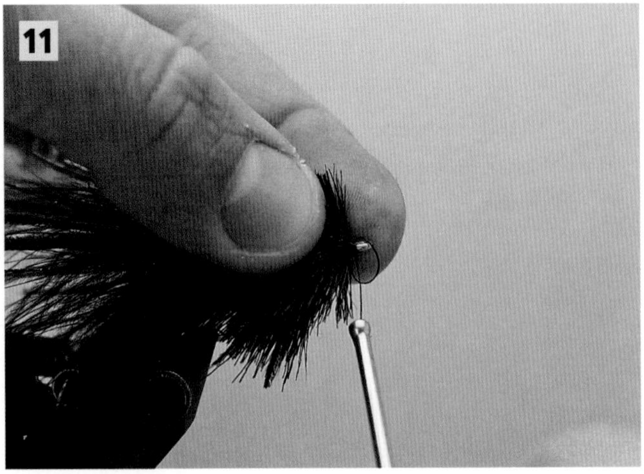


Help the loop over the hood eye with your finger and secure your tensioned wraps with a simple half hitch. This step secures the wraps and allows you to hold all the hair out of the way at the same time. Once secured, push back the hair and herl away from the eye of the hook and whip-finish. Cut away the thread and secure the wraps with head cement.

Being careful not to cut the marabou, trim the iridescent head to a slider or cone shape with a razor blade.

13

Although it looks a little strange in the vise, once in the water the fly comes alive. The supple feathers are set in motion by the slightest movement, and the buoyancy of the deer hair head causes the fly to suspend just under the surface and nudge water out of its way as it swims along. Incorporating the same iridescent material throughout the body and head of the fly makes it look natural, only shining when the light is just right.

CHAPTER 11

# Flats McNasty

The Flats McNasty is an impressionistic attractor pattern created with a blend of highly visible colors spun together in a dubbing brush. Let the fly sink to the bottom, and after a pregnant pause slowly start crawling the fly through the weeds. After a few inches, stop the fly and pause again.

### Flats McNasty

| | |
|---|---|
| **Hook:** | #1 or 1/0 Daiichi 2546 |
| **Thread:** | Orange flat waxed nylon |
| **Tail:** | Gold lead eye |
| **Body:** | Rust and bronze Puglisi fiber and copper and orange Wing N' Flash |
| **Antennae:** | 4 strands gold Krystal Flash |
| **Eyes:** | Large amber EP crab/shrimp |
| **Claws:** | Orange and brown Sili Legs |
| **Shell:** | Orangutan Rust Craft Fur |

The Flats McNasty is a prime example of an impressionistic attractor pattern. It was not designed to look like any specific prey item, but more of a shrimp-crab hybrid that would get the attention of preoccupied redfish in thick turtle grass. Since most of the fish I cast to are rooting around like wild hogs with their big copper heads buried in search of forage, I could afford to make this fly a little heavier without spooking them. The weighted dumbbell eyes get the fly down quick to the soft bottom, and when crawled slowly, the fly creates an obvious muddy disturbance. Monofilament crustacean eyes help keep the fly weedless, but they also provide an appetizing shrimp or crab look. The blend of orange and brown Enrico Puglisi fibers is extremely effective at piquing the interest of these inattentive fish–if you can get the fly under their nose. In stained or off-color water, adding finely cut flash makes a big difference. The shimmering glints of copper and rust act like a signal flare to beckon the fish if your cast is a little off. Once you have their attention, the similarly colored rubber legs are the icing on the cake.

When presenting the Flats McNasty to tailing fish, don't worry about spooking them. I try to cast as close as possible; sometimes it looks like I have beamed them with the fly. Once in a while a fish might flee, but most are so preoccupied they do not even notice the fly's impact. Let the fly sink to the bottom, and after a pregnant pause slowly start crawling the fly through the weeds. Pause after a few inches and let the fly rest. This is usually when a fish takes the fly.

Since the fly is heavily weighted, I like a shorter 8-foot leader. My bite tippet is usually 20-pound fluorocarbon. I don't like going much lighter than that because if you get hit by a snook or get dragged across a few oysters, you don't stand a chance.

## Tying the Flats McNasty

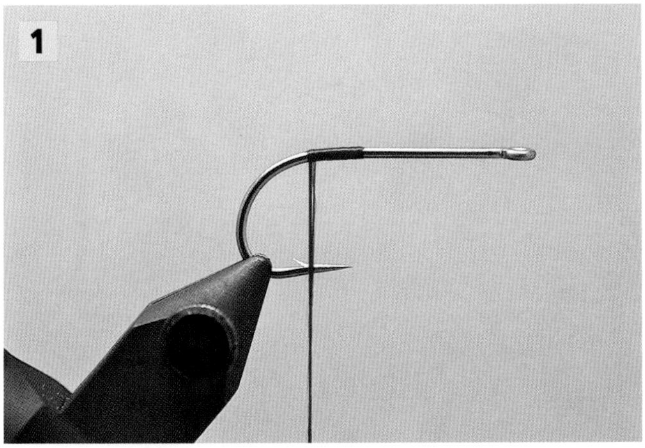


First create a dubbing brush with rust and bronze Puglisi fiber and copper and orange Wing N' Flash. (See page 45 for an explanation of dubbing brushes.) Start the thread at the bend of the hook.

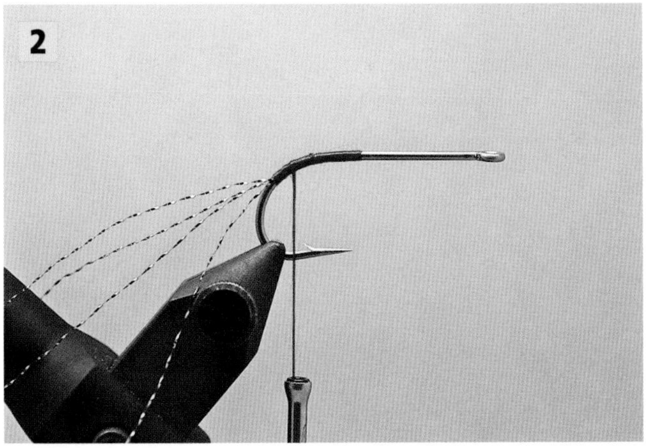


Tie in four strands of Krystal Flash, winding the wraps down the bend of the hook. With the fly riding hook up in the water, the antennae should point up at a 45-degree angle.

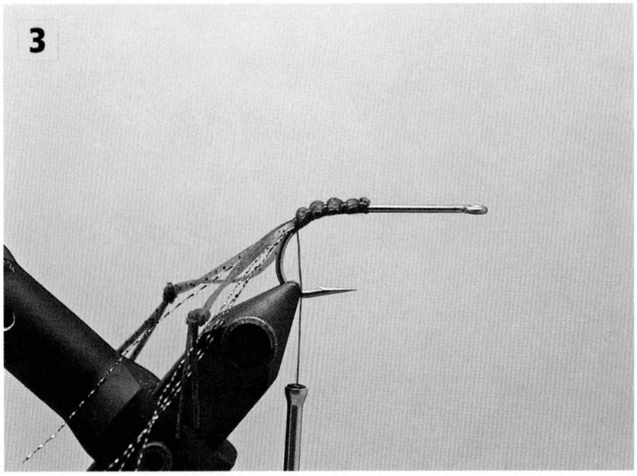


Using two Sili Legs, tie a knot in both ends where the color changes from brown to orange. Trim the orange claws about 1/4 inch. Tie them in on top of the hook, wrapping slightly down the bend of the hook.

Turn the hook over. Taper a 3-inch piece of rust Puglisi fiber at both ends. Tie in a matchstick-size bunch at the middle.

Fold the material back onto itself and tie it down with three or four wraps to secure. Make sure there is an even amount of Puglisi fiber on both sides of the hook.

Tie in the dubbing brush and advance the thread to the eye of the hook.

Palmer the dubbing brush forward with four or five turns. You do not want tight wraps or the fly will be too bulky. Make sure to hold the material back with each forward turn so you do not trap any of the fibers.

Tie off the brush at the eye of the hook and trim away the excess dubbing brush.

Turn the hook over and tie in the gold dumbbell eye on top of the hook slightly behind the eye of the hook with a series of figure-eight wraps.

Turn the fly back over so the hook is up. Using a dog brush, pick out and fluff up the material.

Trim the material to open up the gap of the hook. Make a few cuts from the eye of the hook to the point.

Tie in the EP shrimp eyes directly above the dumbbell eyes. The colored ball should stick out just beyond the bend of the hook.

Cover the eyes with a matchstick-size bunch of rust Craft Fur. Leave 1/4 inch past the hook eye of the hook for a tail. Whip-finish at the eye of the hook and cut away the thread.

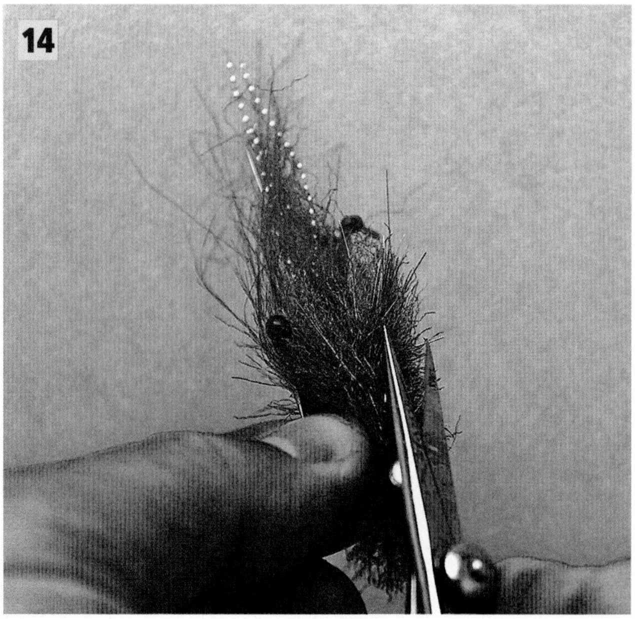


Take the fly out of the vise and trim the bottom of the fly. The fly should have a cone shape with the smaller portion at the eye of the hook, increasing in diameter to the point of the hook. Be careful not to cut off the claws.

Completed Flats McNasty

CHAPTER 12

# 5-Minute Finger Mullet

The 5-Minute Finger Mullet is a dubbing-brush pattern tied completely with synthetic materials. Two large EP crab/shrimp eyes are tied parallel to each other to give the pattern a realistic, wide profile. Long, slow strips or a two-handed retrieve work well to emulate the natural motion of this highly sought after saltwater snack.

**5-Minute Finger Mullet**

**Hook:** #2 or 1 Daiichi 2546
**Thread:** 4-pound mono
**Body:** Steve Farrar's Flash Blend (shrimp, gray, and mullet brown)
**Eyes:** Large black dumbbell or large black EP crab/shrimp
**Head:** Steve Farrar's Flash Blend (dubbing brush gray, mullet brown)

In the late spring and early summer months, the beaches, back bay, and even brackish water are abuzz with schools of finger mullet. These 3- to 6-inch cigar-shaped baitfish are highly sought-after snacks for inshore and offshore predators.

Because finger mullet are such popular food, these vulnerable vegetarians are extremely skittish and tend to find safety in numbers. Their rounded head and cylindrical body push large volumes of water as they swim, and if they are darting around just under the surface, they are easy to spot due to the conspicuous wake they generate. These telling traits are easily reproduced on the tying bench, and predators clearly identify them with food, making finger mullet patterns one of my favorites to tie and fish.

## Tying the 5-Minute Finger Mullet

Start the thread at the point of the hook. Take a matchstick-size bunch of shrimp SF Flash Blend and cut it in half. Taper each end and tie it in at the middle.

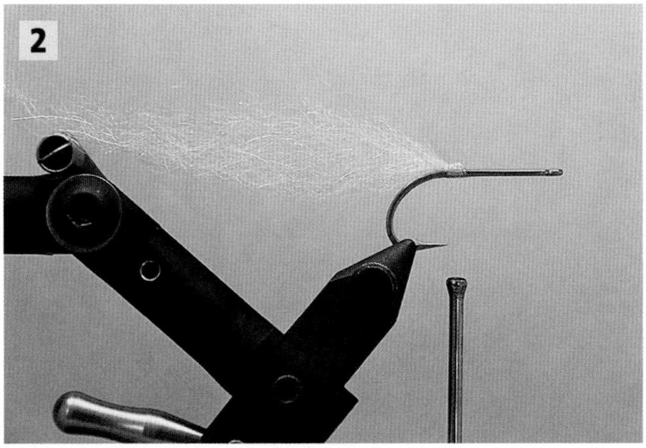


Fold the material back onto itself and tie it down; the material should extend beyond the back of the hook about 4 inches.

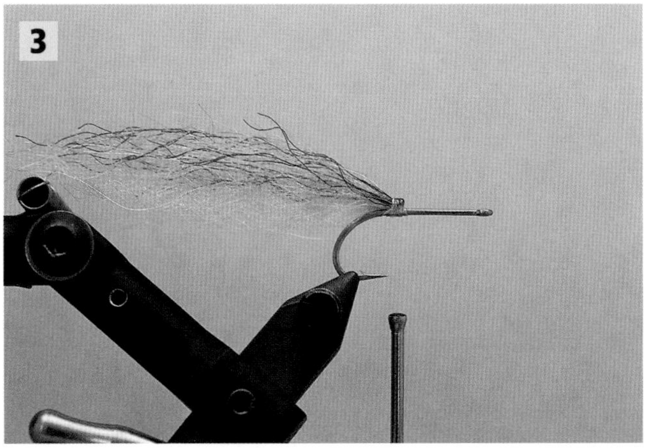


Repeat the same process with gray at the same tie-in point. The gray should be directly on top of the shrimp-colored material. Advance your mono one or two turns past the material so your next tie point will be slightly in front of the last.

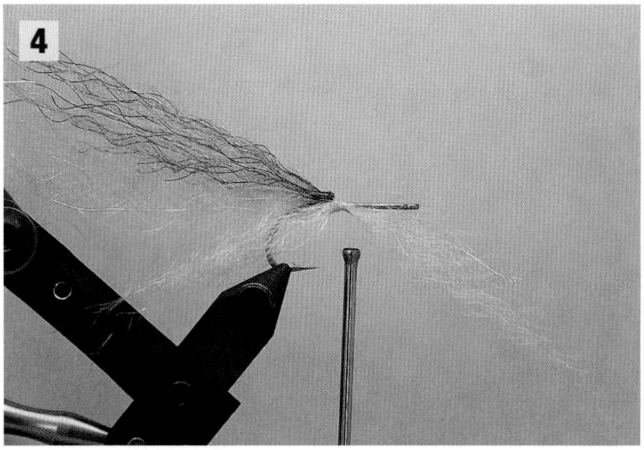


Cut the other half of the shrimp-colored SF Flash Blend, leaving 3-inch and 1-inch sections of shrimp-colored material. Taper each end of the 3-inch piece and tie in at the middle.

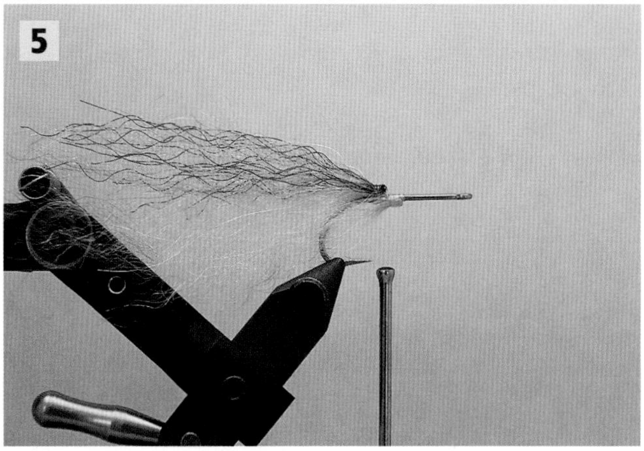


Fold the material back onto itself and tie it down. Repeat the same process with gray at the same tie-in point. The gray should be directly on top of the shrimp-colored material and slightly splayed, giving the back of the fly a wider profile.

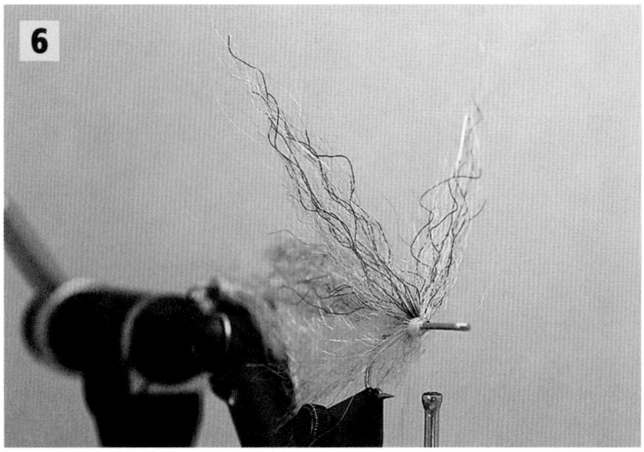


This is how the gray material looks head on. As the next two sections of gray material are added in this fashion, the shoulders of the fly will get more cylindrical.

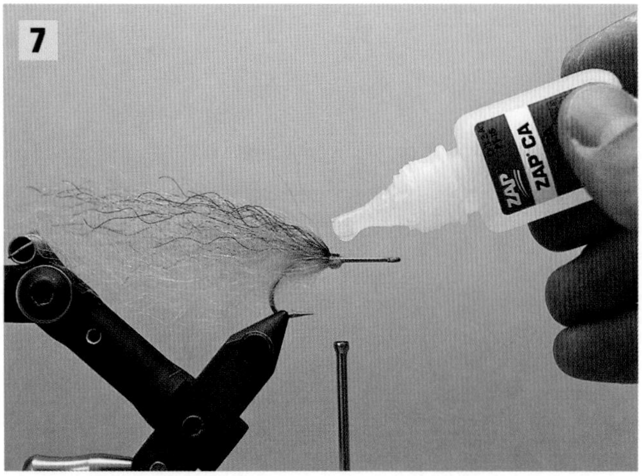


Add a drop of Zap-A-Gap to secure your wraps at various stages when you are tying with monofilament thread.

Repeat the same process with the 1-inch section of the shrimp and gray materials. Slightly less than half of the hook shank should be exposed.

Secure the wraps with a drop of glue, advance your thread one or two turns, and tie in the tip of the dubbing brush securely with four or five wraps.

Advance your thread to about 1/8 inch behind the eye of the hook and tie in the eyes. You can use dumbbell eyes, but I have found that mono eyes cut short and tied in parallel to one another are far more durable and give the head of the fly a wider profile. Secure the eyes with a series of figure-eight wraps. Once the eyes are perpendicular to the shank of the hook, advance your mono to the eye of the hook and add a drop of Zap-A-Gap to your wraps to keep everything in place.

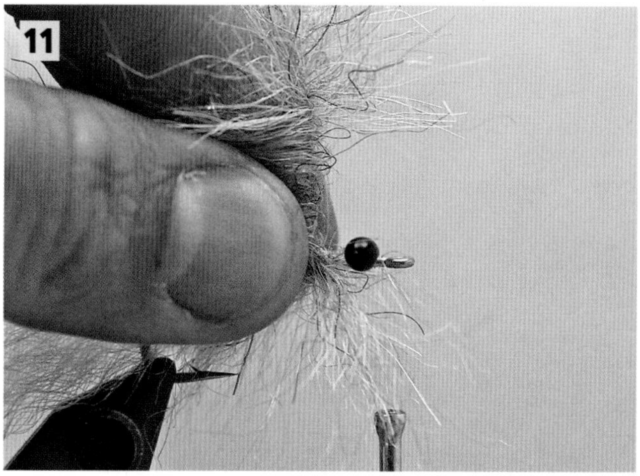

Palmer the dubbing brush forward with tight, concentric wraps. Pull the material back and out of the way with each forward turn so you do not trap any of it.

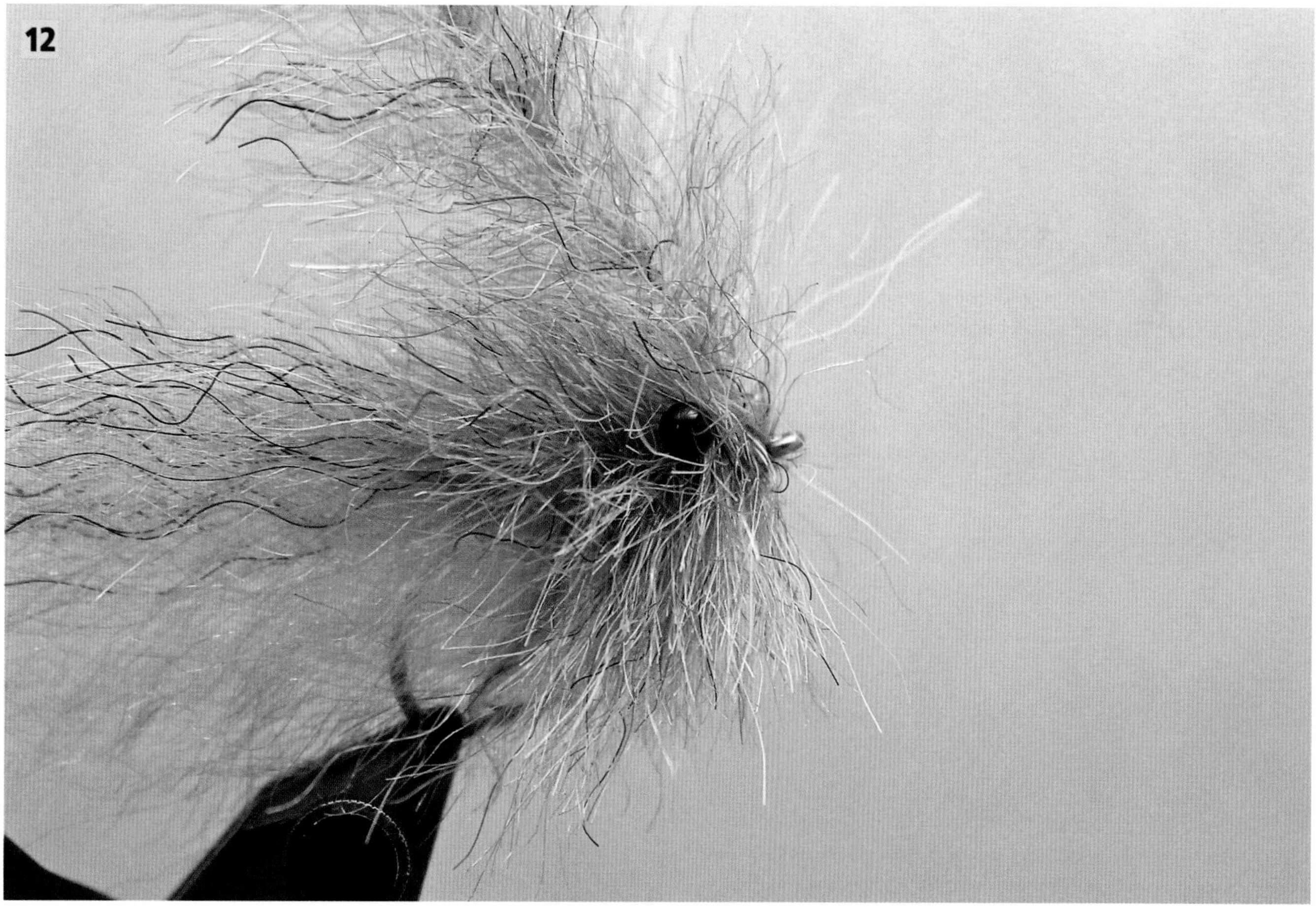

Continue forward until you reach the eye of the hook, and then tie off the dubbing brush. Whip-finish twice and cut away the mono thread. Finish the fly with a drop of Zap-A-Gap to secure your wraps.

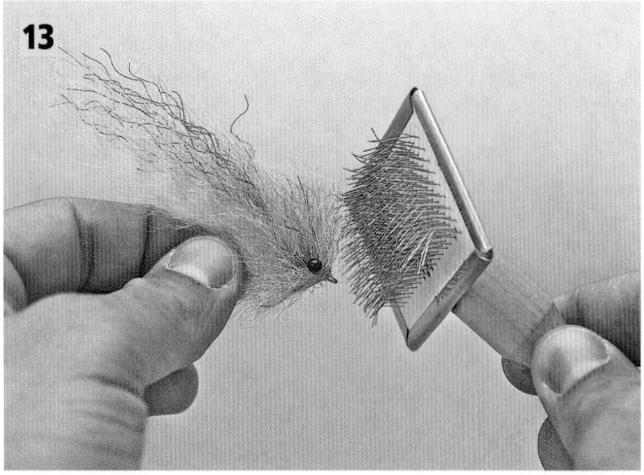


Take the fly out of the vise and use a comb or small dog brush to pick out and fluff up the fibers.

Start shaping the fly by turning it over. Angle your scissors and make a cut from the eye of the hook to the point.

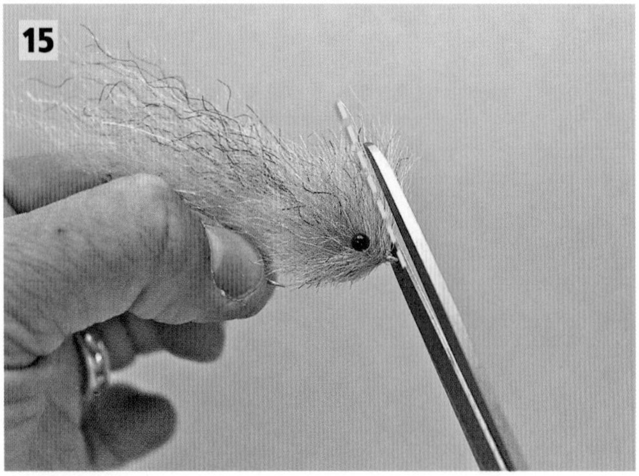


Turn the fly right side up and make a cut mirroring the first. Angle your scissors from the eye of the hook toward the back of the fly at a 45-degree angle.

The shape of the mullet's head should be symmetrical above and below the shank of the hook. The circumference of the head should be about ½ inch.

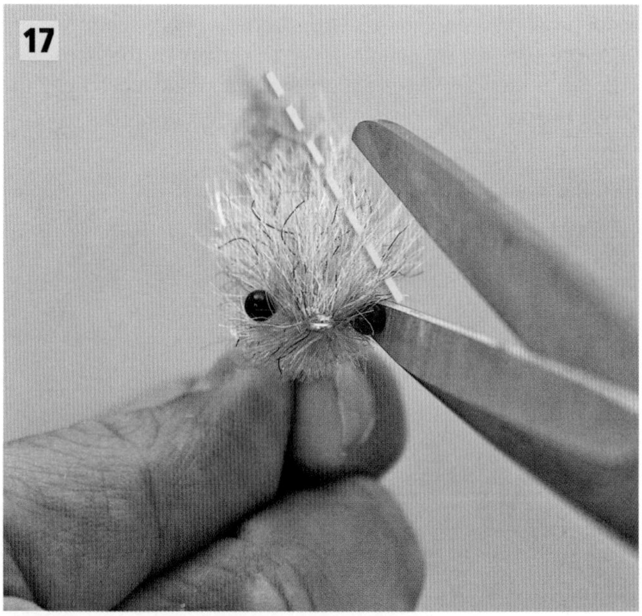


Turn the fly toward you and make a cut on the right side of the fly from the outside of the eye to the tail. Repeat the same process on the left side of the fly. Looking at it from the top, the mullet should have a symmetrical shape like a carrot.

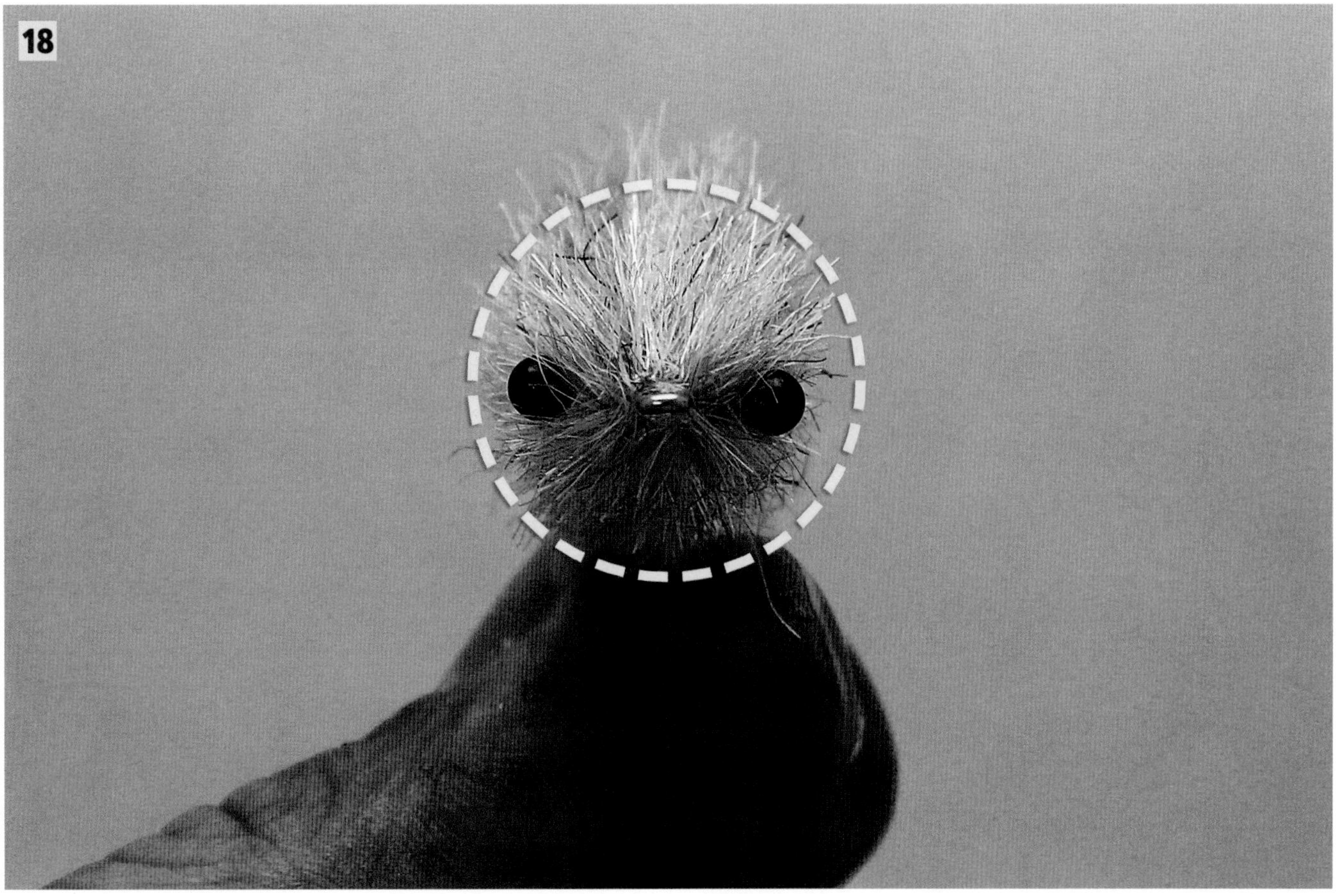


Round out the head with similar cuts from head to tail, keeping the carrot shape.

Turn the fly on its side and comb the fiber of the tail into a thin fan shape.

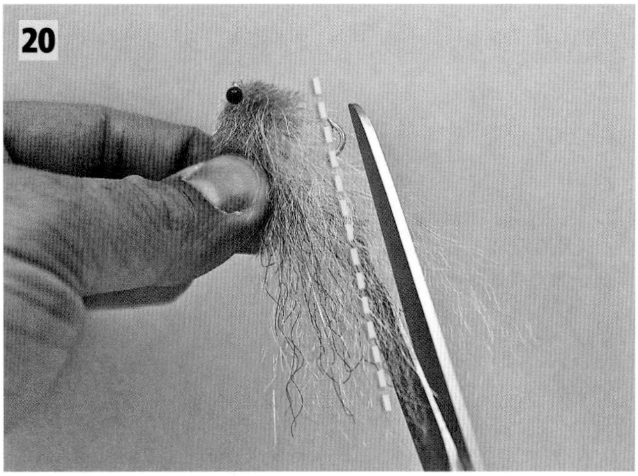


Make a cut on the belly of the fly from the center of the tail to the point of the hook. Start cutting at the point where the two colors of the belly and the back come together.

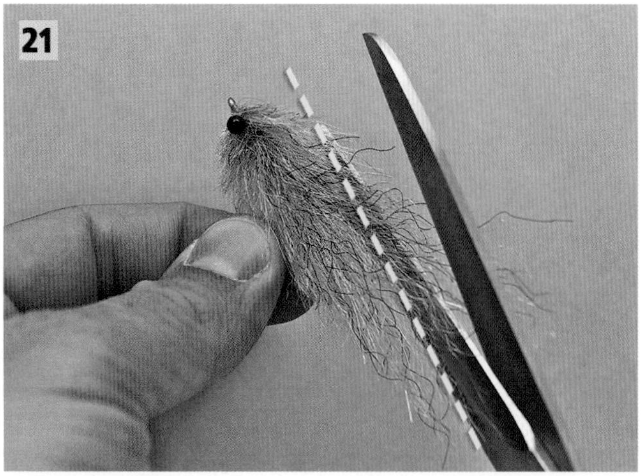

Turn the fly over and make a mirrored cut on the back of the fly. The materials should get more sparse from the head of the fly to the tip of the tail.

The mullet should look completely symmetrical from head to tail.

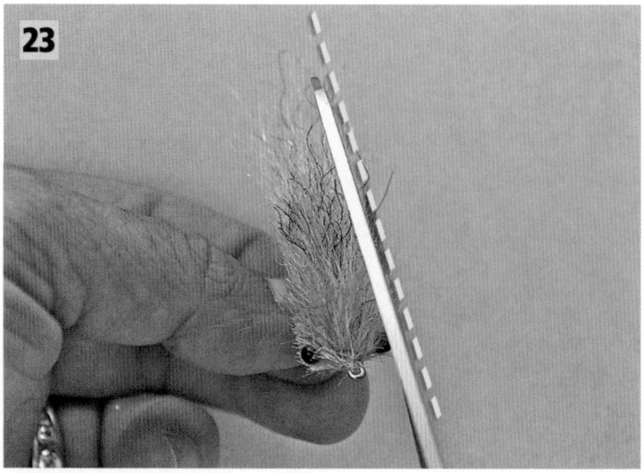

Place the fly in your hand with the hook down so you are looking down on the back of the fly. Fan the material of the back out and make a cut on the right side of the fly from the eyes to the tip of the tail. Repeat the same process on the left.

*Below:* In order to keep the fly from spinning in the water when it is stripped, you need to keep more material on top of the fly than on the bottom. Trimming the round profile to a snow-cone shape will keep your side profile intact while at the same time reducing material.

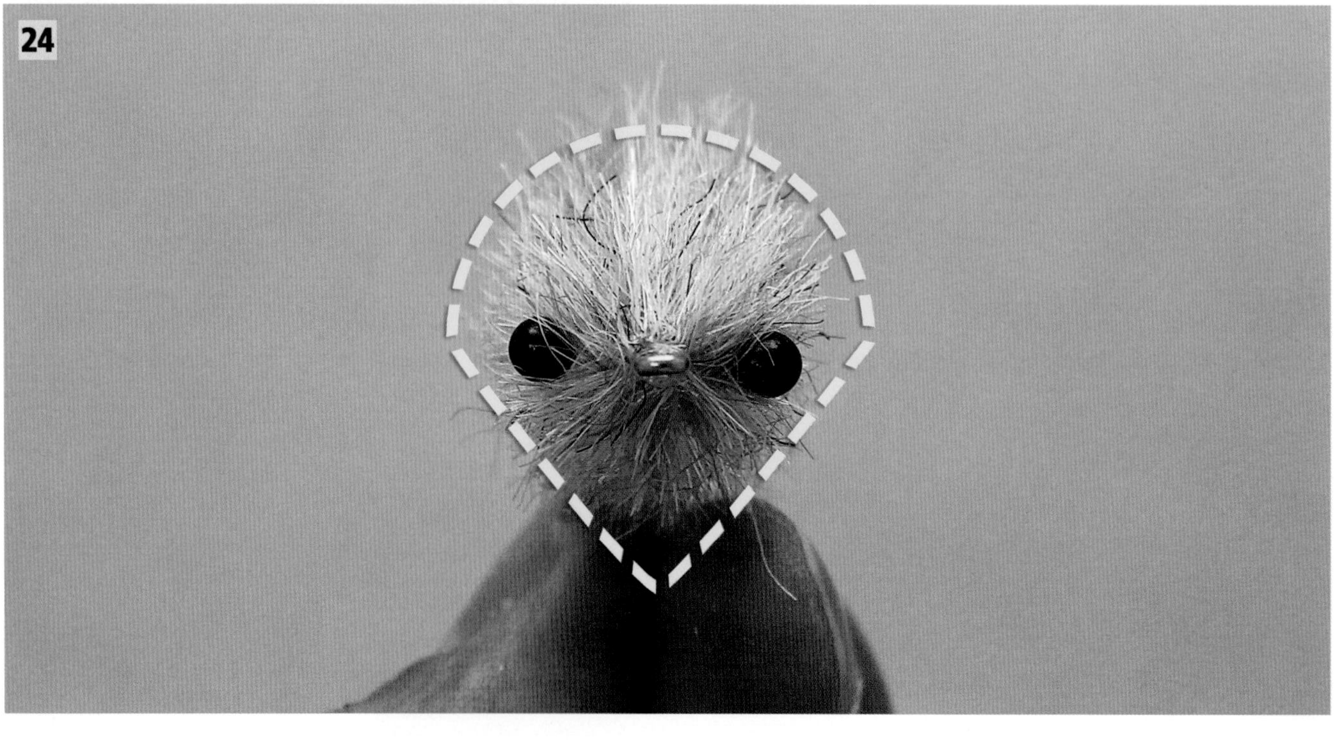

Turn the fly over and angle your scissors to cut the cone-shape belly from the head of the fly to the tail. Repeat on the other side of the belly.

Hold the fly by the hook in your non-dominant hand and give the eye of the hook a few good flicks with your dominant hand. This fluffs up the fly and exposes any fibers that did not get trimmed throughout the process. Trim any longer fibers that do not match the shape of the fly.

Completed 5-Minute Finger Mullet

CHAPTER 13

# GT Pinfish

One of the most prevalent fares for the predators of the flats are the stout 50-cent-piece-size pinfish that swarm the grass flats. The GT Pinfish was designed to mimic their tan and cream colorations and the distinctive violet bands that run along the length of their bodies. A series of long, slow strips with the occasional short, fast pop will generate flashes of gold and violet, tempting even the most scrupulous gamefish.

**GT Pinfish**

| | |
|---|---|
| **Hook:** | #2 or 4 Daiichi 2546 |
| **Thread:** | 4-pound mono |
| **Tail:** | Tan Craft Fur and lavender DNA Holo-Fusion |
| **Belly:** | White saltwater yak hair and blue/pearl Angel Hair |
| **Back:** | Tan saltwater yak hair and gold Angel Hair |
| **Eyes:** | Gold/silver 8 mm Orvis Jurassic eyes |
| **Gills:** | Red saltwater yak hair |

If you have done any flats fishing in Florida, you have most likely used pinfish for bait. Pick them up without paying attention to what you are doing, and you will quickly find out how they got their name. Every fin on these colorful little fish is armed with a needle-sharp spine, but that doesn't stop seemingly every fish on the flats from devouring them.

They are a predominate food source for a number of predators, and tying pinfish patterns to mimic them is nothing new. Enrico Puglisi ties some of the most realistic pinfish flies I have ever seen.

The GT Pinfish is a variation on a number of different patterns. I have tied countless variations using different materials, but this version with tan and white yak hair and lavender DNA Holo-Fusion is by far the most productive.

I was not fly fishing at the time when the idea for this pattern hit me, but rather dead baiting with chunks of ladyfish. The fresh-cut fish is smelly and oily and works well to attract

I was kind of surprised when I caught this brilliantly painted pompano on a GT Pinfish pattern in front of the Sanibel Causeway. There had been reports of significant numbers of them being caught, but I had never caught one on a pinfish pattern. I like to retrieve the fly with short, popping strips to emulate the pinfish that whiz in out of the turtle grass.

cruising redfish in the thickest grass. After letting the bait sit for some time with no action, I reeled it back in to see if it had been stolen or if I needed a fresh one. To my surprise, the quarter-size fish steak was covered in tiny bite marks, and a majority of the meat was eaten away.

I tossed the spent bait over the side of the boat and watched it sink to the bottom. Almost immediately a dozen or so pinfish the size of a 50-cent piece swarmed the chunk like a piranha attacking a cow in the Amazon. They were fast and darted in and out of the thick grass, presenting flashes of gold and violet blue as they did so. They did not have the same green hues that most pinfish have, but rather tan and cream markings and violet bands running along the length of their bodies. And for 2-inch fish they had very stout shoulders and left an obvious wake in the shallow water as they rammed around. That's what these redfish were eating.

It's no secret that my favorite material for tying large-profile flies is yak. Don't get me wrong–I think synthetics are great as well, and there are times when I choose them over natural materials, but this is not one of them. There is something about the way light passes through the material. It's just translucent enough to look alive, and the way it gives up a little of its wiry rigidity when wet allows it to swim and still keep its shape. Synthetics can move water just as well if not better than yak hair, but they have a tendency to trap air and make the fly float, and they just don't look the same in the water. The UV reactivity of white yak hair cannot be beat.

The GT Pinfish has proven to be quite a utility fly, catching a variety of species. Even this little grouper couldn't pass it up.

I wanted to mimic more than just the color, size, and profile of the pinfish I had been seeing on the grass flats. I wanted to mimic the things I could see as well as what redfish experienced right before sucking in the pinfish. These fat little baits were translucent, but they bulldozed water when they moved. The wiry yak hair is a perfect match, and adding the UV DNA Holo-Fusion gives the fly the bluish purple bands of flash and the durability I was looking for. The red throat adds just enough contrast to make this pattern dynamite.

I like to tie baitfish patterns with extra-large eyes because I think it makes a big difference, especially with flies that are translucent or tied sparse. The gold Orvis Jurassic eyes are about as realistic as you can get and match the pinfish perfectly.

## Tying the GT Pinfish

Place the hook in the vise. Start the mono thread in the middle of the hook and make 10 wraps. Cut a pencil-size bunch of Craft Fur and remove any loose fibers or fluff. Tie in the Craft Fur twice the length of the hook with six to eight wraps.

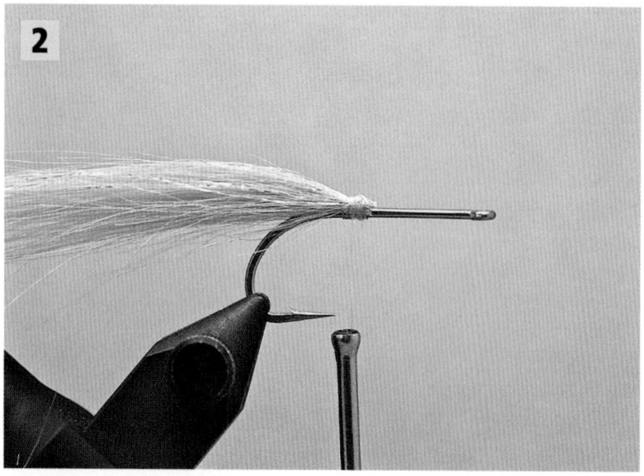

Tie in about 10 strands of DNA in the same place as the Craft Fur and split the material evenly on both sides of the hook. The DNA should be slightly shorter than the Craft Fur.

One trick I like to use with any type of synthetic material or flash is to cut a small notch in the corner of the package. That way I can fish out the amount I wish to use with my scissors, and the rest of the material stays protected in the package.

Mix a matchstick-size bunch of white yak hair with four or five strands of gold Angel Hair. Cut a 4-inch piece and taper it at both ends. Turn the hook over in the vise and tie in the blended bundle with four or five tight wraps. Whip-finish twice and secure the wraps with a drop of Zap-A-Gap or UV acrylic.

Fold the material back onto itself and secure it with four or five wraps. The bulk of the materials should be about half the length of the Craft Fur tail when doubled back. Since you tapered the ends, a few strands of yak hair will be longer, which is OK. Make sure the material is distributed evenly on both sides of the hook.

Mix a matchstick-size bunch of tan yak hair with four or five strands of gold Angel Hair. Cut a 4-inch piece and taper it at both ends. Turn the hook back over in the vise and tie it in with four or five tight wraps.

Fold the material back onto itself and secure it with four or five wraps. As with the white yak hair, the bulk of the tan materials should be about half the length of the Craft Fur tail when doubled back. Don't worry if a few strands of yak hair are longer.

Using the white yak hair and blue/pearl Angel Hair blend, cut a 3-inch piece and taper it at both ends. Turn the hook over in the vise and tie it in with four or five tight wraps.

Fold the material back onto itself and secure it with four or five wraps. Make sure the material is distributed evenly on both sides of the hook and the shank of the hook is covered on the side.

Cut a 3-inch piece of the blend of tan yak hair and gold Angel Hair and taper it at both ends. Turn the hook back over in the vise and tie in the blend with four or five tight wraps.

Fold the material back onto itself and secure it with four or five wraps. Make sure the material is distributed evenly on both sides of the hook and the shank of the hook is covered on the side. Repeat this process with a 2-inch piece of each of the colors.

Turn over the fly in the vise so that its hook points up. There should be a small gap where the hook shank is exposed between the yak hair and the eye of the hook. If you run out of room, carefully push the materials back with your fingers to compress the materials and create some space at the eye of the hook.

Take five strands of red yak hair and double them over, cutting the folded end and combine the two halves. Repeat this process four times until you end up with about 80 strands of ½-inch long yak hairs. On the throat of the fly directly behind the hook eye, tie this in at the middle with four or five tight wraps.

Fold the material back onto itself and secure it with four or five wraps. Make sure the material is distributed evenly on both sides of the hook and the shank of the hook is covered on the side.

Even out the head of the fly with a 1-inch piece of the blend of tan yak hair and gold Angel Hair. Taper both ends, tie it in at the middle, fold it back on itself, and secure it with four or five wraps. Whip-finish twice and secure the wraps with a drop of Zap-A-Gap.

Lightly trim the top of the fly into a leaf shape. Make sure to cut away any white yak hair that may impede the gap of the hook. Try not to trim the Craft Fur tail.

17

Using E-6000 or a similar thick glue, attach the eyes. The points of the pupils should point forward. Look at the fly from the top and then turn the fly toward you and make sure the eyes are lined up from both directions.

18

Using a brown permanent marker and an index card, bar the fly. Depending on the size of the fly, draw four or five bars ¼ inch apart.

Completed GT Pinfish

CHAPTER 14

# Asphyxiator

The Asphyxiator requires only a few materials and is an extremely simple fly to tie, yet it is surprisingly deadly in back bay environments where the water is brackish and off-color. I like to tie this pattern with a weedguard and fish it up under the mangroves or as close as I can get it. In the winter months when the water temperature has cooled, a short strip with a pregnant pause is tremendously effective.

**Asphyxiator**

| | |
|---|---|
| **Hook:** | #2 or 4 Daiichi 2546 |
| **Thread:** | Black flat waxed nylon |
| **Tail:** | Four grizzly hackles and two strands of root-beer Krystal Flash |
| **Body:** | Two grizzly hackles |
| **Eyes:** | Copper bead chain |

The feathers used to tie the original Asphyxiator have been with me for the last 32 years. They were handed down to me from my father, who skinned the roosters himself. When my father started tying flies in his early twenties, materials were hard to find and there was far less variety than today. Passionate tiers spent a lot of time collecting and processing their own materials.

My father was doing some construction work for a farmer who said he needed to get rid of five roosters. The birds had become overly aggressive and would violently peck the farmer whenever he went into the chicken coop to gather eggs. My father offered to take the roosters, and the farmer told him to come after dark to pick them up, since that was the only time that the farmer could get close enough to catch them.

Getting the roosters into the cages and the cages into the car was tricky especially at night. The commotion the

This handsome redfish was hiding tight to the mangroves when he scarfed an Asphyxiator pattern. It seems to be the perfect size morsel for winter redfish.

The brightly colored foam crab pot floats are a great place to find this prehistoric looking tripletail. Look for the floats with the most algae growing on them; they usually hold the most fish. The fish will usually eat a sparsely tied shrimp pattern like an Asphyxiator or a tan Clouser-style fly tied with yak hair. Short, popping strips will get you bit, but you need to pull them away from the rope fast or you'll get tangled up or broken off.

This is the cape my father worked so hard for. Its stained, off-white color and badger markings make it perfect for small, buggy back-bay patterns like the Asphyxiator.

After a little experimentation I was able to transform this old grizzly cape into what I was looking for. I started by dyeing the cape with coffee to enhance its darker markings and give it an overall stained look. (I have also used a combination of coffee and Kool-Aid to add a more yellow hue to the feathers.) The stained, light yellow color and grizzly/badger markings have proven effective, but I have not been able to find anything like them in any store.

roosters made was enough to rock the car. Once my father got home with the roosters, he covered the cage with a dark blue tarp in an effort to quiet them and keep them calm during the night. This worked for a few hours, but as sunrise approached the roosters' natural inclination to crow kicked in, and something had to be done before they woke the entire neighborhood.

The goal was to harvest the birds quietly without damaging the feathers or staining them with blood . . . so asphyxiation was the best bet. And that's how this fly got its name.

Next I selected the feathers I would use to tie the fly and darkened the quill and center of the feather to give it a badger look. When the feathers are palmered, the darker center portion or badger markings create a darker lateral line like a baby snook, and the grizzly or vertical markings give the appearance of a shrimp, small pinfish, or cichlid.

The Asphyxiator is by far my favorite winter pattern for snook and redfish. I like to tie the fly with a double 20-pound test weedguard and cast it as close to the mangrove as I can possibly get. I vary the strip depending on how cold the water is, but generally keep it relatively slow, with a long pregnant pause between strips. If the fish seem to be feeding more actively, I speed up the retrieve slightly and hop it along with a shorter and more aggressive stripping motion, but I continue to pause slightly to let the fly sink for a second or so.

## Tying the Asphyxiator

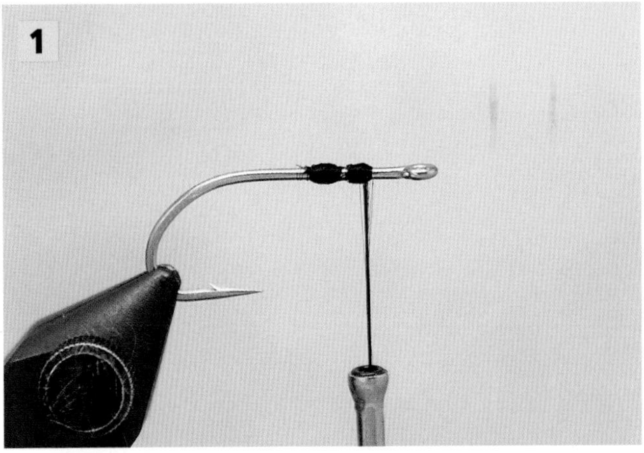


Start the thread on the hook just slightly forward of the middle of the shank. Spin the thread counterclockwise and flatten the thread. Build up a bump of thread. This will act as a backstop of the bead-chain eyes and help stop them from spinning. Advance the flattened thread and build a second bump, leaving a small gap or valley between the two mounds.

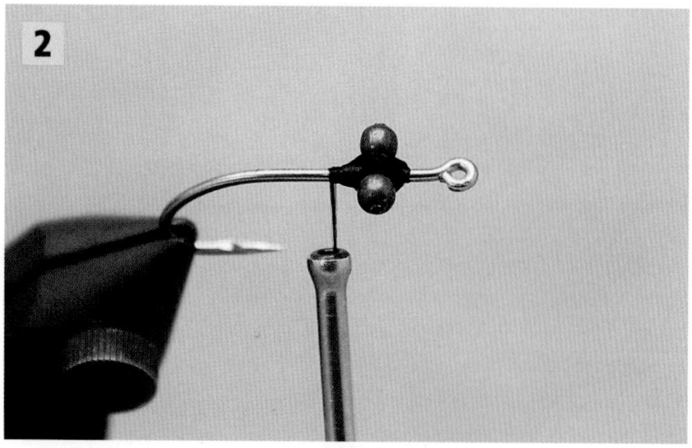


Place the bead-chain eyes in between the two bumps and secure them in place with a series of figure-eight wraps. Apply a small amount of head cement or superglue and tighten the eyes in place by making several wraps underneath the eyes. This will create a wider profile for the head.

Wrap back to the bend of the hook and tie in two strands of Krystal Flash. The strands should extend past the back of the hook about 3 inches.

All feathers have a natural curvature; some more than others. The tying term "praying hands" means that the feathers should line up at the tips with the concave side of the feathers facing each other. When wet, all the feathers come together as one. The opposite of praying hands is splayed, which means that the feathers are lined up at the tips and tied onto the hook with the convex sides of the feather facing each other.

Line up the tips of two pairs of matching hackles in praying hands fashion, not splayed. The feathers should measure 2 inches long. Tie in all four feathers at the hook point.

Select a slightly longer feather than the one used for the tail. The longest barbules of the feather should measure slightly longer than the hook gap. Use a black permanent marker to make a triangle in the center of the feather, following the shape of the feather. When palmered forward, the feather will taper toward the head.

Fold the feather in half so all the barbules are on one side of the quill. Remove any stiff, woody portion of the feather at the base to avoid cracking it when palmering. Tie in the feather at the base of the tail, holding the tip of the feather at its narrowest point and attaching it to the hook at its widest point, with the barbules facing backward.

Advance your thread to the bead-chain eyes and palmer the feather forward, being careful not to trap any of the barbules with each consecutive wrap. Tie off the feather behind the eye and trim the excess tip.

Whip-finish to complete. You have plenty of room in front of the bead-chain eye to add a weedguard. This is extremely helpful since the fly was designed to be fished right up tight to the mangroves.

CHAPTER 15

# Flats Pirate

The Flats Pirate crab pattern is my user-friendly variation of Hiromi Kuboki's 1997 crab pattern. This simpler version uses materials that are easier to find and takes less time to tie. I was targeting redfish when I created this pattern, and I tied later evolutions on larger hooks for tarpon. The beauty of this pattern is that it is easily modified on the water with a few permanent markers, depending on what color the crabs are. Move the fly along the bottom with ultra-slow strips so it's barely moving. Once the fish becomes aware of the fly, don't move it.

### Flats Pirate

| | |
|---|---|
| **Hook:** | #2 or 4 Daiichi 2546 |
| **Thread:** | Tan 210-denier flat waxed nylon |
| **Legs and claws:** | Scud Back colored with permanent marker |
| **Body:** | Spun and clipped deer hair, tan felt pad, and .020-inch lead wire |
| **Eyes:** | Large black EP crustacean |
| **Antennae:** | Natural rabbit |

The Flats Pirate crab is an ultra-realistic crab. Depending on the amount of lead wire and packed deer hair you use, you can fish the pattern in a number of different situations for a variety of species. Originally I believe this fly was intended for permit; however, my intended species was redfish, and later evolutions were tied on larger hooks for tarpon. You can use permanent markers to match the color of the crabs. One of the best ways to find out their color is to check the stomach contents of one of the redfish you have caught and plan on releasing to the frying pan.

When presenting this fly to redfish, you want the fly to sink slowly, so you need to tinker with the amount of lead wire you add to the bottom of the fly so it flutters to the bottom in a natural fashion. If you add too much, not only will the bulky fly be difficult to cast, but it will smack the water like a stone. The balance needs to be correct. The key is trimming as much of the deer hair as possible off the top of the fly, while still maintaining its wide profile. Once you have made your cast to the redfish, move the fly along the bottom with ultra-slow strips. The fly should look like it barely moves. Once the fish becomes aware of the fly, don't move it! This is the most difficult part of fishing crab patterns. When a crab is threatened, it goes in to fight mode. Its claws go up, and it remains perfectly still. If the redfish is interested, he will eat it. Moving the fly as he engages it typically spooks the fish.

Later I scaled this pattern up in an effort to catch tarpon on the surface. I wanted to mimic the 50-cent-piece-size crabs that floated through the passes around the hill tides. The crabs are easy for fish and people to see because the current carries them just under the surface of the water. These floating tarpon snacks are beautifully colored with shades of blue and purple. The tips of their claws and joints of their legs look like they have been dipped in bright orange paint, so they are relatively easy to mimic. When creating your patterns, make sure your hook has a wide enough gap; otherwise the spun deer hair has a tendency to fill the gap of the hook and make it far less effective, and there is nothing more frustrating than missing a tarpon on the surface. Fishing this larger variation of the pattern is fairly self-explanatory. Make a cast, and let the current carry your fly in the same fashion as it does a live crab. When retrieving the crab to make another cast, use long slow strips. Oftentimes you will get a strike within a couple of rod lengths from the boat.

## Tying the Flats Pirate

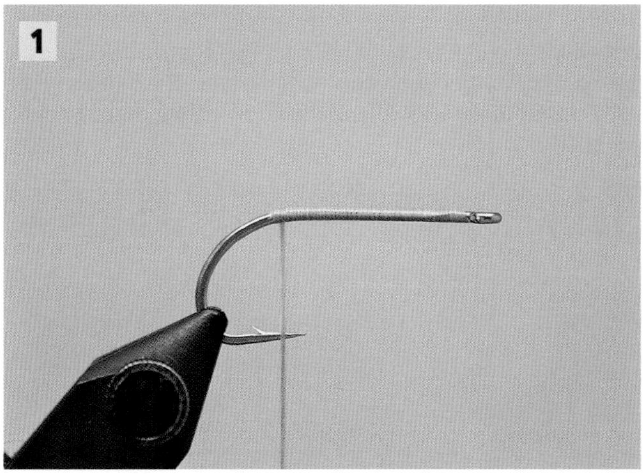


Start the thread at the eye of the hook and wrap back to cover the entire shank. The thread should hang between the point of the hook and the barb.

Select a few similar colors of deer body hair and then stack and clean them. The bundle should be about the size of a pencil. Take extra care to remove as much loose guard hair as possible.

Spin the bundle of hair and advance your thread in front of the flared and gathered hair.

Stroke back the butt ends of the hair and place a half hitch in front to securely lock the bundle in place.

Continue blending and spinning deer hair until the entire shank of the hook is covered with hair. Gingerly pack each consecutive bundle of hair, and don't pack the hair too much for sinking patterns. When the entire hook shank has been covered in hair, stroke back the butt ends and whip-finish, being careful not to trap any of the hair and obstruct the eye of the hook.

Flip the hook over in the vise. Using a new razor blade, trim the hair flat. In order to open the gap of the hook as wide as possible, make your cut close to the shank, being careful not to cut the thread wraps securing the hair.

Using rounded scissors, cut a few hairs at a time in the flattened surface until you have created the rough shape of a crab. Continue cutting deeper into the hair a little at a time until you are past the shank of the hook.

Turn the fly back over (point down) in the vise and trim the top of the crab body with a razor blade. A slightly rounded contour will give the crab a more realistic look.

Once all the long hairs have been trimmed to shape, taper the hair so that it's slightly thinner at the edges. The middle of the body closest to the hook shank should be thicker than the outer edges.

When viewed from the top, the hair body should have a football shape: wider in the middle with a taper at both ends.

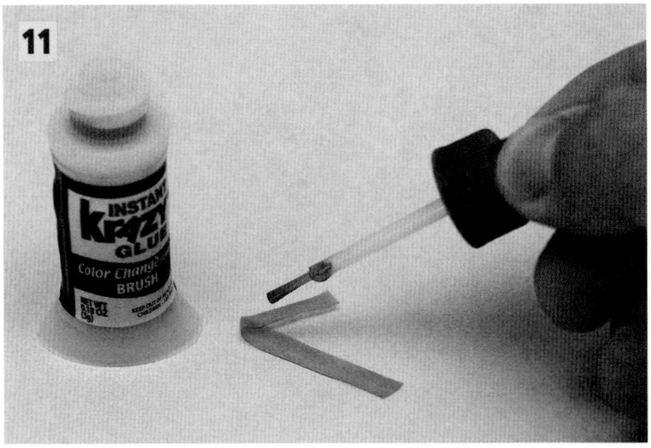


Cut four 2-inch pieces of Scud Back and apply a dot of superglue a third of the way down the material. Fold the material back onto itself at a 45-degree angle and hold it in place until the glue is cured.

Once you have glued all four pieces, lay them out in position. The shorter portion of the Scud Back should be on top so it angles up like claws when the crab is complete.

These Scud Back claws and swim flippers are ready to be colored with a permanent marker.

Trim the claws and swim fins to shape and mark with several colors of permanent marker to add depth and realism to the appendages.

Trace the deer hair body onto a piece of tan felt and cut it to shape. You will also need a 1/4-inch piece of tan Zonker Strip and a pair of black mono eyes.

Tightly coil a 3- to 4-inch piece of lead wire. You may want to experiment with the length and gauge of the wire in order to adjust the sink rate of the fly.

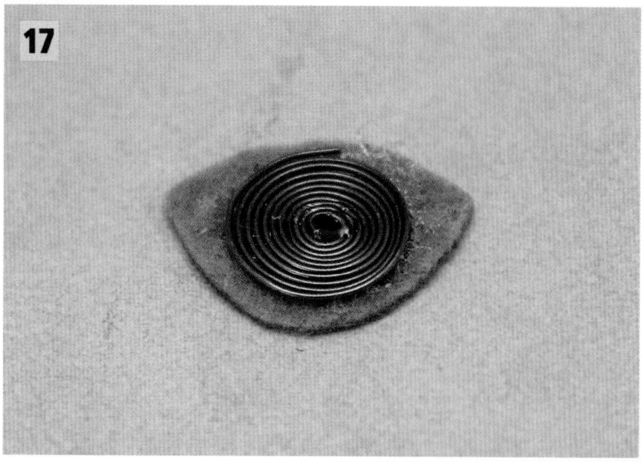

Cover one side of the felt belly piece with a viscous glue like E-6000, Goop, or similar.

Lay the coiled lead wire in the center of the felt pad and press it down into the glue. Apply another application of glue on top of the wire, making sure to cover the majority of the coils.

Trim the leather strip away from the rabbit hair and lay the hair on top of the coiled lead wire. The tips of the hair should stick out ¼ to ½ inch past the felt pad. Trim away the extra mono posts from the eyes, leaving about ¼ inch, and place an eye on either side of the rabbit hair.

Place the claws and swim fins on top of the other materials. The points of the claws should be positioned so they are on either side of the eyes and angled slightly forward.

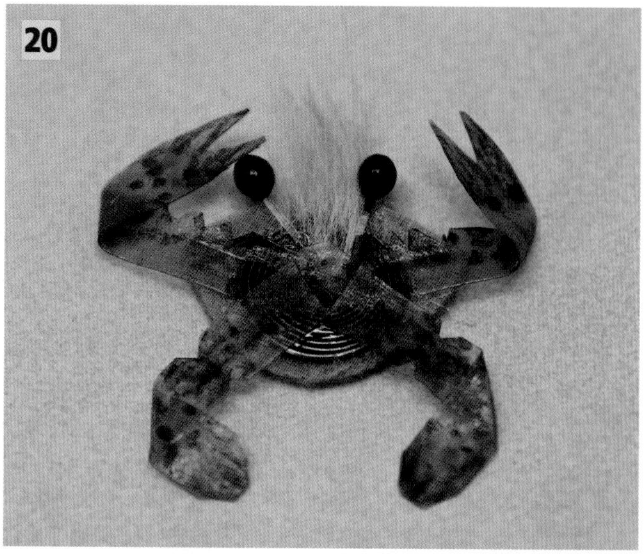

The folded-over portion should be on top so that when the crab is complete the claws angle up in a fighting posture. The flippers should be angled slightly toward each other.

With the hook in the vise point down, thoroughly cover the top of the deer hair body with glue. Work the glue down into the hair with the point of your bodkin.

Place the preassembled body on top of the glue-covered hair and squeeze it firmly into place.

Completed Flats Pirate

# CHAPTER 16 Tuscan Bunny

The current version of the Tuscan Bunny pattern has a a spun foam head instead of spun deer hair. The thin strips of foam allow the fly to maintain its buoyancy without becoming saturated over time. Water flows erratically over the knobby, irregularly shaped head, causing the Zonker tail to swim vigorously.

**Tuscan Bunny**

| | |
|---|---|
| **Hook:** | #1/0 Owner Flyliner |
| **Thread:** | Black 210-denier flat waxed nylon |
| **Body:** | Purple rabbit hair |
| **Tail:** | Magnum Zonker Strip |
| **Head:** | 2 mm spun foam strips |

As I continue to fish my patterns and watch what they do in the water, I analyze how the fish react to them, and usually I end up tweaking how I tie them or adjusting the materials I use. One of the patterns that I use a lot and I really like is a purple and black bunny strip similar to what's used for the Swamp Bunny or Tarpon Bunny pattern. There are a lot of variations on the bunny strip patterns, but the strip is typically a 2- or 3-inch Zonker Strip, and the fly usually has some sort of palmered collar, either crosscut Zonker or a large webby feather like marabou or schlappen of a contrasting color. (Use one of the techniques described on page 21 to keep the fly from fouling.)

The Tuscan Bunny's collar adds movement without the bulk of the Zonker's leather strip, and the collar also helps the fly swim. Anytime you have a wider, stiffer material at the front of the fly and a longer, softer material at the back or tail of the fly, the water must flow around the wider head material, causing the tail of the fly to swim.

The fly makes a nice silhouette and swims well, but if you tie it on a beefier hook, it sinks like a stone. In my experience this black and purple fly is far more effective if it rides just slightly under the surface as opposed to in the middle or lower half of the water column. I want the fish to discover the fly looking up at it so it looks like a finger mullet silhouetted in the sun.

Over the last few years of fishing it, I have changed the pattern. I started out with a deer body hair platform underneath the regular-cut Zonker Strip to keep it from fouling. I tied it on a sturdy, short-shank Gamakatsu hook, and palmered one purple feather over the thread wraps and in front of all the materials. I finished the fly with a classic thread ball for a head at about the halfway mark. If I needed to add a weedguard on the fly, I still had plenty of hook shank for one. But the fly did not track well, and it had a tendency to lean to one side or the other. The deer hair at the back of the fly was not enough to keep the fly from fouling, and the palmered feathers did not move as much water as I would have liked, nor did they impart the tail with any kind of action.

I modified the fly first by going to a hook with a longer shank. This gave me a little more room to make two turns of black crosscut rabbit Zonker for the collar of the fly. I stabilized the tail with a mono loop underneath and stayed with the classic head. The longer shank hook gave me plenty of room for a weedguard even with the added bulk from the palmered Zonker Strip.

The Tuscan Bunny began as a simple version of the classic Tarpon Bunny or Swamp Bunny fly (#1). Black and purple has proven time after time to be an effective color combination for countless saltwater gamefish species.

The first modification to the Tuscan Bunny was a crosscut Zonker collar and a hook with a longer shank to accommodate the extra material. Adding a mono loop underneath the Zonker strip helped keep the fly from fouling (#2).

The third evolution of the Tuscan Bunny was a much bulkier version, and although it looked great in the water, it was a real bear to cast, and it soaked up water like a sponge.

The fourth evolution was much more productive than any of the previous versions. The rabbit hair dubbing loop reduced the weight of the fly considerably, and the spun deer hair head helped to suspend the fly higher in the water. These two critical changes made the fly more productive.

These changes fixed a few of the problems, but they created some new ones as well. The fly had a lifelike breathing movement, thanks to the crosscut rabbit hair. However, as the fly got saturated and the leather on the Zonker Strips got softer and more pliable, the mono loop was no longer sufficient for keeping the fly from fouling. Due to the added weight, the fly would come down on the water with a heavy splat even with several false casts (which I like to avoid) to dry out the material. When larger fish did eat it, the hook ended up bending or straightening out.

For the third evolution I poked a hole through the Zonker Strip about 3/4 inch up the leather and passed the mono loop through the material to keep it from fouling. I learned right away that I needed to go to a magnum-cut Zonker Strip because after a few fish or a series of casts, the Zonker Strip would break off at the hole. As the leather got soft, it weakened, and there was not enough material around the hole to maintain the material's integrity.

In addition to the wider rabbit strip, I also went to a heavier wire hook and added a small piece of foam to the shank of the hook to make the fly neutrally buoyant. I palmered the Zonker Strip over the foam body and spun on a bunch of sculpin wool for the head. I really liked the way the fly looked and acted. It moved a ton of water and swam like it was alive.

The Tuscan Bunny snakes along just under the surface and produces a faint wake just like a contented little finger mullet. This river snook couldn't help himself.

The Zonker tail rarely fouled, and the 2X hook had plenty of backbone to pull the lunkers out of the bushes. The problem was it cast like a tennis ball, and the splat it made when it hit the water was still a problem for laid-up fish.

I discovered the answer to this problem almost a year later when tying bonefish flies for a trip to the Bahamas. I was watching a video of Chris Helm tie a Simram fly he had dubbed with rabbit hair. Instead of palmering a Zonker Strip around the shank of the hook, he made a dubbing loop and cut the hair from the leather and neatly spun it, leaving it long. That was it! No more soggy leather bodies, and the splat was significantly reduced. The second adjustment I made was to swap out the sculpin wool for a heavily trimmed bunch of deer hair for the head. This kept the fly higher in the water column, maintained the shape I was after, and pushed enough water to wiggle the tail of the fly. The fly worked much better, but as the deer hair got more and more saturated with water it lost its buoyancy, and the splat got louder and louder with every cast. Even if I worked the water out of the head and Zonker Strip between casts, it was still too loud and rode too deep in the water column.

Over time I have corrected a lot of this pattern's shortcomings, but I am a firm believer that there is always room for improvement. Feel free to take it from here and make your own adjustments, depending on how you like to fish it.

My latest version has a spun foam head. I experimented with different shapes and types of solid foam, but I just did not like the action, shape, or castability of the solid foam heads. I ran the foam through a pasta cutter to get thin, uniform strips of foam, and then spun them like deer hair. The spun foam head really pushes water and breathes life into the tail of the fly.

The solid foam heads were very smooth and could not be modified easily without altering how the fly tracked. The individual pieces of foam are far less dense than a solid foam head, which allows the fly to sink just a little bit under the surface. When retrieved with a two-handed strip, the fly tracks just under the surface and swims with a snakelike action. Originally I used a slightly longer rabbit Zonker tail, but it did not move as well. I cut away 1/4 inch at a time until I got the action I wanted. A 2-inch strip is perfect for this fly.

Up until the latest version, this fly did not even have a name. I called it the Tuscan Bunny because I used my pasta cutter to slice the sheets of foam into thin, uniform strips that I could easily spin like deer hair to form the head of the fly. This fly works great for ambushing super-skittish fish in shallow water because it doesn't sink and you can get the fly into position well before they arrive. Casting to hyper-sensitive fish in this type of situation is difficult because they tend to blow out well before the fly ever hits the water. Large fish in shallow water key in on any kind of movement above them, and a motion of the rod or the loop in the air is usually more than enough to send them off in a hurry.

The key is to make your cast 4 or 5 yards ahead of the fish on the move and slowly position the fly into its path. Don't move the fly until your target is about 2 feet away, and then only make one or two short strips until you have the fish's attention. If it doesn't attack the fly immediately, a slow steady strip with a constant right-to-left tip waggle will close the deal more times than not.

For snook I like a 10-inch piece of 40-pound mono for a shock tippet, and for tarpon I move up to 60 or 80, depending on the size of the fish and the clarity of the water.

## Tying the Tuscan Bunny

Cut a sheet of 4 mm closed-cell foam into extremely fine strips. Try to make them as uniform and fine as possible. You can use a metal ruler and a razor blade, but it is far easier to run the sheet of foam through a pasta cutter if you have one.

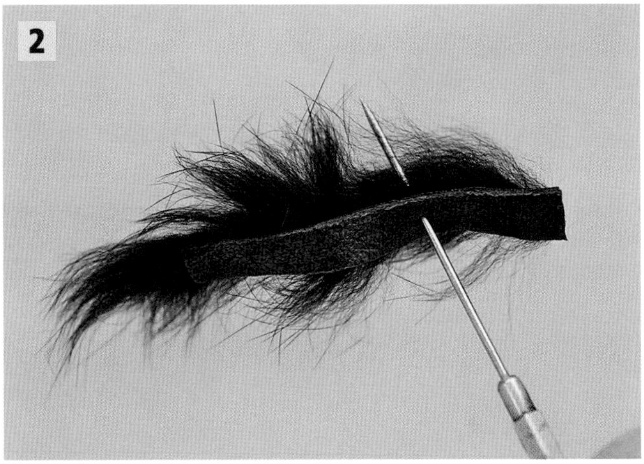


Cut a 2-inch piece of magnum rabbit Zonker and poke a hole through the middle of the strip about ¾ inch up. If you use a thinner cut of Zonker, the tail of the fly will break off after a few casts. The extra width provides durability. The rabbit hair should lie back to the left naturally, and the hole should be on the right side of the strip. Remove the bodkin and immediately slide a 3-inch piece of 20-pound monofilament through the hole. (The tiny hole has a tendency to close up or become difficult to find if you set the strip down and do this step later.)

Start your thread at the middle of the hook shank and wrap back 8 to 10 turns. The thread should hang at the point of the hook to start the fly. Tie down the end of the monofilament on the leather side of the Zonker Strip. The monofilament should be tied directly on the top of the hook shank and curve slightly up.

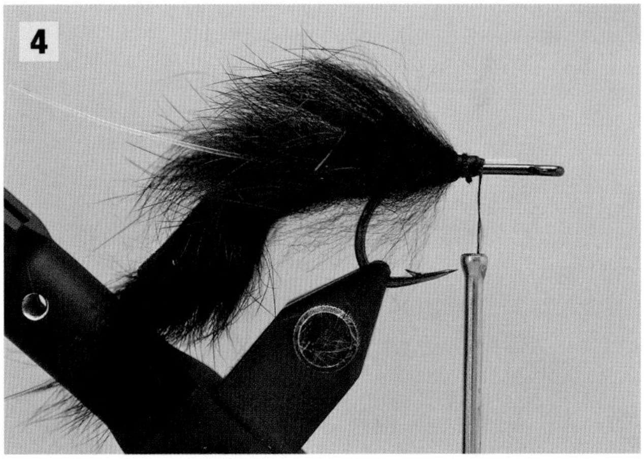


Slide the Zonker Strip down to the hook shank and tie down securely. Make sure the strip is centered directly on top of the hook and not off to the side. This is important, because it affects the way the fly tracks in the water.

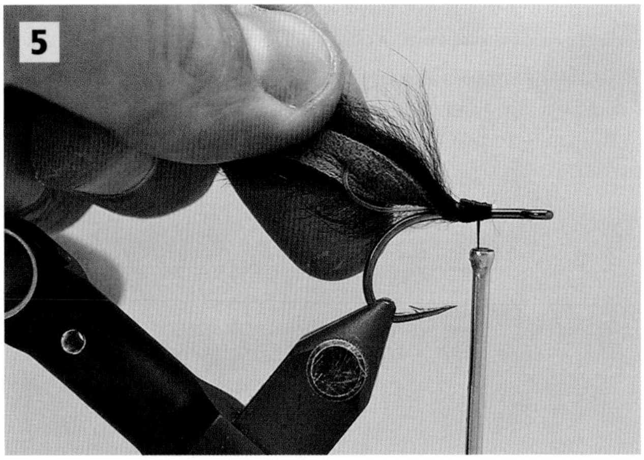


Pull the mono down to the hook shank and tie it in on top of the rabbit strip. The strip should be centered on the loop and slide freely up and down. The loop should hang about ¾ inch off the back of the hook, and it should not pull the strip up or down.

Cut the hair off of a 2-inch strip of magnum Zonker Strip as close as you can to the leather. If you pinch the hair in a bulldog clip, it is far easier to slide into a dubbing loop.

Slide the hair into a dubbing loop and spin it until it is secure. Advance your thread and palmer the dubbing loop forward, making sure to pull the fibers out of the way with each progressive wrap.

Tie off the dubbing loop and make a few wraps backward over the hair to secure it.

Cut the ⅛-inch strips of foam into 12 1-inch pieces. Stack them into a neat pile and spin them onto the head the same way you would deer hair. Advance your thread and whip-finish.

Cut away the thread and trim the foam to shape with scissors. Make sure to cut the bottom of the foam flat and as close as you can to the hook shank without cutting your thread wraps. This will ensure that the fly will ride level in the water and you have not impeded the gap of the hook.

CHAPTER 17

# Mayan Cichlid

*Cichlasoma urophthalmus*, commonly known as the Mayan cichlid, is a flamboyantly colored panfish-shaped gamefish native to Central America. Six to eight vertical stripes, varying in color and distinction, contour the sides of this relatively small yet robust fish. This exceedingly resilient predator was likely introduced to South Florida's waters sometime in the early '80s via aquarium releases or fish farm escapes. The supercharged sunfish lookalikes have flourished in the brackish creeks, lakes, and canals of southern Florida and in turn have become an excellent food source for the resident snook, tarpon, and redfish.

This imitation is meant to emulate the 3- to 5-inch adolescent cichlids that congregate around mangrove roots and riprap. It is tied in a similar fashion as Enrico Puglisi's Peanut Butter Bunker to create a wide profile. The pattern uses saltwater yak hair—mostly for its translucent qualities—but also because its length and wiry texture allows you to create larger flies. The natural yak hair is great for blending because you can easily count the strands of hair. This allows your flies to be more uniform in color and fullness. The coarse hair becomes supple when wet and has a lifelike quality when stripped.

*Above:* This flamboyant imitation emulates the 3- to 5-inch adolescent cichlids that congregate around mangrove roots and riprap. The pattern's bright colors of saltwater yak hair blend for a more realistic look. Originally native to Central America, the cichlids were introduced to Florida in the 1980s and quickly became a favorite food for the resident snook, tarpon, and redfish.

**Mayan Cichlid**

**Hook:** #2/0 Gamakatsu SC-15
**Thread:** 4-pound mono
**Belly:** A blend of white and tan saltwater yak hair and a blend of white and orange saltwater yak hair
**Back:** A blend of olive, chartreuse, and tan saltwater yak hair and a blend of olive and brown saltwater yak hair
**Throat:** Orange saltwater yak hair
**Eyes:** 8 mm orange or yellow doll eyes with post

**Belly Blend #1**
60 strands of white saltwater yak hair
20 strands of tan saltwater yak hair

**Belly Blend #2**
75 strands of white saltwater yak hair
5 strands of orange saltwater yak hair

**Back Blend #1**
50 strands of olive saltwater yak hair
20 strands of chartreuse saltwater yak hair
10 strands of tan saltwater yak hair

**Back Blend #2**
65 strands of olive saltwater yak hair
15 strands of brown saltwater yak hair

## Tying the Mayan Cichlid

Start your mono thread at the point of the hook, using 8 to 10 wraps to secure it. Cut a 4½-inch piece of back blend #1 (olive, chartreuse, and tan). Taper each end until it is between 7½ and 8 inches. Tie in the tapered piece at the middle with eight turns.

Fold back the forward-facing half, and tie it down on top of the rear-facing half. Secure it by wrapping forward with eight wraps. This positions the mono for tying down the folded back half of the material so you do not have to make a large jump with the mono over the bend. You can wrap forward without doubling up your wraps, which gives a clean, sleek look and makes for smoother transition from the top of the material down to the hook shank. Mono is round and slippery and the wraps have a tendency to slide off bulky materials.

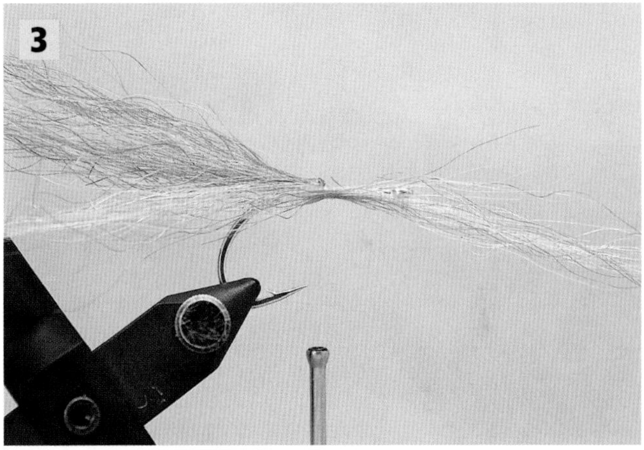


Cut a 4½-inch piece of the belly blend #1 (white and tan), this one 4 inches long and taper it at both end until it reaches approximately 6 inches in length. On the side of the hook closest to you, tie in the piece below the other materials angled slightly downward. Make eight turns, stacking your wraps behind the previous wraps and pushing them forward.

Fold the forward-facing half under the hook shank and back on top of itself. Secure it with eight forward wraps on the far side of the hook. Both sides of the fly should be symmetrical, and you should have a small gap on the sides of the fly where the bare hook shank peeks through the white yak hair. Laying the hair at a downward angle instead of straight back starts to build the profile of the fly.

Cut a 4-inch piece from the back blend #1 (olive, chartreuse, and tan) and taper each of the ends until it is between 6 and 6½ inches. Tie in the tapered piece on top of the hook shank and in front of the other materials at its middle point. Secure the bundle with eight turns, wrapping backward.

Fold the forward-facing half back, but this time instead of securing it directly on top of itself, position the material in a V shape to create shoulders and add width. Each half of the back blend should be angling slightly wider than the first white belly piece.

Next cut a 3½-inch section of the belly blend #1 (white and tan) and divide it into two bundles, one for each side of the hook. Taper each piece until it is roughly 5 inches long. Tie in the first piece on the near side of hook so that it extends slightly longer toward the tail of the fly. This piece fills the material gap and hides the exposed hook.

Fold the forward-facing half of the bundle back on itself and angle it downward to cover the gap of the hook.

Repeat this on the other side of the hook with the other piece of belly blend.

Cut a 3½-inch piece of the back blend #2 (olive and brown) and taper each of the ends until it is between 5 and 5½ inches long. On top of the hook in front of the other materials, tie in the section at its middle, secure it with eight turns, and stack your wraps behind the previous wraps, pushing them forward.

Fold the forward-facing half back, but this time instead of securing it directly on top of itself, position the material in a V shape to create shoulders and add width.

Each half of the back blend should be angling slightly wider than the last.

Cut a 3-inch piece of the belly blend #2 (white and orange) and taper it slightly. Tie it in on the underside of the fly so that the forward-facing portion is slightly shorter than the rear-facing portion. Fold the forward-facing portion back directly onto itself and secure it with eight turns.

Turn the fly over in the vise and use your thumbnail to disperse the material evenly around the bottom and sides of the hook to cover up any spots where the hook is exposed.

Cut a 2½-inch section of the back blend #2 (olive and brown) and taper it to approximately 3½ inches.

Apply this piece on top of the hook in the same V fashion as the previously applied back piece and secure it with seven or eight wraps.

Cut a 1-inch piece of orange for the throat and taper it slightly. Turn the fly over in the vise and tie the piece in on the underside of the fly so that the forward-facing half is slightly shorter.

Fold the forward-facing half back directly onto the rear-facing half and secure it with eight turns. Use your thumbnail to disperse the material evenly around the bottom and sides of the hook. Whip-finish two or three times and coat the nose of the fly with UV acrylic.

Take the fly out of the vise and use a dog brush to comb out any tangles and blend all the colors. Trim each side of the fly to create a wide, flat leaf shape.

Using a brown or olive permanent marker and two index cards as a guide, bar the fly. Depending on the size of the fly, you should be able to fit five or six bars $\frac{1}{4}$ inch apart. Press and hold the marker against the yak hair for a couple of seconds to insure that the ink penetrates the middle of the fly.

Put the fly back in the vise and glue on the dome eyes slightly in front of the hook point, making sure they are aligned from a top view. Turn the fly toward you and double-check that the eyes are aligned from a forward-facing view. Take the time to check from both viewpoints, because if the eyes are out of alignment, the fly will spin when stripped. Once the eyes are completely dry (15 to 20 minutes), take the fly out of the vise and use a long pair of kitchen scissors to trim the fly again to remove any stray hairs and refine the fly to the baitfish shape.

CHAPTER 18

# Bottle Cap Crab

The Bottle Cap Crab is a larger variation of Simon Becker's notoriously effective Hover Crab. In an effort to speed up the process without skimping on detail, I came up with a pretty easy way to reproduce Becker's realistic and symmetrical crab body with a little help from an ordinary beer bottle cap.

### Bottle Cap Crab

**Hook:** #2 Daiichi 2546
**Thread:** Tan 95-denier Lagartun
**Legs:** Floating fly line knotted
**Eyes:** Large black EP crustacean

If you have ever tried to catch a permit on fly, you are acutely aware that the deck is stacked against you. These notorious crustacean crunchers are nefariously critical of any crablike offering, and they are one of the reasons there are hundreds of crab fly patterns today. Most of these patterns consist of a size 2 or 4 hook, 5/32-inch dumbbell eye, a few rubber legs, and a few hanks of synthetic to fill in the middle.

Simon Becker's Hover Crab was the first floating crab pattern designed specifically for super-spooky permit. His design was void of added weight to make the fly sink; instead it had a body of closed-cell foam to make it float. Knowing that the permit would closely scrutinize the fly, Simon took meticulous care constructing minuscule, ultra-realistic replicas, and his handiwork proved deadly. He glued bulbous eyes and segmented legs to the hook shank and cut tiny, jagged points into the forward-facing side of the symmetrical foam discs that made up the body. The jagged points were designed to mimic the anterolateral teeth on the dime-size creatures.

Needless to say, tying a dozen of this exceptional pattern takes a long time. In an effort to speed up the process without skimping on the detail, I have come up with an easy way to reproduce Simon's realistic and symmetrical crab bodies with a little help from a beer bottle cap. How did I come up with this technique? I was walking through the garage one day and saw an upturned bottle cap. I am a huge Parrot Head, and like any longtime Jimmy Buffett fan, I have the lyrics of "Margaritaville" burned into my subconscious, so I immediately conjured up the lyric about stepping on a pop-top in his flip-flop. Laughing at my involuntary thought, I wondered what that flip-flop looked like. Next thing I knew, I was bending bottle caps to different angles and experimenting with 2 mm foam.

## Tying the Bottle Cap Crab

First start with a standard beer bottle cap. (I like Corona, but any will work.) Pinch the cap between your thumb and index finger and apply pressure until the cap starts to bend. Do not overdo it: you only want to slightly bend the cap. About ⅛ inch gives the beer cap a clamshell shape so that the underside or cutting surface will produce a symmetrical oblong shape, just like a crab's body.

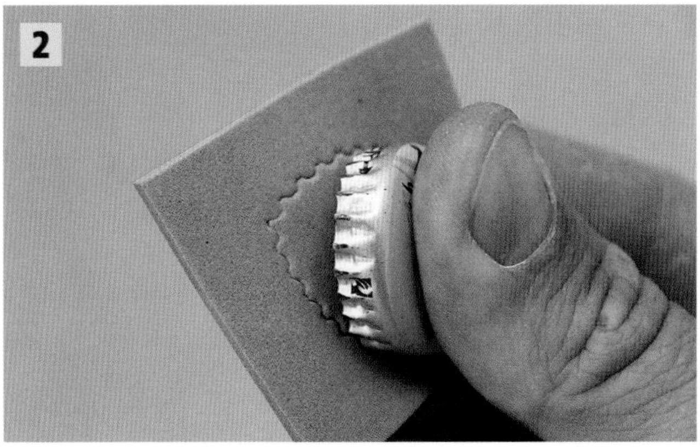


Press the cap into a section of 2 mm closed-cell foam with enough pressure to score the foam nearly all the way through. With an abundance of care, work your fingers around the edge of the cap to make a clean imprint of the toothed edge.

Once the jagged rim of the cap has imprinted the foam, turn the foam and cap over, and with the side of your scissors, firmly trace the notched edge. This will ensure a cleanly cut edge. If you try to cut the foam with pressure alone, the small toothed edges will be indistinct and the finished product not nearly as pronounced. If the crab body is not entirely cut free from the sheet, rework the edge with your scissors until it is completely free. Do not try to pull it loose or you will distort the shape.

Once the disc has been completely cut from the sheet of foam, carefully remove it from the inside of the bottle cap.

Lightly fold the disc in half lengthwise and match up the two corners. Make a slightly curved cut from the corner to the fold in order to trim away one of the jagged edges. This will create a symmetrical and realistic crab shell. If you want a smaller shell, simply make another cut, removing more of the foam.

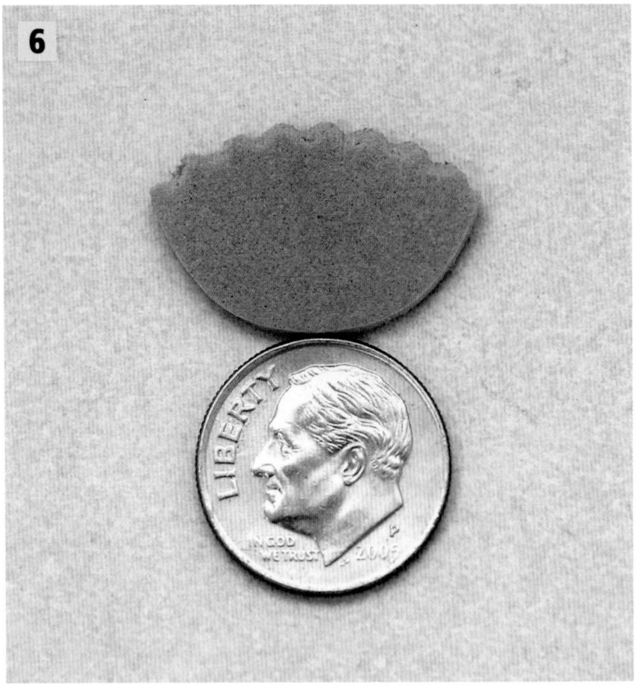


When I travel I like to cut a number of these bodies in a variety of different colors. They do not take up a lot of room and they are easy to modify.

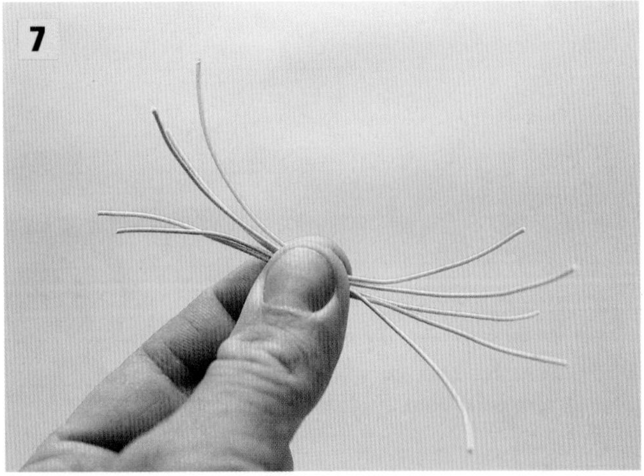


Start the fly by making the crab's swim flippers, cutting old fly line into 4-inch pieces. For a size 2 hook, I like the diameter size of a 7- or 8-weight running line. It is much easier if you cut several in advance and tie all the loops at once. That way you can match the size of the pieces to the fly to represent the crab's swim flippers. It is much more difficult to make your crabs look symmetrical if you tie the legs as you go.

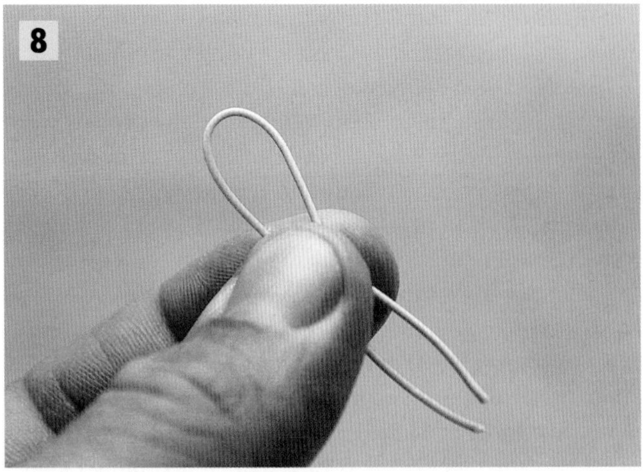


Fold the 4-inch section of fly line in half and line up the tips.

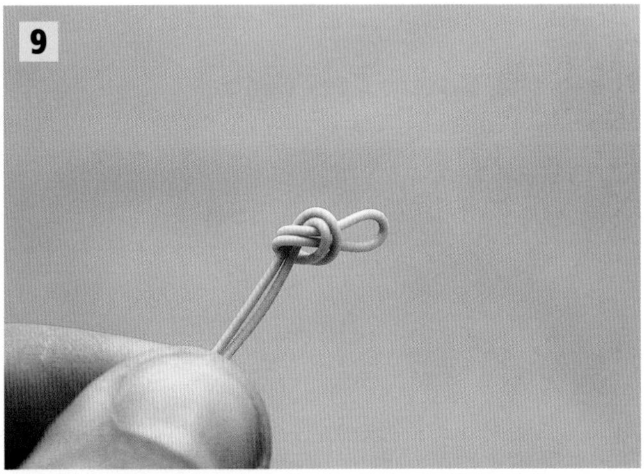


Tie a simple overhand knot with the looped end of the line about $1/4$ inch from the end.

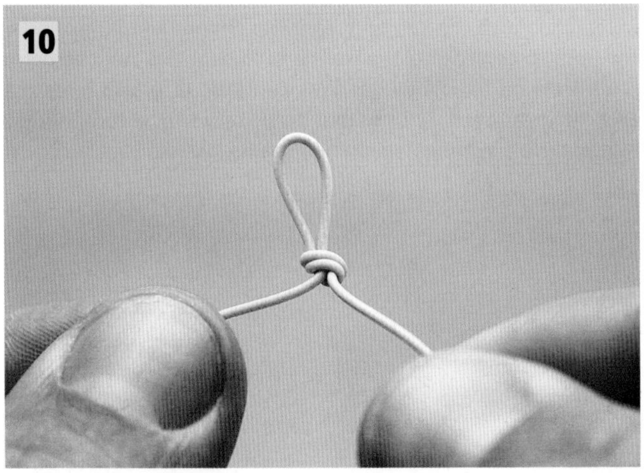


Compress the knot by pulling apart the two tag ends as if you were splitting a wishbone.

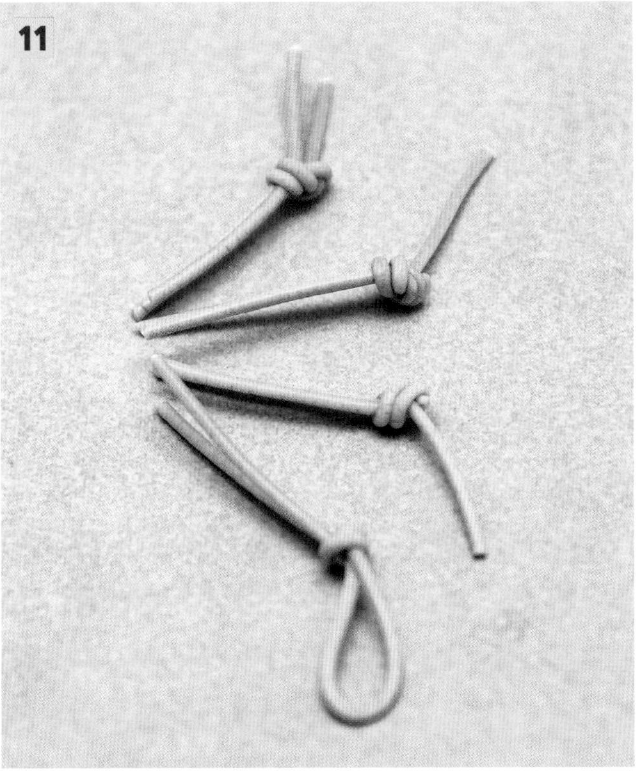

For the claws, simply cut the looped sections and leave two short tag ends or posts on both sides of the knot. To create the legs, cut the loop portion, and remove one of the posts coming out of the knot. The swim flippers are complete.

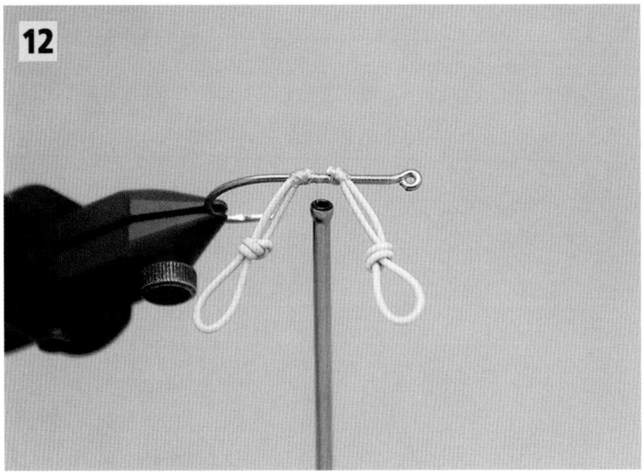

Start your thread at the middle of the hook shank. Attach two of the knotted pieces of fly line with the loops still intact at a 30-degree angle, creating a tent shape. (They represent the swim flippers.) Leave a small gap between the two pieces so the hook gap shows. The gap will allow you to position the claws forward and will be filled in evenly with the butts of the fly line and thread.

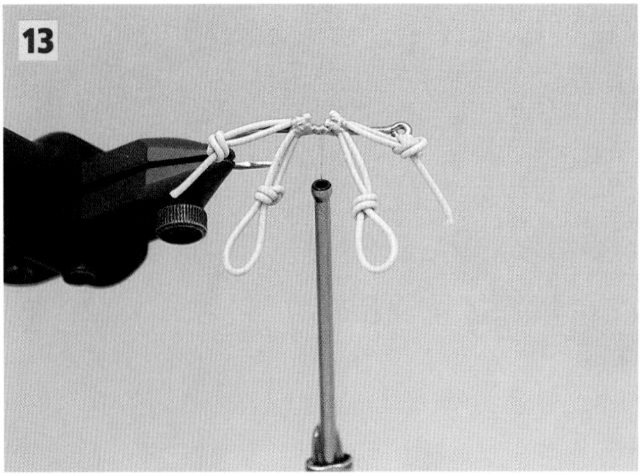

On the far side of the swim flippers, attach a pair of knotted legs, tying them in at the double section. Make sure the single post is pointed down in the same direction as the swim flippers.

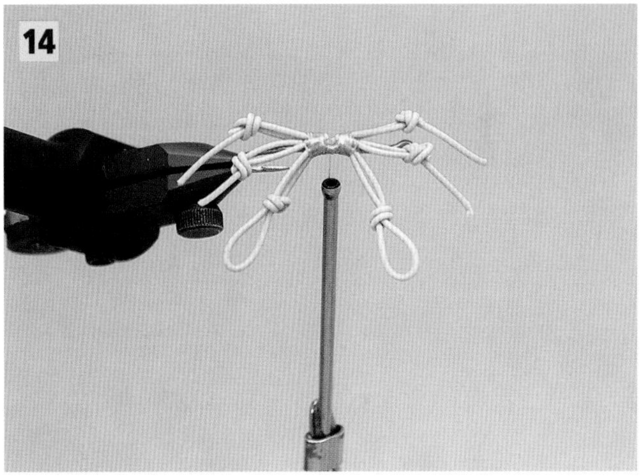

Add another pair of legs the same way you added the last pair, but adjust them so they are slightly shorter. You can judge the length by lining up the knots of all the legs. The knots on the second pair of legs should be slightly inside the knots on the first pair of legs.

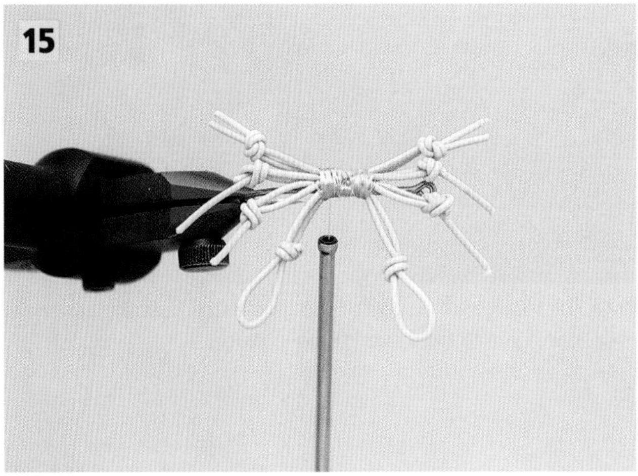

In front of the second pair of legs, tie in the claws. The two posts coming off the knot that represents the claws should be angled forward, not back.

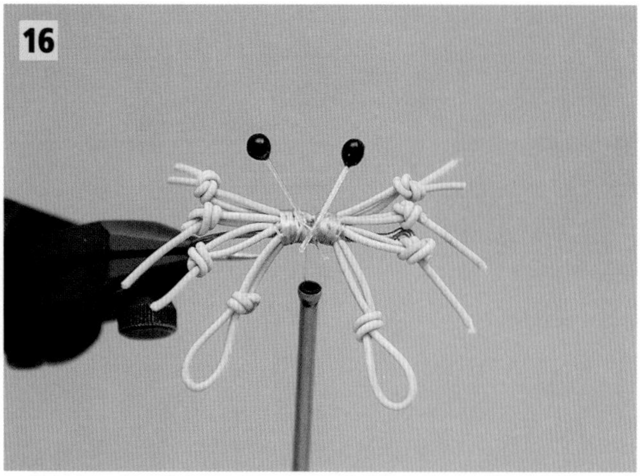


In the middle of all the appendages, tie in the mono eyes with a series of figure-eight wraps. Leave a small portion of the mono stem sticking out from the bottom of the fly. This will help secure the shell by giving two more points to attach to the foam.

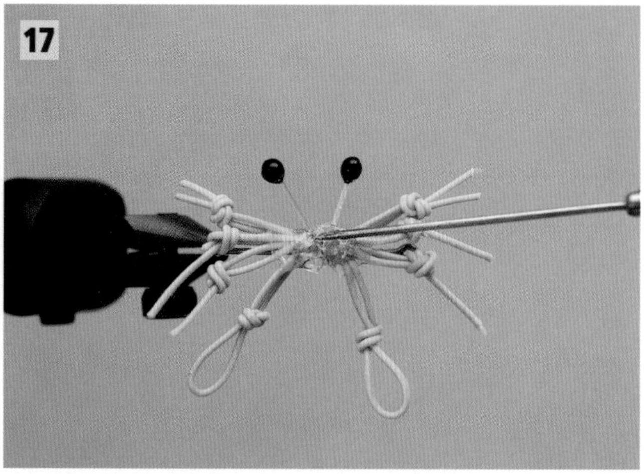


Advance your thread to the eye of the hook and whip-finish. Cut away the thread. At the center of the fly, and on top of all the thread wraps, add a dollop of E-6000 glue the diameter of a dime. It should cover the legs thoroughly almost up to the knots.

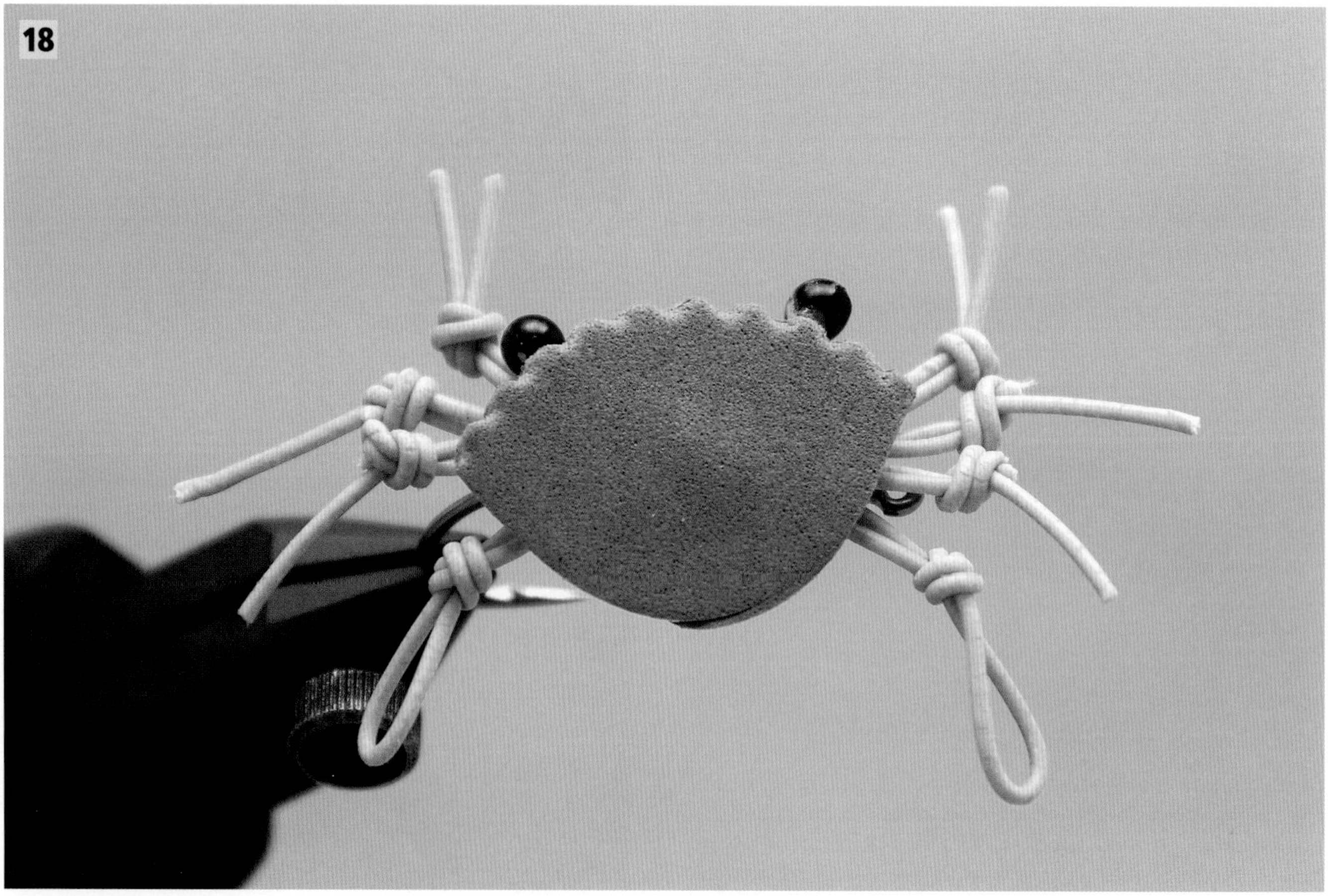


Press the foam shell on top of the glue and adjust the appendages to the desired configuration. Turn the fly over in the vise and add a little more glue to hold everything in place.

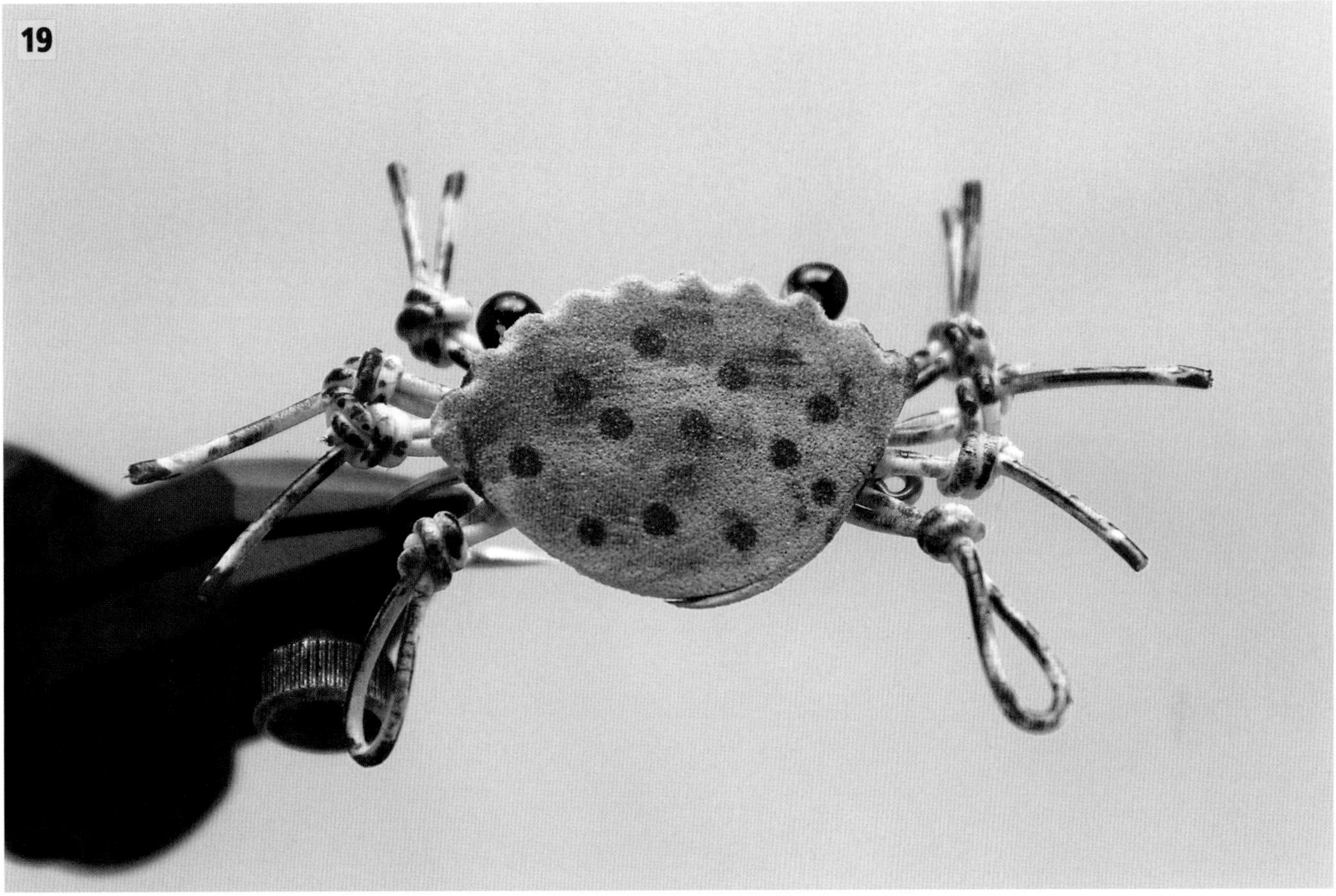

Use permanent marker to add a few dots to the shell and give the legs a mottled look. I like to add red or orange tips to all the appendages, but customize your crustaceans however you see fit.

PART III

# Feather Brains

CHAPTER 19

# Insights from Top Saltwater Tiers

Interviewing such an impressive collection of fly-tying innovators as in the following pages was not only an unforgettable pleasure, but enlightening as well. These individuals have appeared in countless publications and granted interviews to some of the industry's most recognizable magazines. While a typical interview focuses on the fly and how to fish it, I wanted to explore the thought process of why they chose a given material or technique. Each tier was more than willing to talk about their historically productive patterns and graciously shared their insight and theories on pattern development. A few common themes were prevalent in every conversation. The first was pattern evolution, meaning the fly that we recognize as their pattern today is different from earlier permutations. Some were happy accidents that opened their eyes to a new style or technique, but the majority of the flies started out unlike anything we would recognize to be the iconic fly today. Thousands of casts and years of on-the-water testing, tweaking, and sometimes material substitutions were required to achieve the action or attributes they were after.

Another element that was discussed in great detail was the relationship between the fish's strike zone and the fly's drop time. The position and speed in which the fly fell through the water column, and the time it spent in the strike zone, were major factors in the pattern development process. A significant amount of time and thought went into selecting the hook and materials in order to convincingly mimic the natural descent of prey in a given situation for a specific species.

These historically productive patterns have hoodwinked a wide array of species all over the world, but the majority of them were originally designed to target a particular species in a specific fishing situation. Not surprisingly, each of these master tiers possesses a vast knowledge of the fish they are after–especially their feeding habits. It was only after they had achieved repeated success and established a proven track record that they began fishing the pattern as a utility fly.

## Bob Clouser's Clouser Deep Minnow

**When did you come up with the Clouser Deep Minnow?**

Back in the late 1970s, my friend and I pinched split shot on deer-tail streamers to mimic the motion of a jig because, hands down, fishing with a jig is one of the most effective ways to catch fish. We tied the first prototypes of the Deep Minnow on streamer hooks with different sizes of Water Gremlin split shot crimped at the head of the hook. We'd either pinch the split shot on the shank behind the eye and then tie the fly around it or modify a finished fly by pinching the shot on the nose.

These early flies dived and dipped like jigs and caught more fish than the flies without the spilt shot, but they looked so ugly that we didn't want to show them to people. In 1985 Tom Schmuecker of Wapsi Fly company in Mountain Home, Arkansas, sent me a assortment of lead barbell-shape eyes made from molds he developed. I took some of them out of the package and laid them on my fly-tying table and wheels started turning in my mind. These new eyes could add weight and look great on a deer-tail streamer.

In the middle of the smallmouth season in late August 1985, I added these eyes to popular bass patterns such as Wooly Buggers, Zonkers, and marabou leeches and had immediate success. In 1986, I tied more of these flies in different color combinations. The Susquehanna had a bass season of only three months, which doesn't leave time for experimenting with various fly patterns.

In 1987, I added these eyes to my favorite deer-tail streamers, the ones I previously had tied with split shot. With the lead eyes lashed to the hook and painted to look like baitfish eyes, the old patterns took on a new look. The most important component of the new fly was now in place. The eyes provided the weight that made the fly dip and dart in the currents like a natural baitfish escaping a predator. I also slimmed down my original bucktail pattern, because friends who first tested the pattern told me that the sparsely dressed ones were more effective than the heavily dressed ones.

JACK HANRAHAN PHOTO

**What conditions, environments, or situations was the Clouser Deep Minnow designed to be fished in?**
The Susquehanna River near Middletown is perhaps a half-mile wide, with a gentle flow and a bottom paved in limestone rock—perfect habitat for smallmouths.

**Why did you chose the materials you did and the techniques to apply them?**
Deer-tail hair from white-tailed bucks and does is a versatile and effective fly-tying material that works well in the water. I used deer-tail fibers for the wings of my first Deep Minnows back in the 1980s and have yet to find a better substitute for most situations.

When tying baitfish imitations, I do not even the tips of the deer-tail fiber with a hair stacker or other devices. Stacking the hairs aligns the tips perfectly, causing the bundle of hair to look as neat as a paint brush when tied on the fly. This is not the effect I want. Light penetrates uneven tips better than neatly stacked ones, and the fly works better in the water.

**Has the pattern evolved or changed any over time?**
I tied the flies in a few color variations to imitate the local baitfish. Gray and white imitated the silver shiner, and brown and white imitated the golden shiner or sculpin. I tied them all on size 4 hooks, and they were 1¾ inches long, the length of most of the bucktail jigs that worked best on the Susquehanna River.

**What makes the pattern so effective?**
One of the problems with conventional streamer patterns is that they stop moving during the retrieve when the angler is not stripping them. What baitfish would stop when chased by a predator? Predatory fish, especially the older, larger specimens, know when their target doesn't act the way it should. I developed the Clouser Deep Minnow to mimic the movement of a fleeing baitfish. The eyes provide the weight that make the fly dip and dart in the currents like a natural bait escaping a predator. It looks like a minnow, but best of all it's a streamer you can cast easily, and it sinks like an anvil in a swamp.

# Joe Mahler's Straw Boss

I was fishing in Lake Okeechobee with Mark King, and although Lake Okeechobee has great bass fishing, poppers just don't seem to work there. We were fishing up in the cattails. I would throw a popper up there, and I could see the bass come out and look at it, but they just wouldn't commit to it. So I changed flies and we went on to catch a few bass on Woolly Buggers and that kind of stuff, but I went back home thinking, "There's got to be something those fish were interested in eating; they just weren't interested in eating that popper."

I thought back to flies I used back in Indiana, and I remembered a fly called an Everett Drake's wounded minnow. It was a deer body hair fly with a bullet head with deer body hair all the way around. And the beauty of this fly was it would outfish poppers all the time because the deer hair would sink a little bit, and the fly would sit down in the film. So it was doing as much work underwater as it was doing on the top. I was going to tie some of those, but I thought I'd tie some out of bucktail because it's denser and not as buoyant and is going to sink just a little bit. As I was tying it, I folded it back and decided to tie the pulled back hair only on half of the fly and weight it. But when I did and tied the butts in and tightened it down, the butts flared out. I decided to leave them on and make wings out of them. Initially I thought the wings would just add a visual element to the fly, but when I went out and fished, I noticed that as the fly would fall, the wings would make it tilt from one side to another, not in a uniformed zigzag path but kind of irregular. It took a long time to hit the bottom and it took a roundabout way of getting there. So I could see the fish come up and take a good, long look at it as it fell and then charge it. Then I started using it in the salt water, and in the backwater with snook I could watch the fly fall, and then the snook would hit it and disappear.

I designed the fly two years ago. The initial pattern was tied on a size 4 Gamakatsu, a very sharp hook. Then I started going to the swimming pool, and I put my dive mask on and watched the fly fall. The first ones I tied did not have any weight added, and the thread, the hook, and the bucktail gave it a significant sink rate in fresh water. But when I took it to salt water, the fly would not sink so that's when I started wrapping the shank of the hook with lead wire. For a #2 hook, which is usually what I use for snook, I made eight wraps of .30 lead wire, and that is pretty good for the major-

ity of saltwater fishing that I do. I have tied some with double wraps—15 or 16 wraps on top of each other—and I use that lead to build up the bulk for the head.

The bodies have always been bucktail, but originally the little underbelly was squirrel tail, and I used that to separate two pairs of splayed hackles. I found that step to be unnecessary, and I eliminated it. So then I started looking at the underbelly material of the fly. I started using Craft Fur because I love the colors that you can get in Craft Fur. It adds just a little accent to the belly of the fly and it was that bright color that I really liked.

The original one for bass was a tan back with a red underbelly, but the ones that work best for snook on the beach, because of all the glass minnows, are all white with a pearl French braid for the belly or plain white. All white is pretty hard to beat. I like to use a contrasting color, like a darker color for the back or shell, and for the legs a lighter version of the back color. It seems to work well, and I like a lighter color for the underbelly as well, just like a baitfish.

Initially I wanted something that would get down just a little bit, but over time I find myself weighting them more heavily because I realize the power of that fall, and prolonging that fall. The combination of the weight and the wings prolong the fall and make it as dramatic as possible. That's what makes this fly so effective, and most of the time I get the strike after the cast and before the fly hits the bottom. It's amazing how many times I get a hit by doing nothing. Especially in salt water, there are currents and other things influencing the fly in ways that are better and more natural than you can do by stripping.

The colors of the fly changed when I started fishing peacock bass. Peacock bass are cannibals, so I tie most of the flies with a green back, chartreuse legs, and a bright red underbelly. When I initially started fishing for peacocks, I heard that you just have to tie Clousers in bright colors and you were all set. I swear you can watch the eyeballs of the fish follow it right to the bottom. When I tested the Straw Boss, the fish watched it and watched it and then their gills flared and next thing you knew they charged it. So it does tease them and give them more time to think about it.

**How did you come up with the name Straw Boss?**

The bucktail kind of looks like straw, and I wanted a name that had an old Florida feel. Do you know what a Straw Boss is? It's essentially the one who assumes the role of authority, and it was all about attitude. I looked at this fly and said it kind of looks like the guy who says he's in charge.

I have found that in fast-moving water the wings of the fly tend to make it spin. If I fish it in fast water, I do a dead drift, because a retrieve will make it spin. It's a lazy day kind of fly. It was designed for lakes, ponds, and backcountry saltwater fishing when the fish will have a long time to look at it. It's not one of those flies that will go buzzing by the fish's head and the fish reaches out and grabs it out of reaction. From that standpoint, I feel like this tie needs to be tied a little bit better. If a fly is stripped quickly, fish really don't get a good look at it and they tend to hit it out of reaction. Fish are going to take a good, long look at this one and decide to eat it.

The other reason that I think Everett Drake's wounded minnow worked better than a popper was that it had all those little fibers, and I think that the pop that you get or turbulence that is created from natural fibers is different than what comes off a highly glossed cork. I think that like the Everett Drake, when the Straw Boss is stripped, all those little hairs throw off a different vibration and little bubbles, and I think there is something to be said for that.

# Jonny King's Kinky Muddler

I'm always playing with fly designs. After years of freshwater fly fishing, I started using my fly rod in salt water in the late '80s, and in the last 10 to 15 years I have been trying to come up with my own patterns using the same philosophies for striper fishing that I use for trout fishing. My approach is either to match the hatch for the baitfish or I want a fly mechanically to do something.

I was trying to create a bunker pattern, and I was tying with some of Steve Farrar's Flash Blend material. I had just kind of gobbed some on the hook using the hi-tie technique, and I trimmed it too much. But after I trimmed it I realized it created almost the same effect as spun deer hair. One thing you can do with spun deer hair is create dimension on the hook. You can create something that's wide, tall, or cylindrical. There are three differences with synthetic. Unlike deer hair, the synthetic is not opaque; it's translucent, so it's a lot more appealing to most baitfish imitations. Two, it's not totally buoyant because if you were to tie a cigar-shape body out of spun deer hair, it tends to be very buoyant and unless the hook is incredibly heavy the hair will float the fly like a popper. Three, when you tighten deer hair, it flairs at a 90-degree angle to the hook shank.

The way I was tying the kinky fiber, the material was angling back toward the bend.

Why does this matter? Because that permits you to have a smooth transition between the head of the fly and the tail of the fly. Any of the classic flies with spun deer hair heads—even bass poppers—have an unnatural transition between the head of the fly and the body. That always bugged me. You have the head, some kind of a collar, and then a valley or a gap and then the body—obviously not what a baitfish looks like.

One of the things that I learned from Bob Popovics's flies more than anything else is that they have a natural profile. Whether it's a Surf Candy or Silicone or 3D fly or Spread fly . . . more than anything else, they are shaped to have a profile like a real baitfish. When I trimmed that kinky fiber with the spun head of synthetic leaning back, I realized I could make the transition over any kind of tail I wanted, have no interruption between the head and tail, and I can make any kind of shape I want. I tried doing it with that typical up-and-down high tie, but I was always getting the bunker profile—tall top to bottom, but with no dimension side to side. So I started tying it in the V formation or what I call V tying. With a V-tie technique, you just lay the fibers crosswise on the shank, with those on the near side of the shank leaning toward the bend and those on the far side leaning forward toward the hook eye. You then fold the fibers on the far side of the shank back toward the bend and tie them down to create a V. It's a piece of cake. What I realized was by doing that I was creating width in the fly. So I started playing with it and all of a sudden I could make the fly as wide or as tall as I wanted. I have made mullet flies that look as thick as a sausage, and that's a hard thing to do with any other material. If you did that with deer hair, it

Kinky Muddler Variation

Original Kinky Muddler

would never sink. I would not say it's a total joy to cast, but it's still castable and it sheds water much better than any other material.

Here is the other thing about the Kinky Muddler: when I tied it first I tried it with all different kinds of tail materials. Sometimes I just used the Kinky Fibre, and I did not like the way it behaved in the water. While kinky fiber does swim pretty well, it doesn't swim great, and something about having the entire fly tied out of kinky fiber did not let it track as well because the kinky fiber is fairly curly and it traps air. I wanted something at the back of the fly that was a lot more mobile and also absorbed a little more water to help the fly track.

There are a lot of things that influence how a fly will track. You obviously need a hook design or style of hook that will give you an efficient keel with enough weight in the back to make it track properly. So, for instance, the Kinky Muddler is actually used a lot for roosterfish. It holds four world records for roosterfish. The way you generally fish for roosterfish is you will go into a cove and the guide will throw out sardinas–it's not like chumming because they are live sardinas–and maybe you will have a fish blow up 100 feet away from you. Then you turn around and there will be a boil 30 feet behind you and then 150 feet to your right. You will get sporadic blasts all around you and you get one shot, and then you have to rip the fly back as fast as you can, either with a single-hand retrieve or by putting the rod under your arm and doing a two-hand retrieve. So you need a fly that is going to track straight; if it turns up on its side, that's a major fish turn off.

The interesting thing about this fly is that if you do a stop-and-go retrieve, it has a tendency to shoot left and right, but if you do a steady retrieve, it will track dead straight. The way you achieve that is with a proper hook with weight in the keel, and you also need to trim the head the right way. But I found that with the synthetic for the tail, it didn't wiggle enough and it tracked high in the water. So I kept trying different tail designs, and the one that worked best I discovered in January 2008 or late 2007. The first ones had a combination of bucktail and saddles for the tail, so what I did was I made a little platform of bucktail and I tied the saddles over top of the tail and tented them. Tented means that on either side of the bucktail you have the feathers at a 45-degree angle. So they make either side of a triangle and where they meet at the top makes the dorsal surface of the baitfish. The technique is an Atlantic salmon fly-tying technique.

If you look at most baitfish head on, they form a tapered shape. A mullet's pretty cylindrical, but still it has broader shoulders, tapered down to the belly, and above the shoulders it comes to a point along the dorsal surface. A bunker is a much more exaggerated example of this. If you tip those saddles, they will meet at the top edge and there will be a little cavity underneath because their bottom edges are swung out to the sides.

So the design of the Kinky Muddler is based on a basic principle that I observed while fishing and then confirmed with conversations, particularly with Popovics: whenever you have a fly with a bulky head and a long, wispy tail, the shape makes the tail kick. You can test it out yourself by holding your fly out the window next time you are driving along. The breeze will have the same effect on the fly as the water will.

Any time you have a big fat head at the front of a fly and then a long skinny tail, you know the tail is going to kick. The thing that fascinates me most about watching baitfish is trying to get a fly that looks like a baitfish but also behaves like it. So what I wanted was to incorporate that principle to get the tail to kick, but in a fly that looked natural.

Let's say I'm tying on a 2/0 or a 3/0 hook. I would put two or three on each side. I'm not a very uniform fly tier, and every one of my flies comes out a little different. Craft Fur works well on smaller versions, as well as a bunny strip because that swims well. If you are using Craft Fur, keep 50 percent of the base fibers to maintain some of the bulk. What's even better for smaller flies is arctic fox tail.

Soft is good, but the reason bucktail is the greatest fly-tying material is because it's not too soft. It swims great in the water, and it's just stiff enough to keep its shape. I don't like marabou for the tail because it's too wispy. It's great for the tail of a toad or crab feelers, but these suckers get beat up on the beach and I wanted something that would hold together.

I tied some for snook and baby tarpon ones, and a tuft of arctic fox tail works great. The only problem with it is it's prone to fouling, so before tying in the tail I tie in an application of kinky fiber at the bend, and I fold the fibers back on the sides to create a little platform. Then I tie the arctic fox on top and then more kinky fiber on top of that so it looks like the arctic fox is surrounded by a little tunnel of kinky fiber.

Sometimes I think what makes a pattern effective is that people are fishing it, but also it's having a combination of a realistic profile that is uninterrupted, with movement that is natural. That is what I was going for, and I think that is why it works. A fly can be effective for a lot of different reasons. It could trigger strikes because it has a great jigging action, or it could trigger strikes because it has some wild colors on it. I don't think that's what's going on with my fly. I think what's going on with my fly is it looks like the things fish eat, and it behaves like the things fish eat.

## Jon Cave's Wobbler

It was early '80s, and I had kept the pattern under wraps for a few years because I had a couple of patterns stolen in the past. I had been working on this pattern for a few years, and it's kind of an odd story, but up until the Wobbler came out, most people had a tendency to think in terms of size, silhouette, and color of a fly, and very little about how that fly behaved in the water or how it moved. Back then, when Umpqua didn't have much to choose from, some of the saltwater patterns they were selling did not behave properly in the water. They didn't float right or they would spin.

I decided I needed to come up with some kind of an action fly, not with any other thought other than something I would like to fish. It's funny, but I woke up in the middle of the night–it must have been 3 or 4 in the morning–and called a good friend of mine who was also a guide at the time, and I said, "Meet me at the boat ramp in an hour and a half." I had tied up a few flies that were the precursors to the Wobbler using prismatic tape and epoxy, similar to some copies that I have seen today that are copies. We took them out and caught some fish, but they spun a lot and they were not super durable.

I liked the concept I had, though, so I went home and started working on the weight of the fly. I wanted enough weight to make the wobble but not turn all the way over. It took some time to come up with the exact weight to make the fly work right. To add durability to the fly, I changed from the tape to Mylar tubing. The Mylar was thick and durable. If you don't fish a whole lot and you buy one of those things, it will last you a year–especially if you don't mind doing a little repair work on it now and again. If they are tied right, they will last you a long time.

The other thing I didn't like about the prismatic tape was it look a little too much like a lure. It was more of a cut and epoxy job, and to me it looked too manufactured. The other one with Mylar tubing actually had a tying process.

The weight and where it's positioned on the fly is a huge factor in making it function properly. I messed with different lead eyes on it; I put them in front and on the back. I found that dumbbell eyes in sizes up to 1 stabilized the fly, and it would not wobble at all; it traveled through the water column in a straight line.

I tried extra-large bead chain and worked my way back to medium bead chain on some of the smaller ones. I found that, depending on the hook size, finding the proper weight keeps the fly from rotating. It's amazing how fast you can pull those things through the water. They wobble and look like a fast hula dancer when they come through the water.

The unweighted ones have a tendency to ride up closer to the surface. You have to work them really slowly, and I

don't like working them slowly. If a fish gets up behind it, I almost pull the fly away from it. Quite honestly, when I redfish with that thing, I can see the fly as far away as I can cast. You can see the fly flash or if there is a fish behind it, you can really tell what the fly is doing.

Initially in the prototypes, I used prismatic tape and I tried bending the hook, but I found that if you bent the shank of the hook in a C shape, the flies had a tendency to ride up, so I ended up going to a straight shank or bend-back style of hook. The bend backs have a unique movement, and they tend to wiggle a little quicker than the straight shank versions, but I tie mostly on a straight shank hook. I also put a weedguard on the first ones, and I don't do that anymore either in most situations, because of the weight. If

I put the weight on the back, about a quarter of the way down through the bend, the hook point rides up anyway, and it stays pretty much weedless unless you are in really thick grass. I still tie a few with weedguards, but not many.

I have tied the Wobbler up to size 3/0 and experimented with them offshore. I like messing around with what a fish won't eat, rather than what it will eat, and I think you learn a lot doing that. If the fishing is good, and you can find a fly that won't work, it will help you understand what's good or bad about other patterns. The regular Wobbler most people recognize is tied on hooks size 2 through 1/0.

There are two major lures in my opinion: One is a spoon and the other is a jig. The jig was covered by the Clouser Minnow, the Gotcha, and the Crazy Charlie, but nobody had tried to get a wobbling motion out of a fly. So that's what I wanted to do: to try and come up with something that imitates a spoon. I was going to use this fly for redfish because they are notorious spoon eaters. That was my impetus for designing the fly: to come up with that kind of a motion. Initially it was mostly to appeal to redfish, but I have gotten reports from people that have caught fish from northern pike to peacock bass.

I have a version I use for bass fishing and instead of the bucktail on the back I use long saddle hackles, and you can work it really slowly along the bottom. You could also use a Zonker Strip on the back. I have tied a version with a split tail that looks more like a crayfish, and I use that on the St. Johns for fish that hang along the bars looking for crayfish.

For redfish hanging along the edges of Mosquito Lagoon, I have one variation with an eye on each side of the fly, and I cast it along the outside bank where there is a school of fish and let it drop. They often pick the fly up as it's fluttering down to the bottom. A lot of the time I don't even strip it; I just cast it and let it sink and they pick it up then.

I have tried UV acrylic instead of epoxy, but it doesn't work well for this pattern. It worked on the outside as a coating, but on the inside it won't work because the fly has to be wafer thin and it can't have any air pockets inside. You cannot cure the material on the inside of the Mylar. When you slide the Mylar tubing over the hook shank, you fill the tube with epoxy and tie off both ends. For the fly to work properly, both sides of the Mylar have to touch, and there can be absolutely no air pockets inside. You could use acrylic on the outside after you epoxy the fly for better durability, but it will not work internally.

When the Wobbler is tied perfectly, it is actually peanut shaped. If you hold the fly toward you so you can see through the eye of the hook, the silhouette of the fly is peanut shaped and that shape helps it wobble a little bit. When the epoxy is just starting to heat up and set, I pinch the materials with my thumbs and middle fingers and pull out the front and back of the Mylar, the back just a little bit more than I do in the front. It makes the water flow through there an odd way, and that's got something to do with the action of the fly. The fly will work fine if you don't do that, but the peanut shape looks better and it wobbles better too.

The fly is so effective because of its action and its durability. I have not found anything that's better. The Clouser Minnow goes up and down, and the Wobbler goes side to side, but the fish typically eat it when its wobbling on the way down. The weight keeps the fly down, so it allows you to move the fly as fast as you want. It has to be tied with a loop knot or it will stifle the action of the fly. That is key.

## Gary Merriman's Tarpon Toad

The Tarpon Toad was born in gin-clear water of the lower Keys in the early '90s. The pattern quickly became the solution for feeding the lock-jawed giants of the flats.

Years ago after watching some old 3M tarpon VCR tapes that show the fly from the underwater view, Gary was amazed by how much they hopped above and below the fish's track. The trick has always been to keep the fly in the fish's face for as long as possible. The toad is lightweight and, depending on what size hook is used, slow to sink–if not neutrally buoyant–so it tracks in the strike zone instead of rising and falling.

Tarpon Toad Variation

Gary Merriman's Original Tarpon Toad

Merriman wanted a bright pattern that could be easily seen and would capture the tarpon's attention from a great distance. The body of the original Tarpon Toad was constructed using yellow Antron or poly yarn. Inspiration for this body style came from Harry Spear's classic Tasty Toad. Both flies used a series of yarn sections tied perpendicularly to the shank of the hook, much like Del Brown's Del Merkin permit fly. The synthetic yarn floats much better than conventional yarn and contributed to the fly's neutral buoyancy. A chartreuse Zonker Strip tail was tied in upside-down and enrobed with a collar of white marabou. Both materials were selected to give the fly a lifelike movement. The tail was tied in opposite from most flies on purpose. After thinking about how a fish would see his fly, Gary decided to tie the fly from the tarpon's point of view. This decision gave the fly a softer landing and improved the materials' motion in the water. The toad changed the game of tarpon fishing because it could be presented softly and it came alive when barely stripped. You no longer had to land the fly on your quarry's nose like conventional Keys style flies; it could be presented in the path of cruising fish and lay in wait until they discovered it.

Captain Tim Hoover changed the pattern when he ran out of Zonker Strip and substituted long, webby marabou plumes. Proving to be equally if not more effective, the pattern evolved.

**In your opinion what makes the pattern so effective?**
The main reason I think it works is that the fly tracks on a level plane. The toad head makes the fly travel straight and the new lighter and smaller hooks that we are using keep the fly from hopping on the water, unlike the older style Keys flies. Think of it like wings on a plane flying through the water.

## Bob Popovics's Surf Candy

My original Surf Candy was developed in 1972. I made it to withstand bluefish. There were no eyes on it or any kind of decor, just epoxy. I realized that the heads I covered with epoxy on my Blondes always outlasted the rest of the fly, so I decided to carry the epoxy along the entire shank wing. It was popularized later in the early '80s.

The Surf Candy was not designed for anything but durability. A fly that could hold up to bluefish: that was something never achieved before.

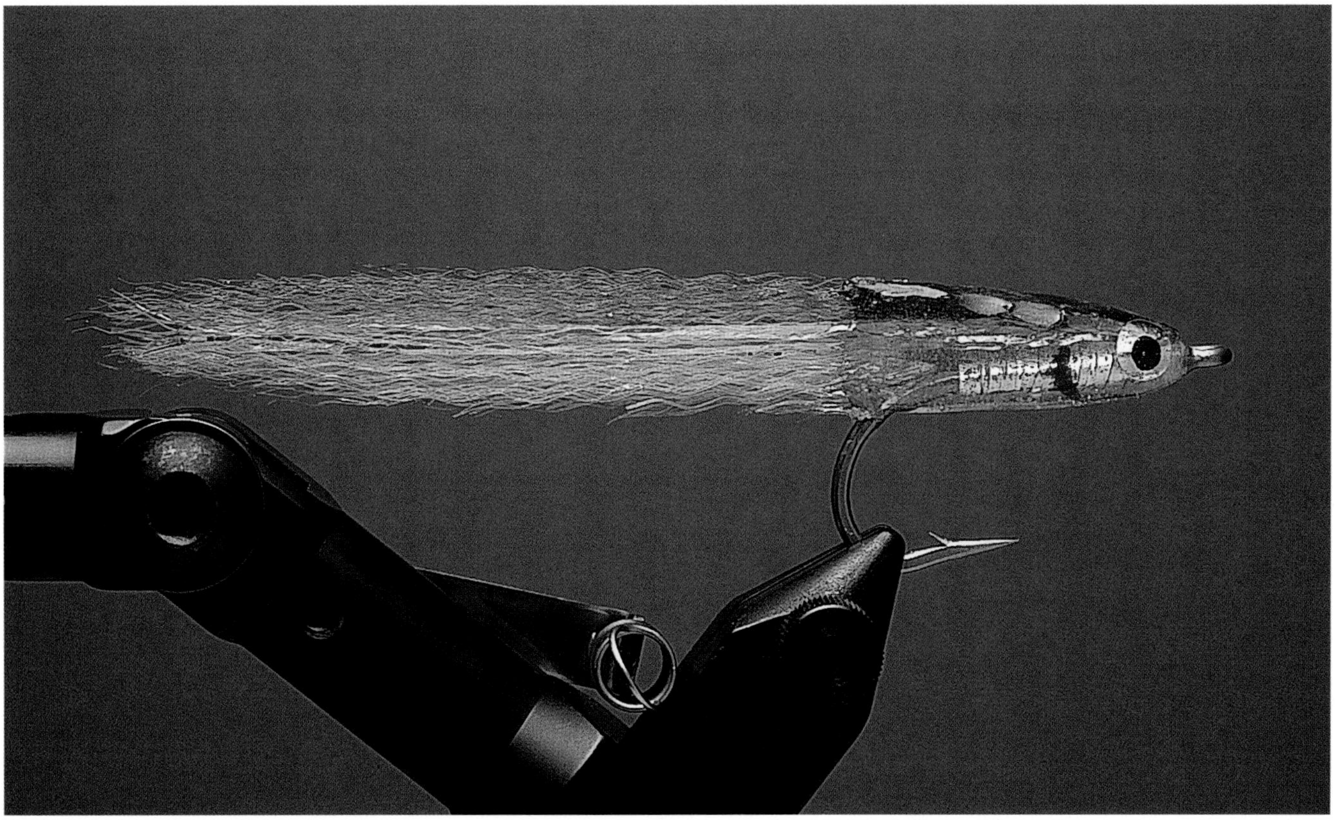

Later design features were nonfouling, then making the fly more realistic. Certain materials such as polar bear and, much later, synthetics provided a translucent feature that the natural baits possessed.

The big material choice is the epoxy. It was manageable, dried quickly, clear, and it was durable. When a durable material like Ultrahair came on the market, putting the two together made a Fleye that could last. I caught as many as 30 bluefish on one Surf Candy, which was unheard of just years before.

The application of epoxy that I used was also unique. I needed the epoxy to hold and protect the wing. No wraps of thread to hold the wing close to the hook and then flare after the hook bend. I wanted a natural and lifelike shape of the bait. Mylar flash was first wrapped around the hook so it showed through the clear epoxy. I held the wing in place till the epoxy hardened.

The Surf Candy has evolved from epoxy to light-cured acrylics. The original Tuffleye is the brand I prefer because it does not use dangerous UV light; it uses blue light that is safe.

These acrylics make the epoxy-type Fleyes much easier to make.

What makes the Surf Candy and its variations so productive is its basic natural shape. It usually represents translucent baits, and the epoxy captures that characteristic.

## Norm Zeigler's Crystal Schminnow

**When did you come up with the Crystal Schminnow?**
I designed the fly in 1995, the first summer that I lived on Sanibel Island.

**What factors led you to design the pattern?**
I was pretty sick at the time and I could not go too far to fish. I did not go much farther than walking down the beach from my house. The water was very clear there and very shallow, and the problem with the Clouser was it kept bouncing on the bottom. It would spook the fish when it landed if I cast too close to them. I wanted the fly to be higher in the water column because a snook has an upward-looking morphology like a pike and it attacks its prey straight ahead or from underneath, unlike a redfish or a bonefish, which is predominantly a bottom feeder. The Schminnow was designed to suspend a few inches below the surface.

**What conditions, environments, or situations was the Crystal Schminnow designed to be fished in?**

The fly was basically designed to be a beach fly, targeting snook in clear, shallow water.

**Why did you chose the materials you did and the techniques to apply them?**

I was catching some fish on the beach with Clousers, chartreuse and white mainly, and I noticed that most of the baitfish were white or silvery colored. I started thinking how I could match the bait better. I know marabou from Woolly Buggers in fresh water, and I don't recall exactly how I came up with chenille. I think I saw some in a shop, and I started out melting monofilament to make the eyes. The first time I used it I had a snook come right up out of the water chasing it, so I knew it was going to be a good fly.

I choose the chenille because it looked so sparkly and the marabou because of how it moved in the water. I could not think of material that moved better in the water. I added the mono eyes to hint at a baitfish, and it has a little shrimpiness as well. It's not exactly duplicating anything. I cut the marabou because doing that is the key to the action. When you strip the fly, the marbou collapses, and when you pause, the marabou flexes open. And if you leave it long, it's snaky like a Woolly Bugger, which is a good action for trout and some other fish, but that pulsation of the marabou when you strip and pause is really one of its keys to success.

I always do a figure eight around the eyes so the thread is covered, and I actually think it helps the eyes stay on a little better and keeps them from breaking off so easily.

**Has the pattern evolved or changed over time?**

When I was experimenting with the fly, I saw that most of the baitfish where small, so I started out tying the Schminnow on different Mustad hooks that were not stainless–they were nickel plaited and made a hell of a mess out of my fly box. They rusted, so I went to the stainless Mustad. I like them for their strength and their price point, and they don't rust. They have a nice sturdy wire and you can catch a big snook and they will not straighten. I started out using ice chenille, and then I found the pearl, which seems to be much better than the plain white. I also use the store-bought black mono eyes now. They show up much better than the melted mono eyes that you try to burn yourself.

**In your opinion what makes the pattern so effective?**

A couple of different things make my fly so effective: First, it is a suspending fly, so when you stop stripping it, it will flutter a little bit, but it will not dive like a Clouser. The second one is clipping off the tips of the marabou tail. When the material flexes open is when most snook are going to hit it.

## Dan Blanton's Flashtail Whistler

I developed the Whistler in 1964. The Whistler was designed to take striped bass in San Francisco Bay. It was not created to imitate any particularly baitfish. Instead I engineered the fly to mimic the look and action of a lead-head bucktail jig–one of the most productive and versatile fish-caching lures ever devised. The local gear guys were kicking our asses with lead-head jigs–all white versions and red and white versions. Our simplistic bucktail patterns of the era just didn't work as well. Of course a bucktail jig and the Whistler emulate a huge variety of baitfish species, fresh and salt, mostly the deeper-bodied bait fishes.

The first pattern I came up with might well have been the first reverse-tied (known today as a Thunder Creek) bucktail, and it looked exactly like a red and white lead-head bucktail jig. Problem was it didn't have much action, although it caught fish.

I kept experimenting. I ended up using an extra-short-shank live bait hook to keep all the weight forward to enhance dipping and diving like a bucktail jig does and to eliminate fouling of the bucktail wing when cast. I added bead-chain eyes to add weight and help the jigging action (another benefit was also more noise and water pushing ability). The eyes whistled when the fly was cast, and that's how the fly got its name. I included a narrow, red chenille collar to simulate gills and also to add more frontal weight and finally a three-hackle collar between the chenille and bead eyes. The hackles were a mix of soft and stiff barbs, which provided extra action and water pushing ability. (Rabbit does not push water, lying down flat when wet.)

The Whistler in the early years (through the mid-1970s) was always tied in the round, often with grizzly feather flanks. Being tied in the round, it always looked right, no matter how the fly turned or twisted in the water. There was no topping of a contrasting color.

The first Whistler was all white with a red bucktail lateral stripe–a white Mickey Finn Whistler; next came the red, white, and grizzly; yellow, red, and grizzly; black and grizzly; ending up with more than 20 color variations. All had names that addressed their color pattern: Black Whistler Grizzly; White Whistler Grizzly, and so on.

In 1971 I started tying them with flash tails using 1/64-inch Mylar strips. I was inspired by a jig Mark Sosin was using to

slay the snook with. He was outfishing me horridly. I went back to camp, tied a Whistler with a flash tail exactly as I do today, and the next day I pounded the snook and Mark too. Today I use various colors of Flashabou in the original saltwater size. My favorite color is a 50:50 blend of pearl and silver Flashabou.

In the early '70s I met Ed Given while fishing on SF Bay. A friend and I were slamming the stripers, and Ed rowed over in his little pram, introduced himself, and asked to see the fly I was using. It was a Whistler. Later he adapted most of the Whistler components into a fly he called a Night Crawler. It was similar to Russ Chatham's Black Phantom fly. I later renamed Ed's fly the Barred 'N Black.

Today I tie the Flashtail Whistler in many color variations, and while I still tie them on a short shank J hook, I now tie most of them on the Targus 9413 hook or the Fly Shop FS5444 60-degree bend jig hook, and I use Spirit River Real Eyes instead of bead chain. Bead chain is still great but it doesn't look as good. All of my Whistlers today are tied as flash tails.

The Whistler was and still is the top jungle river tarpon fly in Central America, and it is also the number one peacock bass fly in Brazil. More than 400 species of fish worldwide have been taken on Whistlers, including several world records. It remains one of the most versatile styles ever created.

In 1964 there was nothing around like it–not nearly as sophisticated doing what it was designed to do. In his book, *Streamers and Bucktails: The Big Fish Flies,* Joseph D. Bates Jr. said the Whistler might well be the greatest fly design ever created. Well, I don't know about this, but it sure turned out to be a damned good fly.

## Chris Helm's Jessie Special

**I borrowed one of your techniques when I was developing one of my latest patterns, the Tuscan Bunny. I was watching a video of you tying a Simiran before I went to Andros, and I was intrigued when you cut the rabbit hair off the Zonker Strip and palmered it around the hook shank with a dubbing loop.**

I did that because it made the fly look a little more streamlined and you don't have that rabbit skin on there. It makes a neater, tighter fly.

**I used the same technique on my Tuscan Bunny fly to make the fly fluffy and impart movement without adding the weight of the rabbit skin. When those Zonker Strips get waterlogged, they get really heavy and have a tendency to come down with a splat!**

There are a lot of little things you can do to improve your fly's action without adding weight. I have a customer who is using marabou in a similar fashion. He has created a dubbing loop with the marabou but not with wire–he uses thread so it does not add any more weight. We put it in the stationary tub, and man, does that thing move! In the water, that thing is dynamite. And we were just testing its action in the stationary tub; we were not out on the river with current.

**What are you thinking about when you are working on improving or modifying patterns or selecting materials and determining what techniques to use to apply them?**

When I modified Lenny Moffo's bonefish fly, I changed several things about it–the color, several of the materials. I started using it in the early '90s down in the Bahamas, and it's another one of those if I only had one fly deals . . . that would be the baby I would use.

One of my customers tied up a bunch of those flies and went down to Mexico for bonefish. Of course when he got there, the guide wanted to see his box and check out the flies he brought before they went out. He took one look at the flies and said, "These won't work here." But my customer told the guide, "I'm going to try them anyway." He put on the Jessie Special and was catching bonefish left and right. He did that the first day, the second day, and on the third day they were out catching bonefish and he spotted a permit. He didn't have time to change flies, so he threw

the Jessie Special and caught a 25-pound permit on it. Here is the kicker . . . at the end of the day they got back into the lodge and the guide said, "I don't want a tip today–I want your flies." The Jessie Special will work anywhere there are bonefish.

I took Lenny's fly, changed the color, and I used a product from krinig, a flat braid that comes in various sizes and thicknesses. I use that and orange and brown Sili Legs, a Krystal Flash tail, and a little orange dubbing where I tie in the legs. I have more of those in my fly box than any other fly.

**So obviously you have years of experience at reading fish and knowing what materials would work in certain situations and how they would look in the water, but what made you pick the materials and modify Lenny's fly the way you did?**

Well that's going back almost 20 years ago, but if I remember correctly, I think it was all about the color. For some reason orange seems to be a great color in attracting fish. Not just saltwater fish but also in fresh water. So I picked the Sili Legs with a little bit of brown and a little bit of orange. I use five legs. The braid is a pale orange color and then Krystal Flash and orange dubbing, bead-chain eyes, and that's all you need. I picked all those materials because of their color. Not that I had tried that color down there–I hadn't. It worked so well I named it after my guide.

**So you know from experience that the color orange is a productive color across the board.**

It's not only for bonefish, it's for grayling, it's for pike, and so on and so forth. And how many times have you heard a guy say he had an orange strike indicator and the fish come up and hit it. I have heard that story 100 times.

**A lot of the fly designers I have talked to will say I always want my flies to move water, so I choose more dense materials for the front of the fly. I like my flies to make noise, so I like to incorporate rattles in my patterns whenever possible. Are there things that you do with your patterns that carry across the board?**

Yesterday I took some flies out to the pond to test them before I head to Canada to fish for pike this summer. There are no pike in this particular pond, but I wanted to see how the fly would move on the surface of the water, and how they would react when I twitched them and retrieved them and so forth. They were perfect. Something I really like is to be able to move the fly and have it undulate and swim back and forth. You twitch your rod tip or give a little strip and then stop it, but the fly will move left and right on its own. I want something that moves kind of slow because sometimes the pike will sneak up slow and then all of a sudden they just zip up on it. These flies do that well. I use a bass worm hook to act like a keel on these bigger flies. The hook also makes the fly effective around weeds as well.

**Are there any techniques you use to keep larger flies from fouling?**

When I tie my Deceiver or Zonker Strip flies, I always put mono loop out the back with the Zonker Strip, and for any type of fly with feather sticking out the back, I always put a bunch of bucktail on first before I put the hackle on. I have never had a problem with any of my flies fouling since I started doing that. It also makes it easier to tie the hackle on as well because you have a wider surface, kind of like a foundation.

The other thing you can use for a foundation is rubber legs. They act the same way and give you a wider surface to tie the hackles onto. The other trick I use when I am tying in hackles is I glue the four feathers together down at the base where I'm going to tie them in. Put a little dab of Bond 527 glue on there, and let them dry for 10 to 15 minutes. It works like a charm.

The other thing you really have to pay attention to is your thread pressure. When you mount those, you want to make all the wraps on your initial tie-in very light. Then when you start back toward the hook eye, you bear down and put a little bit of Zap-A-Gap on there, and it bonds and will never move or roll or twist.

**You mentioned that thread pressure and control are very important. Would you talk a little about thread control and how you use your thread as a tool?**

One of the things that I find when I teach new students, and this is true with what I call intermediate tiers, is that they never change their thread pressure. They wrap the same all the time. If you vary your thread pressure depending on the material and what you are trying to achieve, you will have much more control of the material you are working with. For instance, when I do deer hair bass bugs and I am stacking or spinning the deer hair, I always keep my thread flat, and I use 130-denier gelspun thread. That is important: It's not a strength issue, it's a diameter or width issue. I could get away with 75 denier, but if you have the thread twisted, it will cut the hair quicker than if you were using a larger diameter thread. It allows me to put much more pressure on the hair without cutting it. It will also help to hold it in place.

Another little thing I do, and it's what Dave Whitlock has done for a long time, is to put mono on the hook. I don't put it on both sides of the hook, just the far side, and I only do that on my mouse where I tie the tail in and I use a lot of hair for the butt. I use a 1/8-inch piece of 80-pound mono and cover it with gelspun. It gives you a flat surface to work on so the hair doesn't roll on you.

**Are there any situations when you compress the thread?**

The only time I might do that is when I am dubbing. I like a round thread when I am dubbing. But for the most part I am always counterspinning my thread so it is as flat as possible.

A lot of beginning tiers don't realize that they need to counterspin their bobbin if they are a right-handed tier, and it gives them all kinds of problems. So I spin my bobbin all the time because I want more surface area from the thread, especially if you are tying with deer hair so you don't cut the hair as easily. If its twisted like a rope, it will cut material like a knife.

**You mentioned you have been fishing the Bahamas for bonefish for over 20 years now. Chris, how have your bonefish flies changed or evolved over that period of time? Has your selection in your bonefish box changed much in the last 20 years?**

Hardly at all! The flies that I use work, so I haven't changed them much. I use Charlies, Gotchas, the Jessie Special, and I have a little crab pattern I keep in my box as well just in case. Ninety-nine times out of a hundred I put the Jessie Special on to start, and if it works I don't take it off.

**Have you tweaked any of those stables at all over the years?**

No, but I have tried some other patterns that are like the Jessie, but tied in different colors, or have different colored legs, and they didn't work as well. The Jessie works, and that color combination seems to be the key. I also think it's the rubber legs on top. When you watch that fly go through the water, it looks just like a little crab or shrimp or something. Those legs are moving constantly. You don't want to overdo the legs, though. If you put on too many, you will not get the same amount of movement. Also when I put them on, I make sure I spread them so they are not all bunched together. That's where your thread pressure comes in to play. I make sure my thread is completely flat, and I spread the legs with my wraps. It's important to keep the legs separated to maximize the movement of the rubber legs.

**Thread selection is extremely important to thread control and technique. Are there any other components to selecting materials that is as important?**

Yes, a good example is SLF Hanks, which come in a variety of colors. When you tie flies with them, they look gorgeous, but they are worthless in the water. That material does not move. If you want to tie shadowbox flies that is the stuff to use, but if you're going to tie to fish, you don't want it. You need to select materials that have some life to them. I'm still a great believer in marabou and bucktail. If the materials you use don't come alive in the water, don't bother with them.

**Do you think that natural feathers and fur are more visible to fish than synthetics?**

I think sometime synthetics are too bright in the water. They look unnatural and the fish actually back away from them. You can use synthetics, but sometimes you need to go with a darker, less reflective selection that looks more natural. I think that you can actually have too much flash and too much reflection, particularly in clearer water. The fly has to look like something they would normally eat.

# Index

Page numbers in italics indicate illustrations and sidebars.